MORNINGS

AND

EVENINGS

IN HIS PRESENCE

A LIFESTYLE OF DAILY ENCOUNTERS WITH GOD

BILL & BENI
JOHNSON

MORNINGS
— AND —
EVENINGS

IN HIS PRESENCE

A LIFESTYLE OF DAILY ENCOUNTERS WITH GOD

DESTINY IMAGE® PUBLISHERS, INC.

P.O. Box 310, Shippensburg, PA 17257-0310

"Promoting Inspired Lives."

This book and all other Destiny Image and Destiny Image Fiction books are available at Christian bookstores and distributors worldwide.

Cover design by Christian Rafetto

Compiled by Abigail McKoy

For more information on foreign distributors, call 717-532-3040.

Reach us on the Internet: www.destinyimage.com.

ISBN 13 TP: 978-0-7684-5470-3

ISBN 13 eBook: 978-0-7684-5471-0

ISBN 13 HC: 978-0-7684-5598-4

For Worldwide Distribution, Printed in the U.S.A.

1 2 3 4 5 6 7 8 / 24 23 22 21 20

Contents

Introduction

WELCOME to *Mornings and Evenings in His Presence.* Each day's entry consists of two sections. In the mornings, you will "Rise," meditating on God's Word, reflecting on a short teaching, and speaking out a prayer of empowerment and activation. In the evenings, you are invited to "Rest." There, again, you will encounter a short teaching. Instead of a traditional prayer, though, we have chosen to imagine the words of our tender Father speaking directly to you, bathing you in His love and encouragement as you drift off to sleep. This is a yearlong devotional, and a commitment of this nature requires a sacrifice of time, energy, and focus. Fire always falls on sacrifice. Our prayer is that your year—your life—would be marked by the encounters with God you have in these pages. May His presence go before you, stand behind you, and envelop each and every day.

January

January 1st

*Do not conform to the pattern of this world, but be
transformed by the renewing of your mind.*

—Romans 12:2 NIV

RISE: Many Christians instinctively distrust the mind, thinking it is irredeemably corrupt and humanistic. However, the mind is actually a powerful instrument of the Spirit of God. He made it to be the gatekeeper of Kingdom activity on earth. The great tragedy when the mind goes astray is that God's freedom to establish His will on earth is limited. The mind is not to be tossed out; it is to be used for its original purpose. If the mind weren't vitally important to our walk with Christ and our commission, Paul wouldn't have urged us to "be transformed by the renewing of our minds." In fact, only a renewed mind can consistently bring Kingdom reality to earth.

*Father, help me understand the value you place on my mind. Help me
to see the areas of my life that are being influenced by things other than
You. Thank You that I am being renewed so that I can think like You.*

REST: There is an intense war being waged for our mind and our mental agreement. Every thought and action in our lives speak of allegiance to God or to satan. Both are empowered by our agreement. Renewing our minds means learning to recognize what comes from hell, and what comes from Heaven, and agreeing with Heaven. That is the only way we will complete our divine assignment. God designed our minds to be one of the most supernaturally powerful tools in the universe, but the mind needs to be sanctified and yielded to the Holy Spirit so we can carry out His designs, creative ideas, and plans in our everyday lives.

*I love how you think, My dear one. I love to see what delights you, what
inspires you, what lights up your imagination. Draw near to Me so that
I can heal every lie, wipe away every bit of self-doubt and self-criticism.
Let Me whisper truth into your soul until you see yourself as I do.*

January 2ⁿᵈ

From that time Jesus began to preach, saying,
"Repent, for the kingdom of heaven is at hand."

—Matthew 4:17 ESV

RISE: Renewing the mind begins with repentance. That is the gateway to return to our original assignment on earth. Jesus said, *"Repent, for the kingdom of heaven is at hand."* To many Christians, *repent* refers to having an alter call where people come forward and weep at the altar and get right with God. That is a legitimate expression of repentance, but it's not what the word *repentance* means. *Re* means to go back. *Pent* is like the penthouse, the top floor of a building. Repent, then, means to go back to God's perspective on reality. And in that perspective, there is renewal, a reformation that affects our intellect, our emotions, and every part of our lives.

> *Thank You, God, that You are transforming every aspect of my life. I want to see the world the way You do. Bring to mind any area of my life where repentance is needed so that I can experience Your Kingdom fully.*

REST: Jesus said that *"unless one is born again, he cannot see the kingdom of God"* (John 3:3). What does that mean? Jesus was not saying that we would have visions of Heaven, although I know that happens. He was speaking more practically. He was saying that when our minds are renewed, we will see the Kingdom displayed and proven as He did in His earthly ministry. That what it means to "see" the Kingdom of Heaven. Our souls long to see such things. We have inside of us an unrelenting hunger to watch the Kingdom break into this realm—and not just to watch but to participate, to become the connecting point and gateway for God's power.

> *I know some days feel far away from experiencing My Kingdom, but I am closer than you think. Release your pain and disappointment to Me. Let Me carry them. Let Me show you the glory I long to reveal on the earth.*

January 3rd

Then Jesus answered and said to them, "Most assuredly, I say to you,
the Son can do nothing of Himself, but what He sees the Father do; for
whatever He does, the Son also does in like manner."

—John 5:19 NKJV

RISE: In the New Testament, the very word for *salvation* means healing, deliverance, and forgiveness of sin. The Kingdom brings the complete solution to the whole man, and we have access to that reality even now, just as Jesus did throughout His life. Many believers think miracles and power are for extra-special, anointed people of God. Many get hung up on the idea that Jesus did miracles as God, not man. In reality, Jesus had no ability to heal the sick. He couldn't cast out devils, and He had no ability to raise the dead. He said of Himself, *"the Son can do nothing of Himself."* He had set aside His divinity. He did miracles as a man in right relationship with God because He was setting forth a model for us, something for us to follow.

Jesus, help me to open every area of my life to Your perfect will. I want to
have the same intimate connection with the Father as You did on earth.

REST: If Jesus did miracles as God, we would all be extremely impressed, but we would have no compulsion to emulate Him. But when we see that God has commissioned us to do what Jesus did—and more—then we realize that He put self-imposed restriction on Himself to show us we could do it, too. Jesus so emptied Himself that He was incapable of doing what was required of Him by the Father—without the Father's help. That is the nature of our call—it requires more than we are capable of.

My desire to be close to you is even stronger than yours, My child.
Let Me into every area of your heart and mind. I am safe. Let My
overwhelming love empower you beyond what you could even imagine.

January 4th

Don't you know that you yourselves are God's temple and
that God's Spirit dwells in your midst?

—1 Corinthians 3:16 NIV

RISE: *Dwells* in this verse means "to tabernacle." Jesus *tabernacled* among us—He was the House of God made flesh—the place where God lived. The House of God was not a building, location, or denomination, but a Person. The fulfillment of the House of God began with Jesus. He was the House of God on earth. But this concept did not stop with Him—far from it. He was the initial fulfillment of the House of God, but not the ultimate fulfillment. There is a big difference. For example, your conversion was not God's ultimate intent for you. It was His initial intent that set you up for the ultimate fulfillment, which is that you be filled with His fullness, living the normal Christian lifestyle as defined by what takes place in Heaven.

> *Lord, stoke up my hunger for Your presence. Help me to never settle for*
> *security, but to pursue more of You at all costs!*

REST: We, the Church, the redeemed, are the tabernacle of the Holy Spirit, the eternal dwelling place of God! We are living stones, fitly framed together, building the eternal dwelling place of God (see 1 Pet. 2:4-5). The House of God is us! It is the heart of our very identity. God wants so much to invade this world with the reality of what was purchased on Calvary. But He waits for a people who will live the normal Christian life, putting themselves at risk, constantly tapping into the invisible resources of Heaven that have been standing idle. This is how we function as the House of God.

> *Of all of creation, I have chosen you as My dwelling place, My*
> *inheritance, My prize. And I would choose you again. Allow My fullness*
> *to invade, and watch what we can do together.*

January 5th

*I also say to you that you are Peter, and upon this rock I will build My
church; and the gates of Hades will not overpower it.*

—Matthew 16:18 NASB

RISE: So where precisely are the gates of hell? Where does the devil sit in power? The mind is the gatekeeper of the Kingdom of God. It is the place of access, transition, and power. It follows then that the gates of hell are set up in people's minds. When Jesus rebukes Peter in Matthew 16:23, He didn't say, "Peter, you devil worshiper!" He said, "Your mind is filled with the things of man." A most important thing to remember is that the devil is empowered by human agreement. To say, "I'm only human," is to say, "I'm only satanic." Humanity without Christ at the center is satanic in nature. When we've been given the Spirit of God, we lose the privilege of claiming, "We're only human." We are much more than that!

> *Jesus, help me to truly understand my new nature in You and transform
> my mind accordingly. Fill my mind with Your thoughts!*

REST: The gate of hell is in our minds any time we agree with the enemy. I empower him any time I agree with a man-centered perspective or natural wisdom that does not know God. I empower demonic forces and become a gate to release his power to kill, steal, and destroy in my life. Our goal, then, is to agree with Heaven all the time, to let our minds be the gate of Heaven where angels ascend and descend freely on assignment from God. Whatever is free in the heavenly realm to function needs to be released here. We are to be a gateway people for the free flow of heavenly realities into this planet.

> *The mind I have given you is powerful, but don't be afraid. It is also
> beautiful and creative, like Me. I will guide you, untangling your
> thoughts from the things of this world and introducing you to the ways
> of My Kingdom.*

January 6ᵗʰ

My people are being destroyed because they don't know me.

—Hosea 4:6 NLT

RISE: The nature of revelation is that it opens up new realms of living, of possibility, of faith. It is absolutely impossible to live the normal Christian life without receiving regular revelation from God. The Bible does not say, "My people perish for lack of miracles," or lack of money, or because of bad relationships or bad worship leaders or insufficient nursery staff, or anything else we could list. Proverbs 29:18 says, *"Where there is no revelation, the people cast off restraint."* A more correct and complete translation is: "Without a prophetic revelation, the people go unrestrained, walking in circles, having no certain destiny."

> *Father, help me to prioritize revelation from You. Sometimes I get caught up in trivial details, but I want to see through Your eyes. I want to grab ahold of Your vision and run with it!*

REST: The biblical word *vision* doesn't mean "goals." Goals are fine, but this *vision* is referring to the spirit of revelation coming upon you, giving you a vision of things that are unseen. Revelation is so essential in our lives that without it we perish. This is not a nice vitamin pill we can take or leave. This is what we live by. Without unfolding prophetic revelation that expands your capacity to see life from God's perspective, you will perish. Without seeing your present circumstances through God's eyes, you will spiritually die. Revelation is critical to the normal Christian life.

> *I am not an exacting or stingy Father. I long to reveal My thoughts and secrets to you. Come to Me, seek out My heart, pursue My perspective. I promise that I will not withhold from you.*

January 7th

This is why the Scriptures say: Things never discovered or heard of before, things beyond our ability to imagine—these are the many things God has in store for all his lovers. But God now unveils these profound realities to us by the Spirit. Yes, he has revealed to us his inmost heart and deepest mysteries through the Holy Spirit, who constantly explores all things.

—1 Corinthians 2:9-10 TPT

RISE: The Holy Spirit searches for things that have never been heard by human ears or seen by human eyes. He is the greatest search engine in the whole universe. He searches the greatest reservoir of information imaginable—the heart of the Father. Psalm 139:18 says that God's thoughts about each one of us outnumber the sands on every seashore of this planet, and according to Jeremiah 29:11, all of those thoughts are for your welfare, benefit, and blessing.

Thank You, God, for sending Your Holy Spirit. Thank You for the indescribable gift of Your invitation to know You. Thank You that Your thoughts are for my blessing!

REST: God has been living in the experience of knowing us long before we were ever born. He doesn't just have a few random thoughts about us here and there. For trillions of years, God has been thinking about us, and the Holy Spirit searches that whole archive and brings incredible treasures to us at precisely the right moment—if we're listening. We'll know when He is speaking because it will have a freshness to it. It will always be better than anything we could have thought up ourselves. And, if He gives us new ideas, they will probably be impossible for us to accomplish in our own strength. His thoughts will so overwhelm us that we'll want to draw close to Him so they can be accomplished. .

The way you treasure My word blesses Me. I long to share even more of My heart and My vision for your life. Pull up close to Me, let Me tell you all that I've been dreaming for you.

January 8th

Faith, then, is birthed in a heart that responds to
God's anointed utterance of the Anointed One.

—Romans 10:17 TPT

RISE: Most born-again people know what it's like to be in confusion or trouble and have someone speak a word that brings a supernatural invasion of peace into their soul. You might not even have all of the answers you thought you needed five minutes ago, but for some reason, you don't care. Their words were the spirit of revelation from God Himself. The same way that Jesus became flesh, the Holy Spirit becomes words, and when they are spoken, they bring life. We don't even have to comprehend it to embrace it. We just have to wrap our hearts around it and eventually it will start making sense.

> *Create in me a heart that responds to You, God. Increase my faith so*
> *that I can bring Your Kingdom to the earth as You intended.*

REST: Revelation is for every believer, not just for some "gifted" folks. The greater revelation that a person carries, the greater faith he or she is able to exercise. If I believe it's not God's desire to heal everybody, then my revelation limits me every time a person comes to me who is sick. I have to settle it in my heart—is God's will to heal people? As long as I shun the revelation that God wants everybody to be healed and whole, I have cut myself off from releasing faith in that area. Revelation enlarges the arena in which our faith can function.

> *The amount of faith you have right now is enough. Don't hide it,*
> *though. Take your faith and put it to work. Take a risk in My name,*
> *trust in My word, and watch as your faith grows.*

January 9th

It is the glory of God to conceal a matter,
but the glory of kings is to search out a matter.

—Proverbs 25:2 NASB

RISE: Revelation is not something we can dig out of a theological book or a study guide. It's not even something we can unravel in the Bible all by ourselves. Revelation is locked up in a realm the Bible calls "mystery." A mystery cannot be hunted down and trapped like an animal. It can't be discovered by persistent searching. It must be revealed. We don't unlock mysteries; they are unlocked for us. And they are only unlocked and revealed to those who hunger for them. Jesus said He concealed truth in parables so it remained a mystery to some, but not for others.

> *Help me to see the beauty of Your mystery, Lord. I release any tendency*
> *to try to control what I don't understand. I embrace the unknown,*
> *because I know that You are trustworthy.*

REST: Mystery should be a continual part of our lives. We should always have more questions than answers. If our encounters with God don't leave us with more questions than when we started, then we have had an inferior encounter. A relationship with God that does not stir up that realm of mystery and wonder is an inferior relationship. It would help all of us a great deal if we had to walk out of a few more church services, scratching our heads, wondering what just took place. He is the God of wonder, the God of awe! But tenderness of heart enables us to come into the realm of revelation that unlocks the mysteries of God.

> *I have given you a gift called mystery. If used correctly, this gift will*
> *draw you into the depths of Me, into encounters with Heaven that*
> *surprise you, filling you with awe and wonder. Embrace it!*

January 10th

*You search the Scriptures because you think they give you
eternal life. But the Scriptures point to me!*

—John 5:39 NLT

RISE: Renewing the mind is not merely reading words on a page and having a moment of revelation about a particular verse. Renewal comes as revelation leads us into a new experience with God. Revelation is meant to bring us into an encounter with God and, if it doesn't, it only makes us more religious. Revelation is never given to increase our head knowledge. That's a byproduct at best. To renew the mind, we must not just *think* differently but also *live* differently, experiencing the empowerment of the Holy Spirit in a new way.

> *Holy Spirit, guide me into life-changing encounters so that I may completely transform my life. I pray that You would bypass my head and move my spirit toward an ever-increasing intimacy with God.*

REST: The revelation of the Kingdom is often spoken of as a living seed of another world that carries with it new possibilities. But when a person hears the word but doesn't understand it, the enemy has open access to that seed and can snatch it away (see Matt. 13:19). In our culture, we define understanding as nothing more than cognitive reasoning, coming to conclusions, fully comprehending. But in Eastern culture, which is the culture of Scripture, understanding is an *experience*. It means engaging in activities that involve our five senses. The biblical view of understanding means far more than to give a mental assent; it means to practice in real life what one has come to know by revelation.

> *I want you to know My ways in every fiber of your being. I delight in every detail of who you are. I don't want to connect only with your mind, but rather to engage with every part of you.*

January 11ᵗʰ

Faith empowers us to see that the universe was created and beautifully coordinated by the power of God's words! He spoke and the invisible realm gave birth to all that is seen.

—Hebrews 11:3 TPT

RISE: To understand also means yielding to something before we can explain, define, or describe it. Biblical understanding far surpasses the intellect. We don't have faith because we understand, but we understand because we have faith. In other words, it is imperative to accept and understand things without completely satisfying our intellect. When I read the Bible, I don't always understand what I'm reading. Biblical learning takes place in the spirit first and, as we obey the Spirit of God, our spirit communicates it to our minds so we intellectually understand. But understanding is not required for obedience. A normal Christian is one who obeys the revelations and promptings of the Holy Spirit without understanding.

> *Convict me, Father, in any area where disobedience has manifested as apathy, doubt, or mistrust. Sensitize my heart to the promptings of the Holy Spirit, and give me the boldness to follow.*

REST: Revelation takes us only halfway there; experience leads us all the way. The great tragedy is that if we don't move into experience, that revelation remains locked in our minds so we think it's active in our life. The next time we hear a message about helping the poor we might say, "Amen. The other people in this room need to hear that," even though we have done nothing to help the poor. Hearing without doing has locked us into a form without power. Revelation should change our hearts before we could ever explain what we learned.

> *Everything I do is for your benefit, but it is ultimately so that My glory would be revealed upon the earth. Lift up your face, come near to Me, and allow the truth to transform you.*

January 12ᵗʰ

For they had not understood about the loaves,
because their heart was hardened.

—Mark 6:52 NKJV

RISE: It's not enough to put our revelation into practice; we must also become students of miracles. That means the miracles we experience must shape how we think. Miracles can be dazzling and dramatic, but they are not primarily designed to dazzle us. God gives us miracles to train us how to see differently. A miracle is a school. Or think of it this way: Just as there are nutrients in food, so every situation and encounter with God comes filled with the "nutrients" necessary to make us strong as representatives of God on this planet.

> *Open my eyes to the lessons intertwined in Your supernatural interventions, Lord. Let them transform who I am, teaching me to walk in Your ways.*

REST: Jesus' disciples participated in a mindboggling miracle of a great multiplication of food (see Mark 6). The multiplication actually took place in *their* hands, not in Jesus' hands. He took the small portion they had and divided it into 12 groups, and as the disciples gave it away, it was replenished. But, later that day, Jesus told them to cross over to the other side of the sea in their boat, and He went to a mountainside to pray. There, He saw in His spirit the disciples straining at rowing, almost ready to lose their lives, so He came walking on the sea close enough to check on them. They saw Him and screamed for fear, and He ended up coming into the boat. The winds and waves stopped. The disciples settled down. They were completely amazed. They had obeyed perfectly when carrying out the miracle of the loaves and fishes, yet their hearts still remained hard. They hadn't *seen through* the miracle. It had not transformed them. Because they didn't see their role in the previous miracle, the next time they encountered a problem and Jesus wasn't in the boat, they had no solution. They had missed the whole point.

> *Let My works empower you to do the impossible. My heart is to transform the world alongside you, co-laboring until earth looks just like Heaven.*

January 13th

*While we look not at the things which are seen, but at the things
which are not seen; for the things which are seen are temporal,
but the things which are not seen are eternal.*

—2 Corinthians 4:18 NASB

RISE: When God does a miracle for us, and we get to see it and be a part of it, He is teaching us how to see into the invisible realm. A miracle is a tutor, a gift from God to show us what exists on the other side. If I experience a miracle, and later revert back to the same doubt, complaining, moaning and groaning, it's because I have not allowed the testimony of the Lord to have its full effect on the way I think.

> *Thank You, Father, that You are never distant from me. Help me to increase my awareness of Your presence so that Your reality becomes more real to me than any circumstance.*

REST: Kingdom thinking knows that anything is possible at any time. It's activated when you and I with tender hearts surrender to the thought patterns of God, when we receive His imaginations and say "yes." We want our minds to be full of Kingdom influence. We want miracles, and we want those miracles to have their full effect on us, changing the way we see and behave.

> *I'm not scared of your mind, your will, or your imagination, but I long for you to experience the fullness of your potential in Me. That can only be found as you receive My fullness and allow yourself to be shaped by My Kingdom reality. Come to Me, and see what is possible!*

January 14th

Then the Lord sent a great wind on the sea.... But Jonah had gone
below deck, where he lay down and fell into a deep sleep. The captain
went to him and said, "How can you sleep? Get up and call on your
god! Maybe he will take notice of us so that we will not perish."

—Jonah 1:4-6 NIV

RISE: Which storm are you in? Are you dealing with it the way God wants you to deal with it? Have you let past miracles "tutor" you to a place of faith adequate for your current challenge? Some people face storms because they took a left when God took a right. God brings a storm in His mercy to drive them back. Others face storms because they are in the middle of God's will. He doesn't like the storm, but He wants to train us to use the tools He's given us to calm the storm.

> *Father, help me see the tools that You have already placed in my life to*
> *conquer my current conflict. Thank You that You continue to equip and*
> *empower me for every storm.*

REST: Most of us find ourselves in a storm and instantly conclude our job is to cry out to God to intervene and change our circumstance. But that's not the purpose of the storm; if we only cry out, we are abdicating our role in a miracle. God never allows a storm without first providing the tools to calm the storm. He wants us to use those tools to bring about a miraculous result. He allows problems into our lives so we can defeat them—not only so we can cry out to Him every time. The tools will be in the boat with us, but the enemy will fan the winds of fear to get us to forget where the tools are.

> *Everything the Father gave to Me, I have given to you. Lean into*
> *Me, and I will show you the authority you have in Me to release the*
> *Kingdom and quiet the storms.*

January 15th

So now the case is closed. There remains no accusing voice of
condemnation against those who are joined in life-union
with Jesus, the Anointed One.

—Romans 8:1 TPT

RISE: Too often Christians live under the influence of yesterday's failures, blemishes, and mistakes. When we do, we depart from the normal Christian lifestyle and live under the influence of a lie. Needless to say, this lie halts the renewing of our minds and keeps us from living in the "everyday miraculous" that should be normal for every born-again believer. Why do people receive God's forgiveness but constantly live under the shadow of their failures? We often willingly live under the guilt and shame of bad decisions from yesterday because we think it will help us to walk in humility.

> *Thank You, Jesus, that I can walk in absolute freedom. Thank You that*
> *You have wiped the slate clean, and I am pure in Your sight. Help me to*
> *live that truth every day.*

REST: But living under yesterday's condemnation never makes us more humble. If anything, it keeps us focused on ourselves instead of on the Lord. It's much more difficult to humbly receive forgiveness we don't deserve than to walk in false humility, cloaked in yesterday's shame. When we receive free forgiveness, the one who gave it to us is honored. When He is honored, we are truly humbled.

> *The case is closed. The verdict has been passed. You are now one with*
> *Me, equal participants in My holiness, righteousness, peace, and joy.*
> *I look at you with absolute tenderness and affection. You are My pure*
> *delight, a new creation.*

January 16th

From now on, think of it this way: Sin speaks a dead language that
means nothing to you; God speaks your mother tongue, and you hang
on every word. You are dead to sin and alive to God.
That's what Jesus did.

—Romans 6:11 MSG

RISE: Probably 95% of all counseling that churches undertake is simply to help people stop questioning what God has said and to stop questioning who we are in Christ. We are the people God loves, the people God forgives. We are the House of God, the gate of Heaven on earth. When Moses asked God, "Who am I that I should go to Pharaoh, and that I should bring the children of Israel out of Egypt?" God appeared to ignore the question by answering, "I will certainly be with you" (see Exod. 3:11-12). But that was the answer! Moses said, "Who am I?" God said, in effect, "You are the man God goes with." Who are you? You are the person God hangs around with. You are clean and forgiven. That is your identity!

> *Father, help me to see fully who I am in You. Help that truth to become*
> *unshakable within me so that everything I do emerges from my identity*
> *as the one You want to be with.*

REST: God is never honored when we deny what Jesus did for us. He suffered so we would be free. What parent delights in seeing his or her child suffer? Neither does God delight in seeing us suffer with the effects of guilt and shame. Yet we often ascribe that evil motive to the Father. When Jesus bought you, He also bought whatever problem you're facing. We either believe His provision was adequate or we don't. Unfortunately, many believers constantly battle a phantom self-image from the past with no assurance of their present identity in Christ. Forgiveness seems like a theory or an impractical truth. Yet it is the most practical truth there is.

> *As the Creator of the universe, I chose you to be My inheritance. I chose*
> *intimacy with you above control, above cold perfection, above all else. Stop*
> *fighting away My love, and experience my full acceptance and delight.*

January 17th

*In Him we have redemption through His blood, the forgiveness of our
trespasses, according to the riches of His grace.*

—Ephesians 1:7 NASB

RISE: The death of Christ wiped out our record of sin. This may seem like grammar school teaching, but most people don't live with the realization that they are totally forgiven. They can quote the passage, but they don't live under the influence of its truth. The blood of Jesus wiped out the power and record of sin in your life. Your old nature is dead. It hasn't been put on a shelf, or in a closed room, or imprisoned—it has been crucified. Period. Done deal.

> *Thank You, Lord, that I have been made completely new! Help me to
> never reach back with familiarity to my old nature, but to reach toward
> my full inheritance as a child of God.*

REST: Remember that Jesus addressed believers as saints. We tend to think sainthood is acquired after years of sacrificial service. Wrong. We went from rotten sinners to born-again saints in a single moment when we accepted salvation. Once the blood of Jesus has wiped out our sin, we can't get any cleaner. That doesn't mean we can avoid the hurdles and issues that come with changing our lives and renewing our minds. Maturity is a process. But, as Kris Vallotton says, "You are not a sinner; you are a saint. It doesn't mean that you can't sin; it just means that you are no longer a professional." That's the story of your life.

> *I have changed your name for eternity. It is not through your own effort,
> but by My grace that this transformation occurred. Embrace it. Live
> from this new identity. I will remind you as often as you need to hear it
> that you are pure, you are chosen, you are clean, you are Mine.*

January 18th

For I am persuaded that neither death nor life, nor angels nor principalities nor powers, nor things present nor things to come, nor height nor depth, nor any other created thing, shall be able to separate us from the love of God which is in Christ Jesus our Lord.

—Romans 8:38-39 NKJV

RISE: It's difficult if not impossible to demonstrate the will of God "on earth as in Heaven" if we don't think of ourselves as truly forgiven, and if we hang on to a false view of our identity. It effectively cancels out most of our potential in ministry. Some people reduce each day to, "I hope I survive" instead of, "What will God do today through me?" You and I were designed to triumphantly demonstrate the reality of the King and His Kingdom. Our first thought of each day should instead be the reality of the Kingdom. We are forgiven! There's nothing anybody can do to change that.

Forgive me, Jesus, for any way that I have settled for surviving instead of partnering with Your victory. Open my eyes to the reality of Your Kingdom.

REST: When the enemy brings up sin from our past, he is talking about something nonexistent. It's completely legal for us to say, "I didn't do that. The person who did that is dead." Either the blood of Jesus is completely effective, or it's not effective at all. His blood has the power to completely transform us into a new creation in Christ. There is no power on earth that can separate us from the love of God. Although Paul mentions the present and the future, he doesn't mention the past, because the past can separate us from *our awareness* of the love of God, if we let it become our present identity. Jesus bought our sin, not to bring it up again but to destroy it so we don't have to think about it anymore.

My tender love is chasing you down. Receive My love. I paid the highest price so that you could live in victory. Receive My victory.

January 19th

O how I love and treasure the revelation of your word;
throughout the day I fill my heart with its light!

—Psalm 119:97 TPT

RISE: It's easy for our minds to stray into natural thinking only, for our faith to erode so subtly that we don't notice it happening. Little by little we can begin to think "practically," leaning on natural wisdom instead of Kingdom reality. One of the great tools for keeping a Kingdom mindset is to meditate on and remember God's Word, devising ways of reminding ourselves of His promises to us, and then passing those promises and remembrances on to the next generation of believers. Without taking practical steps to remember and meditate on the truth, we will easily forget what God has promised. By degrees, we will become earthly minded, and that's what we must avoid if we're to successfully live the normal Christian life.

> *Today, I turn away from any thinking that has excluded Your marvelous*
> *works from my awareness, God. I commit to putting Your truth before*
> *me daily!*

REST: In Eastern occult religions, meditation means emptying the mind. But biblical meditation is the opposite—it's filling the mind with God's truth. Some Christians don't like the idea of meditation because they've only seen it demonstrated in a corrupt way through diabolical religions. But if you've ever worried about something, you already know how to meditate! Every person, saint and sinner alike, meditates every day. The question is, what are you meditating on?

> *Remember who I am, all that I have been to You, and trust in Me. In*
> *this way, we will be able to cross into the promised lands of your life,*
> *inhabiting these new realms together.*

January 20ᵗʰ

*You will keep him in perfect peace, whose mind is stayed
on You, because he trusts in You.*

—Isaiah 26:3 NKJV

RISE: Say you've got a problem with your finances. A person with a renewed mind derives joy even in that circumstance because joy comes not by what is seen but by what God says. God is not a liar and He will keep His word. But a little voice called worry steals in and reasons with you, saying, "Years ago you disobeyed the Lord financially, and now you'll reap what you sowed." That might sound like a pretty good argument, and it might cause you to shift your meditation from God's Word to worry. Soon that little voice has grown so big it's like a megaphone in your ear. Perfect peace means divine health, prosperity, wellness of being, soundness of mind. *Stayed* or *fixed* means "braced, lodged in an immovable position."

> *Jesus, I long for Your perfect peace. Help me fill my mind with so much of You that nothing else will fit.*

REST: When we listen to worry, we become "unfixed." Why does worry shout so loudly for our attention? Because if we look at it long enough, it will gain our trust. Pretty soon we begin praying out of fear, and eventually we quit praying and start looking for sympathy. We have trusted that other voice, and it won the affections of our heart. We must get our minds set on spiritual things because as long as we fill our minds with what's happening in the natural, we restrict our effectiveness. We may rise up now and then and score a victory with the gift of faith, but we won't have the continual influence of Kingdom transformation flowing through us. What's the solution? To meditate on the Word and give ourselves every opportunity to remember what is true.

> *I am worthy of your trust, but it is up to you to remember. Fix yourself in My faithfulness. I will not let you down.*

January 21st

Then Joshua set up twelve stones in the midst of the Jordan, in the place where the feet of the priests who bore the ark of the covenant stood; and they are there to this day.

—Joshua 4:9 NKJV

RISE: God invites us to engage Him in this way and to review the circumstances of our lives before Him so that through this interaction we are transformed. When Israel crossed the River Jordan, the leaders of the tribes each took a stone and made a pile on the Promised Land side of the river. The stones were to trigger their memories about what God had done. But they also served to remind God of their condition, their need, and their obedience. Memorial stones that we put before God—in the form of prayer and generosity—remind Him of our condition, our need, and our obedience. Is it possible that God has chosen not to know certain things so that He could discover them in His relationship with us? He gives us a stunning privilege of putting before Him stones of remembrance to remind Him of our past faithfulness.

Bring to mind practical tools, Father, that would help me to remember all that You've done in my life. You have been so faithful to me, but sometimes, when the storm comes, I forget. Help me to remember.

REST: Renewing the mind becomes possible when we remember, record, review, and remind ourselves and God of what He has done in the past, and of our obedience. It is a sure way to solidify your identity in Him, and to mold your mind so it conforms to the mind of Christ.

I am not self-centered; the act of remembering My deeds is for your benefit. Rehearse the ways My love has broken through your fear and doubt. I long to do it again.

January 22ⁿᵈ

With my whole heart, with my whole life, and with my innermost being, I bow in wonder and love before you, the holy God!

—Psalm 103:1 TPT

RISE: One of the toughest lessons a Christian can learn is how to trust and praise God in the uncertain time between a promise and its fulfillment. It is a powerful act of spiritual warfare to stand in the middle of death and disease, conflict and unresolved issues, and to cause our spirits to rise and give thanks to God. Our troubling circumstance may last days, months, or years, instead of just an hour or two, but our approach should be the same: We must declare the goodness and faithfulness of God even in the midst of our trial, before we have an answer.

> *Jesus, help me to focus on Your nature, Your goodness, Your beauty no matter what circumstance I am in. I want to give You the gift of praise in the midst of pain, chaos, and confusion.*

REST: In Revelation, we see the gates of Zion called praise and discover that each one is made out of one solid pearl (see Rev. 21:21). Think for a moment. How is a pearl formed? Through irritation and conflict. A granule of sand gets inside an oyster shell, and a pearl forms around the granule to keep it from doing harm. The Bible's pairing of praise with irritation is not coincidental. When we are stuck in conflict and uncertainty, and yet we praise Him without manipulation, it is a sacrifice. It means we are reacting in a way that produces something beautiful. In that moment a gate is formed, a place of entrance where the King of glory can invade our situation. That gate—that place of praise in the midst of conflict—is where His presence rests, where the King Himself dwells. The gate is formed when we move above human explanation and into a place of trust.

> *Do you know how beautiful you look to Me when you choose to praise in the middle of trouble? My child, praise Me in the middle of whatever you are feeling. Don't hide your heart from Me. I see your sacrifice and nothing can stop Me from rushing in to be close to you.*

January 23rd

God is not a man, that He should lie, nor a son of man, that He
should repent; has He said, and will He not do it? Or has
He spoken, and will He not make it good?

—Numbers 23:19 NASB

RISE: When some Christians find themselves in a place of uncertainty with no answer for their problem, they change their view of God and ascribe to Him character traits that are totally anti-biblical. They might convince themselves that He won't help them out of a financial hole because He isn't intervening in their affairs, though the Bible says, *"And my God shall supply all your need according to His riches in glory by Christ Jesus"* (Phil. 4:19). They may claim He won't heal them, though the Bible says He heals all your diseases and forgives all your iniquities (see Ps. 103:3).

> *Forgive me, Father, for all of the times I've allowed myself to define Your*
> *character by my circumstances. Thank You that You're the same always!*
> *I lay my right to understand at Your feet, trusting that You are who You*
> *say You are.*

REST: Uncertainty causes some people to misunderstand who God is. They begin to deny God's true nature and embrace sickness and disease, poverty and mental anguish as gifts from God. That is a devastating lie from hell. It's actually blasphemous to attribute to God the work of the devil. But many Christians want answers so badly during times of uncertainty that they invent theological answers to make themselves feel good about their present condition. In doing so, they sacrifice the truth about God on the altar of human reasoning.

> *I know it makes you feel safer to understand when things get scary, but*
> *when your rationale turns Me into the source of pain and lack, it only*
> *serves to drive you away from Me. Come back. Sink into the safety of My*
> *embrace, and leave all of your questions here with Me.*

January 24th

For I consider [from the standpoint of faith] that the sufferings of the
present life are not worthy to be compared with the glory that
is about to be revealed to us and in us!

—Romans 8:18 AMP

RISE: God is good all of the time. The devil is bad all of the time. We do ourselves a tremendous service to remember the difference between the two. Healing, salvation, wholeness, provision, and joy have already been given to us. They can't be recalled or returned. They are facts of Kingdom living. They were paid for by Jesus on the Cross. The suffering referred to in the Bible means living between two conflicting realities and trusting and praising God through it all. Anybody can declare the greatness of God after they've won the *Reader's Digest* sweepstakes. But when we live in the middle of a conflict—of having a promise that is not yet fulfilled, or having a problem that seems to never get resolved—we rise above circumstance and declare that He is good all the time, no matter what.

> *Thank You for changing every aspect of my reality when You died for Me, Jesus. I never want to forget everything that You paid for with Your sacrifice. You are so good.*

REST: We may find ourselves facing problems and not knowing where the tools are to bring about the solutions. But that doesn't mean the problem is insurmountable. There is power in resolving in our hearts that God is good all of the time, and that His will for healing and wholeness does not change, despite what we see in the natural. We can rest knowing that two things are guaranteed to us. First, in every situation in which we suffer loss by the devourer, all things will work together for good. Second, our God is a God of vengeance. The devil never has final say in anything.

> *Take My promises and wield them like a mighty sword against any lies that come to steal your resolve. Take My promises and wrap them around you like a thick, warm blanket. I am with You, and My word is true.*

January 25th

Let us acknowledge the Lord; let us press on to acknowledge him. As surely as the sun rises, he will appear; he will come to us like the winter rains, like the spring rains that water the earth.

—Hosea 6:3 NIV

RISE: Questions are allowed in the Kingdom, but lack of answers must not interrupt our heart-communion with God. If we demand answers from God, then we are walking in the spirit of offense. In Hosea, those words *press on* can be translated "hunt." That's a picture of how we should passionately pursue the Lord, in spite of not fully understanding Him or His ways. We are to run after Him even in the time of potential offense. The answer is always on the other side of our offense. Getting through the difficulty—without becoming defiant or demanding with God—will take us into the very thing God promised.

> *I promise to never let offense steal me away from my communion with You, Lord. I give to You my need for answers, fully trusting that You will take care of me.*

REST: When we find ourselves in an uncertain time—and we surely will at some point—we remember that we can create a gate of praise by lifting our hearts and our voices to God. We are to persistently pursue fellowship with God even though our uncertainty feels deep and endless, and no answers have materialized. The suffering will last but a moment in God's grand plan for our lives. So, we can be thankful for the opportunity to persevere. And we can be assured—better times are on the way!

> *My mind is filled with thoughts of how to bless you, encourage you, and help you achieve My dream for your life. My heart is filled with adoration for you, My beloved child.*

January 26th

*And so, dear brothers and sisters, I plead with you to give your bodies
to God because of all he has done for you. Let them be a living and
holy sacrifice—the kind he will find acceptable.
This is truly the way to worship him.*

—Romans 12:1 NLT

RISE: The mind has been undervalued in some Christian circles, but the same is true of the physical body. Many see the body as evil in itself, something to be ignored, pushed aside, tolerated but never really used for Kingdom purposes. But God designed the human body to be more than a tent that you dwell in. It is an instrument of God that recognizes His presence and discerns what is happening in the Kingdom realm.

*Thank You, Lord, that my body has been hard-wired to commune with
You. Increase my sensitivity to Your presence, Holy Spirit.*

REST: We encourage people to offer their bodies as a living sacrifice by volunteering at a rescue mission or at a retirement home—by going somewhere or doing something with their bodies. I've heard people teach that when we raise our hands or dance or kneel or lie prostrate in worship, we are offering our bodies as a living sacrifice. All of those applications are true and correct. But I'd like to suggest that this passage is also speaking about our physical bodies' role in recognizing and working with God.

*I was the one who knit together every part of your body in your mother's
womb. Every single cell within you knows My voice, My breath, My
presence. Honor your physical form, for it was made to respond to Me.*

January 27th

O God, You are my God; early will I seek You; my soul thirsts for You;
my flesh longs for You in a dry and thirsty land
where there is no water.

—Psalm 63:1 NKJV

RISE: David had 30 to 40 years in which he came freely before the actual, manifested presence of God that was upon the Ark of the Covenant. God's glory radiated visibly from it. The Bible makes it clear that David was immeasurably impacted by God's presence. I don't think that he was speaking purely metaphorically about his body in Psalm 63. He was declaring that he'd been so affected by the presence and the glory of God that his body itself ached and cried out for more.

> *God, I want to know You like David did. I want to encounter You with*
> *my whole being—spirit, soul, and body.*

REST: What was true for David is true for us. In the same way that you and I might hunger for food or thirst for water, our physical bodies—not just our emotions, intellects, and spirits—can ache for God. And if we can hunger for God physically, then we can be satisfied by God physically. There is no such thing as hunger without the potential of fulfillment. We don't have an appetite for things that are nonexistent. Rather, God has put within our makeup the capacity to recognize Him and His activities with our physical bodies.

> *I will never tease you. I have placed the hunger for Me within every*
> *aspect of your being because I long to fulfill your desire for My presence.*

January 28th

He saw the disciples straining at the oars, because the wind was
against them. Shortly before dawn he went out to them, walking
on the lake. He was about to pass by them.

—Mark 6:48 NIV

RISE: God's first language is not English. He communicates with us in various ways, through impressions of the heart, mental pictures, feelings, emotions, and physical sensations. When we ignore our bodies, we are at least sometimes ignoring the voice of God. This is important because when we neglect the physical signs of the Kingdom, we can miss what God is doing. Sometimes Jesus walks by our boat and does not intend to get in the boat, figuratively speaking. He is nearby, but the only way He'll get in the boat is if we request it strongly. He puts Himself within reach, but doesn't make it automatic. If we don't perceive that He is there, we will miss the opportunity. One day it will be normal for all Christians to discern the Kingdom with their five senses. But to get there, we have to train our senses.

Help me, Holy Spirit, to train my senses to know the presence of God.
Heighten my awareness of You so that I can learn Your every move.

REST: How do you react when God comes into the room in a special way? How do you manifest the presence of God? How do you feel, sense, or perceive God when He is moving around you? We need to know the answers to these questions to fully live the normal Christian life. Without understanding that God moves and communicates with us in the physical realm, our minds cannot fully come into line with Heaven's reality.

I am speaking to you constantly. I want to communicate with you even
more than you long to hear from Me. Lean into that reality, and learn
the unique ways that I connect with you, My treasure.

January 29th

*So don't be proud of your allegiance to any human leader. For
actually, you already have everything! It has all been given for your
benefit, whether it is Paul or Apollos or Peter the Rock, or whether it's
the world or life or death, or whether it's the present or the future—
everything belongs to you!*

—1 Corinthians 3:21-22 TPT

RISE: A spiritual inheritance enables the next generation to start where the previous generation left off. It's the intent of the Lord for us to wake up to this, one of the most significant yet overlooked principles in the Christian life. He wants generations to pass on their spiritual inheritances. You see, with an inheritance, we get for free what someone else paid for. Sometimes we inherit graces from the Lord where we don't have to go through some of the processes a previous generation went through. That doesn't fit the do-it-yourself motto of the age, but it's the way it works with God.

*Father, open my eyes to all that You have given me as my inheritance. I
want to access everything that You have for me!*

REST: A spiritual inheritance is about making us more effective and efficient in our representation of the King and His Kingdom. It is not for our gratification. It's delightful, it's enjoyable, it's pleasant, it's encouraging, but it's not simply for personal consumption. It is to open doors so that the King and His Kingdom have influence in more places than before. A spiritual inheritance pulls back the curtain and reveals what we already have permission to possess. Receiving a spiritual inheritance is like learning that years ago somebody put ten million dollars in your bank account. You had the money all along, but now you are at liberty to spend it, because you have knowledge that the money is there and belongs to you.

*Every part of your inheritance is available to you. Everything I've given
you is designed to bless you, but is ultimately for My glory. Seek it out;
don't leave anything in the bank.*

January 30th

When an impure spirit comes out of a person...it says, "I will return to the house I left." When it arrives, it finds the house swept clean and put in order. Then it goes and takes seven other spirits more wicked than itself, and they go in and live there. And the final condition of that person is worse than the first.

—Luke 11:24-26 NIV

RISE: The tragedy of history is that revival comes and goes, and subsequent generations build monuments around the achievements of the previous generation, but do not completely occupy their inherited spiritual territory. Perhaps they don't want to pay the same price their forefathers paid, or perhaps they end up forming organizations around past movements to preserve and defend the idea but not the practice of revival. In either case, they inherit territory for free, but do not pay the price to develop it, and so they lose it.

Holy Spirit, give me a revelation about the price that was paid for the spiritual freedom that I get to live in. Help me to never get comfortable but to advance God's Kingdom with all boldness.

REST: The quickest way to lose something is to take a defensive posture where we maintain what we have instead of working to increase it. This principle is illustrated in Luke. When a person gets set free, there is a moment when he is absolutely clean and purged from filthiness. From that moment on he has the responsibility of managing that liberty. Jesus used a house to illustrate it. The house is clean and swept, there's no furniture, no inhabitants there, but it's newly renovated and beautiful. It's now the owner's responsibility to set up the furniture, to dwell in it, to occupy that home. One of our greatest problems is the failure to occupy the inheritance that we've been given.

The soldiers in My army were never made for retreat but for ever-advancing dominion. Hear My battle cry, and press forward!

January 31st

So all of us who have had that veil removed can see and reflect the glory of the Lord. And the Lord—who is the Spirit—makes us more and more like him as we are changed into his glorious image.

—2 Corinthians 3:18 NLT

RISE: Every generation of revivalists, so far, has been fatherless as it pertains to the move of the Spirit. Every generation has had to learn from scratch how to recognize the presence, how to move with Him, how to pay a price. The answer to this tragedy is inheritance, where you and I receive something for free. What we do with it determines what happens in the following generations. God is serious about returning for a glorious Church. He's serious that nations should serve Him—not just a token representation from every tribe and tongue—but entire nations, entire people groups apprehended by God Himself.

> *Father, I thank You that You are taking us from glory to glory. I am a part of a victorious army advancing Your Kingdom every day.*

REST: We must understand and embrace our spiritual inheritance. We were never intended to start over from scratch every two or three generations. God wants to put each generation at a higher level than the previous one. Every generation has a ceiling experience that becomes the next generation's floor. We dishonor our forefathers and the great price they paid to get their breakthrough by not maintaining and expanding what they accomplished. They attained by tremendous risk and persevering under ridicule and rejection. The things we take for granted today cost the previous generation tremendously. Inheritance helps us to build truth on top of truth. Instead of starting over each generation, we inherit certain truths that allow us to move forward into new areas.

> *I have built My Kingdom on the foundation of family. Look to your spiritual mothers and fathers, honor their breakthrough, and their victories will become yours.*

February

February 1ˢᵗ

Don't you have a saying, "It's still four months until harvest"? I tell
you, open your eyes and look at the fields! They are ripe for harvest.

—John 4:35 NIV

RISE: There are natural principles we live and work by in the things of the Spirit. We understand spiritual things through natural pictures. We compare evangelism to a harvest, because we are familiar with the process of plowing a field, making the dirt tender so it can receive seed, then planting, watering, tending, and harvesting. Those are the natural principles of harvest. But Jesus wants us to understand spiritual realities that have no natural picture. He meant that with a superior revelation not bounded by the natural order, every day is harvest day.

> *Thank You, Jesus, that I am not limited by the laws of nature. I live by*
> *the laws of Your Kingdom. Give me the vision to see the fullness of my*
> *inheritance in You, and give me the courage to act upon it.*

REST: We must lift our eyes to see from His perspective. I don't care if we're first-generation believers, or if our families have been in the church for generations. By revelation, we have access to an inheritance that is beyond our wildest imaginations, beyond our wildest dreams. We owe it to the generations in the past to occupy that territory because they paid a great price to bring it to us. We owe it to our parents, our grandparents, and to our great-grandparents. We owe it to our children, and their children. Before Jesus returns there will be the community of the redeemed walking under the influence of their inheritance. There will be a generation that steps into the cumulative revelation of the whole gospel. There will be a generation that lifts their eyes and sees that supernatural season in which every person is harvestable now, and have the anointing necessary to carry it out.

> *I am God—all-powerful, all-knowing, and ever-present—and you*
> *are My child. All of the authority of Heaven has been released to you*
> *through Jesus Christ. Grasp that reality and run with it. Let My*
> *Kingdom come upon the earth through you.*

February 2nd

*Jesus Christ is the Son of God...and he has never been both a "yes"
and a "no." He has always been and always will be for us a resounding
"YES!" For all of God's promises find their "yes" of fulfillment in him.
And as his "yes" and our "amen" ascend to God, we bring him glory!*

—2 Corinthians 1:19-20 TPT

RISE: Jesus is the divine yes of God. He reveals the most complete picture of God in all history. Jesus Christ is, Himself, perfect theology. Anything you think you know about God that you can't find in the person of Jesus, you have reason to question. Jesus is the fulfillment of all the hopes and dreams of all humanity throughout all time. He modeled life for all who would believe on His name. But God's will on earth is incomplete without His character, love and power working in each of us who confess Him as Lord.

*God, my gratitude for Jesus overwhelms me. Thank You for sending
Your Son, for giving us such a tangible revelation of Your goodness.*

REST: God has countless promises for us, and they are all yes in Jesus. But that is something I would expect, as He is good, and He always has our best in mind. He constantly overflows with words of hope and promise for His people. The stunning part is that the equation is not complete without our "amen!" This means that it is His grace that makes it possible for us to have an effect on the outcome of matters, simply through our agreement, as evidenced by our amen. Things that happen right in life do not just happen because they are right and true. They happen because someone on earth said "amen" to what God was saying in Heaven. Therein is the divine partnership—co-laboring.

*I have invited you into a relationship, not only with who I am, but also
with My vision for the earth's redemption. Your role is not a small one;
you are crucial to manifesting My heart to this world.*

February 3rd

Now you [collectively] are Christ's body, and individually [you are]
members of it [each with his own special purpose and function].

—1 Corinthians 12:27 AMP

RISE: Make no mistake. God is capable of doing everything the gospel requires all on His own. It's obvious that He can preach better than we can; He can heal and deliver better than we can; and He is absolute perfect holiness. His love is completely unselfish in every way, without shadows and hidden agendas. His love is beyond our comprehension. He does not need our help. He does not need us, as He has no needs. Yet He desires us and has great value for enabling us to become His dream come true.

> *Father, Your desire to work with me to change the world is hard to comprehend and beautifully humbling. I need Your heart for the world and for myself; equip me fully for the task at hand.*

REST: We are what God dreamed of in eternity past. Jesus is the head of His Church, the Body. We are His Body on earth. To think of ourselves in any other light is to fall short in our thinking in a way that ultimately undermines our purpose in this life. We are a generation for such a time as this.

> *I make no mistakes. I have never wanted a different person for this exact moment in time other than you, experiencing the fullest expression of yourself. Trust Me, find yourself in Me, let Me speak to you about who you truly are and My plans for us.*

February 4th

*You live fully in me and now I live fully in them so that they will
experience perfect unity, and the world will be convinced that you
have sent me, for they will see that you love each one of them with the
same passionate love that you have for me.*

—John 17:23 TPT

RISE: So much of the gospel, as it is preached in our day, is aimed at satisfying the needs and desires of the individual believer. That's not necessarily wrong; it's just incomplete—dangerously incomplete. Independence is common, and those who think of the group (big picture) are often thought to be religious or bound by tradition. Yet there are aspects of the life of the believer that can never be discovered by the one. They must be embraced by the whole. Some things are much too precious for God to give to one person only. They must be imparted to a body of believers; otherwise, the temptation for pride will become the beast that devours.

*Jesus, help me to turn from my natural independence toward Your spirit
of unity among believers. Fill me with Your grace so that I can receive
all that You have intended for Your Church.*

REST: The Scripture says, *our* Father, not *my* Father. It says, "*we* have the mind of Christ," not "*I* have the mind of Christ." It says He is returning for a spotless bride (body), not a spotless individual. The list goes on. Thinking only of our well-being by reducing the Gospel to a personal cure-all—not the transformational force on the earth that God intended—is in some ways the roadblock to what we all long for. Thankfully, although God intends the power of the good news to strongly affect the individual, His intent is to bring ultimate transformation on a much bigger scale: that of all culture and society.

*I long to pour out My blessings on My children so that the world would
see My goodness, My provision, My wondrous ways. Draw near to your
brothers and sisters in Christ. I never meant for you to live apart from
community.*

February 5th

Declare His glory among the nations, His wonders among all people.
—Psalm 96:3 NKJV

RISE: The transformation of society starts with the transformation of the mind of an individual. It begins with the one. But it is the acorn that becomes a tree that produces a forest. A transformed mind transforms a person. And a transformed person transforms a city. And transformed cities bring about the desired domino effect over a nation, bringing about what we historically call a reformation. This is the heart of God.

> *Help me to expand my vision, Holy Spirit! Fill me with Your dreams for my family, my city, my nation, and beyond.*

REST: He still loves people and has plans for our cities and nations that are good. To yield to the power of unrighteousness, by not expecting the power of the gospel to have its full effect in our lifetime, is a disgrace to the power of the Cross. This must not happen on our watch. Jesus didn't go through everything He went through so we could do church until He returned. If He can deliver a person from sin or disease, He can deliver a city, a nation, etc. It's time for the brilliance of the renewed mind to take center stage and for us to not allow ourselves to be overcome with the hopelessness that prevails in the hearts of those who don't know Him. It's time.

> *Dream with me for the nations! Tell the world who I am—all that I have done in your life—and watch as My presence enters into every environment and fills the atmosphere with My mercy and grace.*

February 6th

The Lord is not slow about His promise, as some count slowness, but is
patient toward you, not wishing for any to perish
but for all to come to repentance.

—2 Peter 3:9 NASB

RISE: Our mistake is often seen when we create explanations to tragedies and difficulties that God is not causing. This kind of reasoning appeals to the minds of those who have not yet settled into a lifestyle that treasures mystery. Mystery is as important as revelation. Strangely, the sovereignty of God is the one carpet that most unanswered questions get swept under. The sovereignty of God is one of the most valuable truths in Scripture. Perhaps this is why the enemy works so hard to pervert it. God is all-powerful and independent of all others. He thinks and acts completely of His own mind and will and has full authority to carry out anything He wants without having to give an explanation to anyone. But He has revealed Himself in very endearing ways throughout Jesus' life and ministry, giving reasoning, examples, a model to follow, and ultimately bringing us into a divine partnership where we actually co-labor with Him to bring about His intended plans and purposes on earth.

God, help me to hold a space for Your mystery in my thinking. Help me to
never minimize or explain away who You are in an effort to protect myself.

REST: We are written into the equation as an expression of His sovereignty, not in violation of it. Some things He will do with or without us. And then there are some things that are in His heart that will not get done if we don't do our part. For example, Jesus is going to return, whether we vote yes or no. It is established. But on the other hand, He is not willing that any should perish, but that all should come to repentance. His will is for all to come to Him. But without our co-laboring by preaching the gospel of the Kingdom, it simply won't happen—even though it is God's will.

It is a great expression of My sovereignty that I chose to partner with
you, allowing My nature to be revealed in My creation. I know what
I'm doing. Won't you join Me?

February 7ᵗʰ

Your kingdom come, your will be done, on earth as it is in heaven.
—Matthew 6:10 NIV

RISE: The salvation of every citizen within a community does not necessarily mean that that city will automatically be like Heaven on earth. It's a painful realization, but seldom does it feel like Heaven on earth when we step into most of our churches. There's something more that must be embraced and practiced for that aspect of His will to be fully realized. It starts with the supreme value of Heaven, and that is His presence. Everything is attached to the presence of the Lord, which in biblical language means His face. The regard for the presence of God must have practical application for church life for us to have His intended will to be done here on earth.

I long for Your presence above all else, God. Help me to keep Your face always in front of me, forever my first priority.

REST: His world works differently than this one. He gave us both permission and a command to seek for His world to shape this one. It's a revolutionary position that we have been assigned. His intended purposes and plans include the transformation of culture and society. But there is no transformation of the world around us if there is no transformation of the world within us. We will always re-create around us the reality that exists within us. That is both good news and bad, depending on how well we have dealt with the issues of our hearts. Realizing that God has a plan and purpose for our city should affect the way we think and act. It is a partial evidence of the mind being renewed, as we think, plan, pray, and live according to His desires and dreams for our lifetime. Discovering His purposes fills our days with possibility-thinking, not thinking focused on evil or calamity.

I created you to be a dreamer, a problem-solver, a creator like Me. There is no darkness within the world that is a surprise to Me, nor any problem that I do not already have a solution for.

February 8th

Your lives light up the world. Let others see your light from a distance,
for how can you hide a city that stands on a hilltop? And who would
light a lamp and then hide it in an obscure place? Instead, it's placed
where everyone in the house can benefit from its light.

—Matthew 5:14-15 TPT

RISE: God is looking for a generation that He can use as builders to bring about His intended purposes for cities and nations. This kind of transformation of society doesn't happen by us being on the outside. It happens from within.

Open my eyes, Lord, to the gifts and talents that You've intentionally
placed within me to give to the world. Help me to steward them, to
develop them, and to execute them with excellence in whatever area You
have called me. Give me favor among men so that I can show Your true
nature to the world.

REST: We are the light of the world. As such, we are to be the city set on a hill that attracts lost people to come and find salvation, healing, and safety. This ministry attracts people to us. It is vital and needed.

You are My light to the world. You don't have to muster up your own
brilliance, though. I will pour My light into you. You simply receive it,
and you will always have more than enough to share with the world.

February 9th

You are the salt of the earth; but if the salt loses its flavor, how shall
it be seasoned? It is then good for nothing but to be thrown out and
trampled underfoot by men.

—Matthew 5:13 NKJV

RISE: We are also the salt of the earth. We are to add flavor to life in our communities. As long as we keep to ourselves, hoping the world will find their way into our meetings and embrace our values, we are the salt that is effectively tasteless. We must be sprinkled into the systems of this world to have full effect. Interestingly, the word *tasteless* means "to be foolish." I'd like to suggest that the picture of the Church being tasteless is a picture of the Church that fails to bring the influence of wisdom into the environments that God has assigned us to. Foolishness is in obvious contrast to wisdom. God has a purpose in the last days that is way bigger than anything any of us would ever think of: the transformation of the world around us.

Jesus, I pray for the wisdom and the courage to bring flavor to the world.
Fill me with all of the attributes of You that every person hungers for.

REST: Our role is multifaceted. It includes living a holy life, being filled with compassion, and demonstrating His power. But one more thing must be added for us to bring about God's purposes on the earth: wisdom. God is looking for us to become the servants of all, bringing the flavor of His wisdom into the systems of this world, that people might see and taste of His kindness. For it is still true that it is His kindness that leads to repentance. (See Romans 2:4.) This is the greatest hour for evangelism in all history, being set up with the greatest tool in all history—the people of God becoming all that God intended to give credibility to the message we preach.

You must fill your heart with holy affection for your city before you
set out to change her. Love the world as I do. It has always been My
kindness that leads people to a change of heart.

February 10th

No longer do I call you slaves, for the slave does not know what his
master is doing; but I have called you friends, for all things that I have
heard from My Father I have made known to you.

—John 15:15 NASB

RISE: Toward the end of His earthly life, Jesus gave His disciples the ultimate promotion. He told the twelve that He no longer called them servants, but friends. To be
in the same room with Him, or even to admire Him from a distance, was more than
they could have asked for. But Jesus brought them into His life. They had proven themselves worthy of the greatest promotion ever experienced by humanity—from servants
to intimates. With this promotion, the disciples' attention would now shift from the
task at hand to the One within reach. They were given access to the secrets in the heart
of God.

> *Thank You, Jesus, that I get to be Your friend! I want to spend time with*
> *You, to hear Your thoughts and know Your heart.*

REST: When Jesus gave His disciples this promotion, He did so by describing the
difference between the two positions. Servants don't know what their master is doing.
They don't have access to the personal, intimate realm of their master. They are task-ori-
ented. Obedience is their primary focus—and rightly so, for their lives depend on
success in that area. But friends have a different focus. It almost sounds blasphemous
to say that obedience is not the top concern for the friend, but it is true. Obedience
will always be important. But friends are less concerned about disobeying than they
are about disappointing. The disciples' focus shifted from the commandments to the
presence, from the assignment to the relationship, from "what I do for Him" to "how
my choices affect Him." This bestowal of friendship made the revolution we continue
to experience possible.

> *My heart is open to you. I want to be so close to you that our hearts*
> *impact one another. I'm not scared of disappointment; I love you, and*
> *I long to be close to you.*

February 11th

And Jesus answered and said to her, "Martha, Martha, you are
worried and troubled about many things. But one thing is needed,
and Mary has chosen that good part, which will
not be taken away from her."

—Luke 10:41-42 NKJV

RISE: Several paradigm shifts take place in our hearts as we embrace the promotion from servants to friends. First, *what we know* changes, as we gain access to the heart of the Father. Second, our *experience* changes. Encounters with God as an intimate are quite different from those of a servant. Third, our *function* in life radically changes. Instead of working *for* Him, we work *with* Him. We work not *for* His favor but *from* His favor. Fourth, our *identity* is radically transformed. Our identity sets the tone for all we do and become.

> *Father, help me to truly understand who I am in You. I don't want to*
> *perform for love anymore; I want work from Your favor.*

REST: The classic example of the difference between servants and friends is found in the story of Mary and Martha. Mary chose to sit at Jesus' feet while Martha chose to work in the kitchen. But Martha was making sandwiches that Jesus never ordered. Doing more for God is the method servants use to increase in favor. A friend has a different focus entirely. They enjoy the favor they have and use it to spend time with their friend. To say we need both Marys and Marthas is to miss the point entirely. And it simply isn't true. I've heard it said that nothing would ever get done if we didn't have Marthas. That, too, is a lie. Mary wasn't a non-worker; she just learned to serve from His presence, only making the sandwiches that Jesus ordered. Working *from* His presence is better than working *for* His presence. A passionate lover will always outperform a good servant in pleasing Him.

> *Come close to Me, My precious child. Let Me whisper into your heart*
> *how dear you are to Me, how accepted you are, how much I delight in*
> *you. Let those words ring in your ears forever.*

February 12th

Draw near to God and He will draw near to you.

—James 4:8 NKJV

RISE: We usually think of the will of God as something static—fixed and unchangeable. We primarily associate it with specific events at certain times. The element missing in our understanding of this subject is our role in the unfolding of His will. When God was going to destroy Israel, He told Moses to get out of the way, because He was going to kill the people that Moses had led out of Egypt into the wilderness. Moses then reminded God that they weren't his people—they were God's, and not only that, he didn't lead them out of Egypt, God did! God responded by basically acknowledging he was right, and then promised not to kill them. The astonishing thing isn't so much that God changed His mind and spared Israel; rather, it was that He expected Moses to come into the counsel of His will, and Moses knew it.

> *I long to know You as well as Moses did, God. Give me an understanding heart so that I might know You more.*

REST: Abraham was another covenant friend of God who held an awareness of God's expectation that His friends would be involved in the demonstration of His will, influencing the outcome of a matter. They understood that the responsibility rested on their shoulders, and they must act before God to get what people needed. The priestly role of an intercessor was never more clearly illustrated. The primary focus of His will wasn't whether or not to destroy Israel; it was to bring Moses in on the process. His will is not always focused on events; it is focused on His friends drawing near into His presence, standing in their roles as delegated ones. The will of God is as much process as it is outcome—often fluid, not static.

> *My will is never separate from My character. My desire is that you would know My heart so well that you would reflect it back to Me when we talk, confidently standing before Me as a beloved friend.*

February 13th

*This [is what] I command you: that you love and
unselfishly seek the best for one another.*

—John 15:17 AMP

RISE: Surrounding their promotion to friendship, Jesus gave His disciples a blank check of sorts that they were to live by and use throughout their lives for the expansion of the Kingdom. For us to properly receive what Jesus has offered us in verses like the one above, any robotic understanding of what it means to be a follower of God has to change. God never intended that the believer be a puppet on a string. God actually makes Himself vulnerable to the desires of His people. In fact, it can be said, "if it matters to you, it matters to Him."

> *Thank You so much, Jesus, that I don't have to be a robot in order to please You! Thank You that, in fact, You want me to be fully myself when I come before You. I want to believe everything You say about me, but I need Your help.*

REST: While much of the Church is waiting for the next word from God, He is waiting to hear the dream of His people. He longs for us to take our role, not because He needs us, but because He loves us. God joyfully makes Himself vulnerable to the desires of His people.

> *You are Mine, every part of you. As you spend time with Me, lean into those things you daydream about even if they seem too big, too scary to talk about out loud. I am a God of the impossible. Share your wildest dreams with Me; I want to know every part of you.*

February 14th

You did not choose me, but I chose you and appointed you so that you might go and bear fruit—fruit that will last—and so that whatever you ask in my name the Father will give you.

—John 15:16 NIV

RISE: There is no question that spending time with God changes our desires. We always become like the one we worship. But it's not because we've been programmed to wish for the things He wants us to wish for; it's because in friendship we discover the things that please Him—the secret things of His heart. It is the instinct of the true believer to search for and find, that which brings pleasure to the Father. Our nature actually changes at conversion. It is our new nature to seek to know God and to please Him with our thoughts, ambitions, and desires.

My nature is changing as we speak! Thank You, Jesus, that I am becoming more and more like You.

REST: The question should not be, "Are my desires from God?" The question should be, "With what, or with whom have I been in communion?" I can commune with God or with the enemy. If I take time to ponder an offense I experienced some years ago, and I begin to wonder if God ever judged that person, the desires of vindication and retaliation will stir up in my heart. Why? Because I have been fellowshipping with the *father* of bitterness, and those desires are the *children* formed in my heart. If fellowshipping with evil can produce evil desires in us, how much more should it be said that time with God forms desires in us that have eternity in mind and ultimately bring Him glory? The thing to note is this: these desires are not there by command; they are in our hearts because of our fellowship with God. They are the offspring of our relationship with Him.

The dreams of your heart are one of the ways I have designed You to impact the world. The enemy would be delighted if his critical lies silenced you, but nothing can stop us when we dream together.

February 15th

If you ask anything in My name, I will do it.

—John 14:14 NKJV

RISE: Many believers discount their desires, automatically trying to get rid of everything they want in order to prove their surrender to God. Their selfless approach overshoots the will of God and actually denies the fact that God is the Father of the dreams and abilities within them. It sounds good on the outside because of its selfless religious appeal, but it works against God's purposes on the inside. Most still don't see the difference between the entrance to the Kingdom, and life in the Kingdom. We enter on a straight and narrow road, saying, *"Not my will but Yours be done."* The only door is Christ Jesus. The only way to find life in Christ is to come in complete abandonment to Him.

Jesus, help me to trust so much in Your transformational work in my life that I dream freely and confidently with You!

REST: But life in the Kingdom, which is past the narrow entrance of salvation, is completely different. It's bigger on the inside than it is on the outside. It is here we find the Lord saying to us that we're no longer servants, but friends. It's in that context He says that the Father will give us whatever we want. The emphasis is on *what you want*. Granted, we can't forget the context, or we'll just create more selfish people who confess Christ. Just as the Cross precedes the resurrection, so our abandonment to *His will* precedes God attending to *ours*. But the opposite emphasis also has dangers—if we never become people of desire, we will never accurately and effectively represent Christ on the earth.

You have been given a new identity as My sons and daughters, and I want you to explore the freedom within your dreams with Me. It may take practice to begin dreaming. That's OK. Let's start today.

February 16th

When hope's dream seems to drag on and on, the delay can be
depressing. But when at last your dream comes true,
life's sweetness will satisfy your soul.

—Proverbs 13:12 TPT

RISE: Solomon gave us this amazing statement. If there was anyone qualified to discuss fulfilled personal desires it was Solomon. We can't allow his disobedience later in life to deter us from the profound lessons learned through his obedience early in life. He experienced the power of having his heartfelt desires accomplished.

> *Father, let Your blessings pour out on me. Let everyone around me see*
> *Your hand on my life in such a way that they stop and marvel at how*
> *good You are.*

REST: Solomon's words revisit the subject of the tree of life found in Genesis. It connected Adam and Eve to eternity. (After eating the forbidden fruit, the angel of the Lord guarded the way to the tree of life so that Adam and Eve could not eat its fruit; it made eternal whatever it touched. It would make their sinful condition permanent—an eternal, unredeemable state.) Here we are told that a believer will experience the tree of life as their desires are fulfilled. This implies that those who taste the wonder of fulfilled desires in Christ will be given eternal perspective and identity through that fulfillment. The process of surrender, personal transformation, and fulfilled desires is the training ground for reigning with Christ forever.

> *Like any dear friends, as we spend time together, our hearts become*
> *more and more alike. Express your longings; share with Me your desires.*

February 17th

*He said, "Blessed be the Lord, the God of Israel, who spoke with His
mouth...saying, 'Since the day that I brought My people Israel from
Egypt, I did not choose a city out of all the tribes of Israel in which to
build a house that My name might be there, but I chose David to be
over My people Israel.' Now it was in the heart of my father David to
build a house for the name of the Lord, the God of Israel."*

—1 Kings 8:15-17 NASB

RISE: An extraordinary example of fulfilled dreams is illustrated in Solomon's building of a temple that his father, David, had planned. The building and consecration of
Solomon's temple is one of the most significant events in the Bible. Yet at the temple's
dedication, Solomon shared that God hadn't chosen a city, He chose a man, and the
idea for a temple was in the heart of the man. God basically said: The temple wasn't my
idea. *David* was my idea.

*Sometimes it feels so scary to dream, Papa. Help me to trust in Your
power, Your provision, and in Your delight. Help me to dream again!*

REST: David's creativity and desires helped write history because God embraced
them. David gave us many Kingdom principles, which set the direction in which we are
to live. It is as if he said, "Dreamers! Come! Let's dream together and write the story
of human history." You are God's idea, and He longs to see the treasure that is in your
heart. As we learn to dream with God we become co-laborers with Him.

*I have chosen you, not for what you can accomplish, but for who you are.
Come, open your heart, and place your dreams into My steady hands.*

February 18th

*So the Lord God formed from the ground all the wild animals and all
the birds of the sky. He brought them to the man to see what he would
call them, and the man chose a name for each one.*

—Genesis 2:19 NLT

RISE: In the Garden of Eden, God assigned Adam the task of naming all the animals.
Names had much richer meaning in those days because they represented the nature
of something. I believe that Adam was actually assigning to each animal its nature, its
realm of authority, and the dimension of glory it would enjoy. In reality, Adam's assignment was to help define the nature of the world he was to live in. This co-laboring role
was a creative role, complimentary to God the Creator.

*Father, open my eyes to the places in my own life where You've given me
authority to co-labor with You. Give me the wisdom to use that creative
power wisely and for Your glory.*

REST: God brings us into these situations, not because He can't do it Himself. He
delights in seeing all that He made come into its identity in Him by embracing its
divine purpose. To embrace the privilege of creative expression is consistent with being
made in the image and likeness of our Creator.

*Have you ever watched a child create a whole world from a few blocks
and a couch cushion? I'm in that. I've given you the gift of creative
imagining with Me. Some of you will need to relearn this skill, but
that's alright—the children will lead you.*

February 19th

*This is the reason I urge you to boldly believe for whatever you ask for
in prayer—believe that you have received it and it will be yours.*

—Mark 11:24 TPT

RISE: We are to pay attention to our desires *while we're enjoying the presence of God in prayer.* Something happens in our time of communion with Him that brings life to our capacity to dream and desire. Our minds become renewed through divine encounter, making it the perfect canvas for Him to paint on. We become co-laborers with Him in the master plan for planet earth. Our dreams are not independent from God, but instead exist *because of* God. He lays out the agenda—*On earth as it is in Heaven*—and then releases us to run with it and make it happen!

> *Thank You, God, that You care so much about my dreams. I trust You to
> shape me in every way so that my dreams align with Your heart.*

REST: As we grow in intimacy with Him, more of what happens in life is a result of our desires, not simply receiving and obeying specific commands from Heaven. God loves to build on our wishes and desires, as He embraced David's desire for the temple. This truth is risky from our perspective because we see those who live independent of God and only want Him to validate their dreams. True grace always creates a place for those with evil in their heart to come to the surface through increased opportunity. But the richness of this truth is worth pursuing in spite of the perceived danger, because only this truth enables the Church to come fully into her destiny through co-laboring with the Lord.

> *I am not scared of selfish dreams. If you're heading in the wrong direction,
> I will correct your path. Don't stand still in fear of My discipline. I am
> not a punisher. Fly freely, dream as big as you can, and tether your heart
> with Mine. I won't let you go.*

February 20th

For if we have been united with him in a death like his, we will
certainly also be united with him in a resurrection like his.

—Romans 6:5 NIV

RISE: One of the most natural parts of being created in the image of God is the ability to dream. It's a God-given gift. Yet many believers, in their attempts to please God, kill the very capacity He gave them. If we pursue that line of thinking for long we end up with neutered believers. Self-mutilation need not be physical to be a perversion. Anytime we try to cut away at what God placed in us, we are entering a form of spirituality that the Scriptures do not support, and are contributing to a spirit that works against us having a truly effective witness. It is not wise to crucify the resurrected man and call it discipleship. The Cross is not for the new man; it's for the old man.

Jesus, I have been both crucified and resurrected with You. Let me never
act like what You did was not enough for my total transformation.

REST: Many have even prayed, "None of me, all of You." God had none of us before we were born and didn't like it. He created us for His pleasure. A better prayer would be, "All of me covered by all of You!" Even John the Baptist's statement, "He must increase but I must decrease" is often misapplied in order to endorse the self-depreciating form of Christianity. Look at the context; he was passing the baton to Jesus. His job was to prepare the way for the Messiah. It was important for him to be out of the way, as he closed out the Old Testament prophetic ministry. Jesus would bring about the fulfillment of all the prophets had announced and initiate God's manifest dominion on the planet. John the Baptist passed the baton to Jesus, who has passed it on to us *that we might increase.*

I created you to be the biggest, brightest version of yourself. That's the
version the world needs and the one I delight in partnering with.

February 21st

*Put on the new self, which in the likeness of God has been
created in righteousness and holiness of the truth.*

—Ephesians 4:24 NASB

RISE: The outpouring of the Spirit always brings an increased awareness of our sinfulness. Some of the greatest hymns of confession and contrition have been written during such seasons. But the revelation of our sin and unworthiness is only half of the equation. Most revivals don't get past this one point, and therefore cannot sustain a move of God until it becomes a lifestyle. It's difficult to build something substantial on a negative. The other half of the equation is how holy He is on our behalf and who we are as a result. When this is realized, our identity changes as we embrace the purpose of our salvation by faith. At some point we must go beyond being simply "sinners saved by grace." As we learn to live from our position in Christ, we will bring forth the greatest exploits of all time.

*Open my eyes, Holy Spirit, to my new reality of Christ in me. Help me
to fully grasp what it means that I have God's righteousness now.*

REST: Throughout much of church history people have been stripped of their God-given gifts, talents, and desires, under the guise of devotion to Christ. This stripped-down version of Christianity removes the believer from ministry, and relegates that privilege to a certain class of Christian called "ministers." The regular believer's role is reduced to financial and emotional support of those in public ministry. To work without fulfilled dreams and desires is to partner with the religious spirit that exalts routine without purpose, and calls it suffering. The honor of giving to promote ministry must not be devalued, but its emphasis should never be at the expense of each individual carrying their own creative expression of the Gospel through realizing their God-given dreams and desires.

*You are a minister of the gospel no matter where you are called to work.
Follow your passions and develop your skills with excellence; represent
Me well wherever you are planted.*

February 22nd

God's heavenly throne is eternal, secure, and strong,
and his sovereignty rules the entire universe.

—Psalm 103:19 TPT

RISE: Our heavenly Father is the Creator of all, and the Giver of all good gifts. His children should bear His likeness, which means they should be creative. When unbelievers lead the way in inventions and artistic expressions, it is because the Church has embraced a false kind of spirituality. It is not living in a true Kingdom mentality, which is the renewed mind. The renewed mind understands that the King's dominion must be realized in all levels of society for an effective witness to take place. Someone with a Kingdom mindset looks to the overwhelming needs of the world and says, "God has a solution for this problem. And I have legal access to His realm of mystery. Therefore, I will seek Him for the answer!" With a Kingdom perspective, we become the answer in much the same way Joseph and Daniel were to the kings of their day.

Help me, Father, to see problems in my family, my city, and my nation
as invitations for Your presence to invade through my renewed mind.

REST: To be free to dream with God, one must learn to be a co-laborer. The desire of the true believer is never independence from God. The goal is not to find ways to shape God's thinking, as though He needed our input. Instead it is to represent Him well. Learning to display His heart instinctively and accurately is the passion of true lovers of God. His heart is to redeem all people, and the tools He uses to display His goodness are gloriously vast, reaching into the heartfelt needs of every individual. Only divine wisdom can meet that challenge. Learning the dreams of God for this world is our beginning place. Dreaming can be expensive. We know that the Father's dream of redeeming humanity cost Him the life of His Son. However, partnering with Him in His dreams will release in us a new capacity to dream like Him.

I will never be dethroned. My Kingdom is ever-advancing, but My
desire is to work with you to bring practical, surprising solutions into
every arena. There's no issue that I do not care about.

February 23rd

*When He set for the sea its boundary so that the water would not
transgress His command, when He marked out the foundations of the
earth; then I was beside Him, as a master workman.*

—Proverbs 8:29-30 NASB

RISE: Wisdom and creativity are related subjects in the Bible. In fact, creativity is a manifestation of wisdom in the context of excellence and integrity. Wisdom is personified in Proverbs 8, and is the companion of God at the creation of all things. Therefore wisdom and creativity must not be separated in the mind of the believer. They are the essential tools needed to complete our assignment of being an effective witness to the lost. It is wisdom that makes our role in this world desirable to them.

> *If I've ever thought of myself as not creative, Lord, I repent. I am Your
> child, so I am creative by nature. Help me to see this reality become
> manifest in the world.*

REST: The six days of creation saw the most wonderful display of wisdom and art imaginable. As God spoke, the worlds were made. Light and beauty, sound and color, all flowed together seamlessly as wisdom set the boundaries for creation itself. Wisdom is given an artisan title of "master workman." Wisdom is not stoic as it is so often pictured. It's even more than happy; it is celebratory in nature and finds pleasure in the act of creation. But its greatest delight is in us! It has found perfect companionship with humanity. We were born to partner with wisdom—to live in it and display it through creative expression.

> *Let's go on a journey together to discover the unique style of creativity
> that I've placed in you. As My child, you are creative, but don't limit
> that to painting or drawing. Let's explore the many aspects of wisdom's
> workmanship that I've planted in your heart.*

February 24th

*And I have filled him with the Spirit of God, in wisdom, in
understanding, in knowledge, and in all manner of workmanship.*

—Exodus 31:3 NKJV

RISE: The first mention of a person filled with the Holy Spirit in Scripture was Bezalel. He was called upon to head up a building project for Moses. His assignment was to build God a house that He might dwell among His people. God revealed what He wanted that house to look like, but it would take a special gift of wisdom to know "how" to get it done. That is where Bezalel came into the picture. He was given supernatural wisdom to complete the task with artistic excellence. It was wisdom that qualified him to take on this assignment, and it was wisdom that enabled him as an artisan or master craftsman to design and build what was in God's heart.

> *I need Your wisdom, Father, to run after the dreams in my heart. I can't
> do this without You. Fill me daily with Your creative, wise Holy Spirit.*

REST: Later in this chapter of Exodus, artistic design, excellence, and inventive work are listed as a few of the characteristics of wisdom. That is part of what being filled with the Spirit looked like in Moses' day. The New Testament adds the power element, because every believer now has access to the miracle realm through the outpouring of the Holy Spirit. This new emphasis does not abolish the original revelation of the subject, but uses it as a foundation to build upon. If we combine the two we end up with believers who walk in wisdom, making practical contributions to the needs of society, who also confront the impossibilities of life through the provisions of the Cross, bringing solutions through supernatural display of miracles, signs, and wonders. Perhaps it is these two things working in tandem that should be considered *the balanced Christian life.*

> *Pay attention to what frustrates you about your city, your job, your
> home, but don't stop with annoyance. It's often there that I desire to
> meet you with supernaturally creative solutions.*

February 25th

*These are the horns that scattered Judah so that no one could raise
their head, but the craftsmen have come to terrify them and throw
down these horns of the nations who lifted up their horns against the
land of Judah to scatter its people.*

—Zechariah 1:21 NIV

RISE: This is one of the more alarming passages in the Bible. Not because it deals with spiritual warfare, but because God's tools for victory are not common knowledge for most of us today. In these verses, the people of God are being terrorized and scattered by abusive authorities and powers. Hopelessness is the theme of the day, and the confidence that God is with them is at an all-time low. The God of all wisdom illuminates a truth that is to awaken the people of God to His end-time plans. He sends forth His army to tear down the military strongholds. Who are His soldiers? Craftsmen! Not since God first sent a choir into war has there been such an outlandish strategy for battle. This is a plan that only Wisdom could design.

*Fashion me into one of Your craftsmen, Lord. I want to lead the charge
against the enemy with excellence and creativity!*

REST: When creativity is the normal expression of God's people there is something that happens to all who oppose Him. They become disheartened. The devil himself has no creative abilities whatsoever. All he can do is distort and deform what God has made. God is made known through His works. When His works flow through His children their identity is revealed, and there is an inescapable revelation of the nature of God in the land. He is irresistible to those who have eyes to see. Craftsmen are not simply woodworkers and painters. Nor does that title belong only to actors and musicians. Everyone, doing their God-given task with excellence, creativity, and integrity is a craftsman in the biblical sense.

*If failure was not an option, what's the thing you would do? Do that
with all of your might unto Me.*

February 26th

*So when the queen of Sheba saw the [depth of] Solomon's wisdom,
and the house which he had built, and the food of his table, the [vast]
seating order of his officials, the attendance and service of his ministers
and their attire, his cupbearers and their attire, and his stairway by
which he went up to the house of the Lord, she was breathless.*

—2 Chronicles 9:3-4 AMP

RISE: The world's definition of wisdom is focused on the attainment and use of knowledge. It's not wrong; it's just misleading. The Church has adopted their incomplete definition, pursuing a wisdom that has no soul. Biblical wisdom sees with divine perspective, and is the creative expression of God, bringing practical solutions to the issues of everyday life. Besides Jesus, Solomon was the wisest man to ever live. He caught the attention of his entire generation. People were in awe of his gift. The royalty in other nations envied his servants who had the privilege of being exposed to his gift on a daily basis.

*I want an understanding mind like Solomon, Lord. Let me never
forget that You have a solution—one You want to share—to every single
problem on the earth.*

REST: The effects of Solomon's wisdom brought Israel into the greatest time of peace and prosperity they had ever known. Wisdom, through one man, changed a nation. The wisdom of God will again be reflected in His people. The manifestations of wisdom are varied. Its nature can be seen in three words—integrity, creativity, and excellence. Divine wisdom springs from integrity, and becomes manifest through creative expression with excellence as its standard. Wherever we find ourselves operating in any of these three expressions we are being touched by divine wisdom.

*Imagine a world where millions of My children were embracing this
gift to live life as My favorite creative expression, bringing hope and
solutions to insurmountable problems. Imagine the difference, and
realize that this is possible!*

February 27th

So don't hide your light! Let it shine brightly before others, so that the commendable things you do will shine as light upon them, and then they will give their praise to your Father in heaven.

—Matthew 5:16 TPT

RISE: Many people feel disqualified from creativity because they have narrowly confined it to the world of art and music. They fail to realize that everyone has some measure of creativity, which should be consistently expressed throughout life. There are others who feel disqualified because they think that creativity always means we are to make something new or do something novel. In reality, most great ideas are actually the offspring of other concepts. It is wisdom that can take something that is an everyday item or concept and build upon it creating something new and better.

> *Father, help me to embrace the fullness of Your freedom. You have qualified me; that is all that I need to move forward in the direction of my dreams.*

REST: There is a misconception that often exists in the artistic community; creativity must come from pain. There's no question but that some of the greatest works of art came from people who were troubled with life, or experienced some of the worst tragedies. The reality is this—it often takes trauma to launch a person into a place of seeing the true priorities for life. The believer doesn't need that experience. Having our old nature crucified with Christ is the only tragedy needed to launch us into our proper roles of creative influence.

> *The world hasn't even begun to tap into the fullness of beauty and wisdom that I am prepared to release. Come into My presence and prepare to release the sounds, ideas, and visions of Heaven over the earth.*

February 28th

But the natural man does not receive the things of the Spirit of God,
for they are foolishness to him; nor can he know them,
because they are spiritually discerned.

—1 Corinthians 2:14 NKJV

RISE: The Church has a clear assignment: we are to exhibit the multifaceted wisdom of God, now! It must permeate all we are and do. This neglected element is at the heart of our call to disciple nations. It is a part of the "witness" that turns people's heads in the same way as the nations were impacted by Solomon's wisdom. It's our connection to wisdom that clearly manifests our eternal purpose of reigning with Christ. When we walk in wisdom, we mirror the reality of Heaven here on earth, and actually give Heaven a target for invasion. In the same way agreement with the devil empowers him to kill, steal, and destroy, so agreement with God releases God to accomplish His purposes in and through us to the world around us.

I want people to be drawn to Your heart through my life, Jesus. Help me
to walk in the fullest expression of Your wisdom.

REST: A reformation has begun. And at the heart of this great move of the Spirit is the total transformation of the people of God as they discover their true identity and purpose. Great purpose elicits great sacrifice. Up until this time, many of our agendas have failed. Our attempts to make the Gospel palatable have had a serious effect on the world around us. The world has longed for a message they could experience. Yet many believers have simply tried to make the good news more intellectually appealing. The natural mind cannot receive the things of the Spirit of God. The wisdom of God is foolishness to men. It's time to be willing to appear foolish again, that we might provide the world with a message of power that delivers, transforms, and heals. This is true wisdom. It alone satisfies the cry of the human heart.

Be careful that you do not turn Me into a kind but harmless version of
Santa Claus. I am Love, but I am also Jehovah.

March

March 1st

Before you do anything, put your trust totally in God and not in yourself. Then every plan you make will succeed.

—Proverbs 16:3 TPT

RISE: Many are discouraged because their dreams have failed. In their pain and frustration, they oppose the message that a believer has the right to dream. Here is a higher reality: when people pursue dreams but fail to see them fulfilled, they prepare the way for others who carry the same dream to eventually get the breakthrough that they were seeking. It is hard for many to take comfort in this thought, but that's because we usually think it's all about us. There is no failure in faith.

> *Bring to mind, Father, any moments in my life when I've felt failure. Will You show me how You see them?*

REST: Often a tragic loss here on earth is viewed quite differently in Heaven. What is honored in Heaven is frequently pitied or mocked here on earth. When a person dies while trying to live out an expression of faith, people often criticize the foolishness of their decision. Few realize that their loss became the soil in which someone else could eventually realize their dream, because their loss actually paved the way to a breakthrough. To our detriment, we have lived without the consciousness that a failed attempt at a dream often becomes the foundation of another person's success. Some water, others plant, and still others harvest. We all have an important role to set the stage for the King of kings to receive more glory. It's all about Him, not us.

> *Do not limit Me by your definition of success. I can see the big picture. If you feel defeated, come to Me. I will show you how proud I am of your faithful decisions.*

March 2nd

Everyone was impressed by how well Jesus spoke, in awe of the
beautiful words of grace that came from his lips. But they were
surprised at his presumption to speak as a prophet, so they said among
themselves, "Who does he think he is? This is Joseph's son,
who grew up here in Nazareth."

—Luke 4:22 TPT

RISE: An intellectual gospel is always in danger of creating a God that looks a lot like us; one that is our size. The quest for answers sometimes leads to a rejection of mystery. As a result, mystery is often treated as something intolerable, instead of a real treasure. Living with mystery is the privilege of our walk with Christ. Its importance cannot be overrated. If I understand all that is going on in my Christian life, I have an inferior Christian life. The walk of faith is to live according to the revelation we have received, in the midst of the mysteries we can't explain.

Expand my experience of You, God. Go past my logical understanding!
I want to encounter You in ways that leave me hungry for more.

REST: Not understanding is OK. Restricting our spiritual life to what we understand is not. It is immaturity at best. Such a controlling spirit is destructive to the development of a Christlike nature. God responds to faith but will not surrender to our demands for control. Maturity requires a heartfelt embrace of what we do not understand as an essential expression of faith.

Bring your questions to Me with a humble spirit. Leave them at My
feet. This is a relationship. I am not intimidated by your mind, but I
long to show you more than your mind can fully comprehend.

March 3rd

*And the peace of God, which surpasses all understanding, will
guard your hearts and minds through Christ Jesus.*

—Philippians 4:7 NKJV

RISE: Our spirit is where the Holy Spirit dwells. Our spirit is alive and well and is
ready to receive great things from God. When I filter everything through my mind and
remove what isn't immediately logical, I extract much of what I really need. Only what
goes beyond my understanding is positioned to renew my mind. If we can learn more
about the actual voice and presence of the Lord, we will stop being so paranoid about
being deceived by the things we can't explain.

> *Jesus, help my spirit to rise up and take its rightful place of leadership
> over my mind and body. My heart is yielded to You, even when I do not
> understand.*

REST: Our hearts can embrace things that our heads can't. Our hearts will lead us
where our logic would never dare to go. No one ever attributes the traits of courage and
valor to the intellect or the strength of human reasoning. Courage rises up from within
and gives influence over the mind. In the same way, true faith affects the mind. Faith
does not come from our understanding. It comes from the heart. We do not believe
because we understand; we understand because we believe. We'll know when our mind
is truly renewed, because the impossible will look logical.

> *I have designed every aspect of you to respond to My presence, to yield
> to My voice. Take My hand; trust that I will lead you better than your
> own discernment ever could.*

March 4th

And without faith it is impossible to please God, because anyone who comes to him must believe that he exists and that he rewards those who earnestly seek him.

—Hebrews 11:6 NIV

RISE: What we don't understand is sometimes as important as what we do. It's one thing to obey when He has given us understanding about a matter, and quite another to obey while facing questions and circumstances that seem to contradict what we understand. So many fail at this point, and then bring the Bible down to their level of experience. Many do this to feel better about the fact that they are living in compromise—a compromise of their revelation from Scripture. Our challenge is instead to bring our lifestyle up to the standard of God's Word.

> *Father, I want to be so connected to You that my obedience to Your direction is immediate and natural. Holy Spirit, empower me with God's grace to live in holiness and truth.*

REST: To embrace revelation with one hand, and embrace mystery with the other, forms a perfect cross. This is a cross that everyone who is hungry to do the works of Jesus will have to carry. God must violate our logic to invite us away from the deception of relying on our own reasoning.

> *Can you imagine the number of stars in your galaxy? Now, try to imagine the number of galaxies that I have set in the universe. The way your mind is stretching right now is the way I want to stretch your heart. There are so many wondrous things I want to show you, but you'll need to trust Me enough to follow Me into the unknown.*

March 5th

To Him who [always] loves us and who [has once for all] freed us [or washed us] from our sins by His own blood (His sacrificial death)— and formed us into a kingdom [as His subjects], priests to His God and Father—to Him be the glory and the power and the majesty and the dominion forever and ever. Amen.

—Revelation 1:5-6 AMP

RISE: It is the mercy of God to withhold revelation from those who have no hunger for truth, because if they don't hunger for it, the chances are they won't obey it when they hear it. Revelation always brings responsibility, and hunger is the thing that prepares our hearts to carry the weight of that responsibility. By keeping rev- elation from those without hunger, God actually protects them from certain failure to carry the responsibility it would lay on them. And so, He conceals. Yet, He doesn't conceal from us; He conceals for us!

Thank You, Father, that You care enough about my heart to protect me from revelation that I'm not ready for. I open my heart to You—prepare and mold me for greater understanding of You.

REST: But there's another part to this equation— "it's the glory of kings to search out a matter"! We are kings and priests to our God. Our royal identity never shines brighter than when we pursue hidden things with the confidence that we have legal access to such things. Mysteries are our inheritance. Our kingship, our role in ruling and reigning with Christ, comes to the forefront when we seek Him for answers to the dilemmas of the world around us.

It is natural for you to search for answers because that is how I've designed you. Pull close to Me in your hunger, seek out the treasures of My truth, and I will not disappoint you.

March 6th

*Let us be glad and rejoice and give Him glory, for the marriage of the
Lamb has come, and His wife has made herself ready.*

—Revelation 19:7 NKJV

RISE: It is very hard to imagine the Church bringing answers to the issues of life when much of our eschatology anticipates world conditions getting worse and worse. When we also believe that the darkness of world circumstances is the signal for Christ's return, we have a conflict that ultimately costs us a practical vision—to invade and transform the world system.

> *Holy Spirit, guide me into Your view of our world. Give me wisdom as
> I navigate various sources of information that seem to be shouting bad
> news. Fill me with Your hope!*

REST: Jesus is returning for a spotless Bride, whose Body is in equal proportion to her Head. If my faith for His return has its anchor in the darkness of the world around me, then I will do little to change it. Being made in His image gives us the privilege and responsibility to reflect His greatness to the world around us. The nations are looking for a people who can bring the answers to the issues facing our world.

> *Rise up, My child, take your rightful place with Me. Learn the ways
> of Heaven so that you can release My nature upon the earth. You were
> never made to shrink back or watch the world from the shadows. You
> are a reformer, a world-changer, because You are Mine.*

March 7th

Most assuredly, I say to you, he who believes in Me, the works that I do
he will do also; and greater works than these he will do,
because I go to My Father.

—John 14:12 NKJV

RISE: We don't need more people without authentic Kingdom experiences telling us what we can and cannot have in our lifetime. Those who walk out their faith with an experiential paradigm understand that we will always live in the tension of what we have seen and what we have yet to see, and that we are always moving on to more in God. This is an understanding by experience issue.

Fill me with boldness, Lord. I need to encounter You in ways that open
my mind and heart to what You deem to be possible. Help me to not be
limited by my own fear or even my own experiences. I want You—and
only You—to define my reality.

REST: Someone has to go beyond the boundaries of historical accomplishments and attempt something that has been considered impossible by their contemporaries. The Church is often known as the group that changes not. Very little of what exists today would exist at all if those who preceded us did not seek to surpass the boundaries experienced by their predecessors. And so it is with the Church. It is this adventure that God has called us to. And it is this adventure that we call the normal Christian life.

Many things have been considered impossible until the moment they
were accomplished. But My people are not hedged in by popular opinion
or the fear of failure. They hear My voice, calling them out on the water,
and they step out of the boat. Keep your eyes on Me; let's adventure
together.

March 8th

By God's will we have been purified and made holy once and for all through the sacrifice of the body of Jesus, the Messiah!
—Hebrews 10:10 TPT

RISE: A yielded imagination becomes a sanctified imagination; and it's the sanctified imagination that is positioned for visions and dreams. There is great paranoia over the use of the imagination in the Church of the Western world. As a result; unbelievers often lead the way in creative expression—through the arts and inventions. They have no bias against imagination.

> *I repent for any way I've limited my imagination because of fear or a religious spirit. I long to meet You in my daydreams, God. Inspire my imagination with Your wisdom and creativity.*

REST: The imagination is like a canvas to a painter. If it's clean, the artist has much to work with. God would love to use our imagination to paint His impressions upon; He just looks for those who are yielded. However, those who are preoccupied with "not being worthy" are too self-centered to be trusted with much revelation. At some point it has to stop being about us long enough to utilize the benefits of being in Christ for the sake of those around us. Such a position gives us unlimited access to the mysteries of God that enable us to touch the needs of a dying world.

> *I accept you. I am proud of you. You have been chosen by Me forever. Settle into the foundation of My love so that we can build together. Don't look back in doubt. Accept My acceptance once and for all, and let's release the Kingdom onto this broken world.*

March 9th

And Jesus came up and spoke to them, saying, "All authority
has been given to Me in heaven and on earth."

—Matthew 28:18 NASB

RISE: We have been given authority over this planet. It was first given to us in the commission God gave to mankind in Genesis (see Gen. 1:28-29). and was then restored to us by Jesus after His resurrection. But Kingdom authority is different than is typically understood by many believers. It is the authority to set people free from torment and disease, destroying the works of darkness. It is the authority to move the resources of Heaven through creative expression to meet human need. It is the authority to bring Heaven to earth. It is the authority to serve.

> *Father, my heart breaks for the brokenness I see all around me. Help me*
> *to step into the authority You've given me so that I can see Your heart*
> *manifest in each situation.*

REST: As with most Kingdom principles, the truths of humanity's dominion and authority are dangerous in the hands of those who desire to rule over others. These concepts seem to validate some people's selfishness. But when these truths are expressed through the humble servant, the world is rocked to its core. Becoming servants to this world is the key to open the doors of possibility that are generally thought of as closed or forbidden.

> *Let your heart be broken. Let yourself be stirred with compassion for the*
> *pain and suffering you see in the world. But don't stop there. Heal the*
> *sick, comfort the brokenhearted, bring freedom to the captives, raise the*
> *dead, release all that I've put inside of you!*

March 10th

For even the Son of Man did not come expecting to be served by
everyone, but to serve everyone, and to give his life as the ransom price
in exchange for the salvation of many.

—Mark 10:45 TPT

RISE: Neither our understanding of servants or of kings can help us much with this challenge for both are soiled in our world, probably beyond repair. That is where Jesus comes in. He is the King of all kings, yet the Servant of all. This unique combination found in the Son of God is the call of the hour upon us. As truth is usually found in the tension of two conflicting realities, we have an issue to solve. Like our Master we are both royalty and servants. Solomon warns of a potential problem, saying, *"the earth cannot bear up under a slave when he becomes king"* (Prov. 30:21-22). Yet Jesus contradicted Solomon's warning without nullifying the statement, by being effective at both. *Jesus served with the heart of a king, but ruled with the heart of a servant.* This is the essential combination that must be embraced by those longing to shape the course of history.

> *Holy Spirit, shape my heart. Knock off any rough areas of insecurity,*
> *seal up the truth of my identity in my heart so that I can serve like Jesus*
> *did.*

REST: Royalty is my identity. Servanthood is my assignment. Intimacy with God is my life source. So, before God, I'm an intimate. Before people, I'm a servant. Before the powers of hell, I'm a ruler, with no tolerance for their influence. Wisdom knows which role to fulfill at the proper time.

> *You have been made in My image—ruler, servant, tender-hearted*
> *friend. Model yourself after Me as seen in the life of Jesus. He is perfect*
> *theology—united with the God the Father, powerful over the enemy,*
> *and the servant of all.*

March 11th

Whoever can be trusted with very little can also be trusted with much,
and whoever is dishonest with very little will also
be dishonest with much.

—Luke 16:10 NIV

RISE: There is no such thing as secular employment for the believer. Once we are born again, everything about us is redeemed for Kingdom purposes. It is all spiritual. It is either a legitimate Kingdom expression, or we shouldn't be involved at all. Every believer is in full-time ministry—only a few have pulpits in sanctuaries. The rest have their pulpit in their areas of expertise and favor in the world system. Be sure to preach only good news. And when necessary, use words!

Open my eyes, Lord, to see all of the opportunities You've placed in front
of me to express Your Kingdom. Destroy every box I've inadvertently
placed around Your presence, and help me to share Your heart with
those around me.

REST: The call of God is important, not because of the title it carries (or doesn't carry). It's valuable because of the One who called us. An assignment to be in business is as valuable in the Kingdom as is the call to be an evangelist. The privilege to be a stay-at-home wife and mother is equal in importance to being a missionary. Embrace your call with the faithfulness and thankfulness worthy of the One who has called you. Our eternal rewards do not come because of how much money we made, how many souls were saved, or how many homeless people we fed. All rewards are given based on our faithfulness to what God has given and called us to be and to do. The honor we give to one another must not be only to those who have obvious spiritual occupations. Honor must be given to those who are faithful in the call, no matter what it is.

How dull this world would be if all of My children wanted to follow
the same path. I've infused the world with diversity on purpose! Only a
diverse world can begin to express My multi-faceted nature.

March 12th

*Beloved ones, God has called us to live a life of freedom in the Holy
Spirit. But don't view this wonderful freedom as an opportunity to set
up a base of operations in the natural realm. Freedom means that we
become so completely free of self-indulgence that we become servants of
one another, expressing love in all we do.*

—Galatians 5:13 TPT

RISE: The goal for all ministry is the transformation of society itself by invading the systems of the city in order to serve. Serving for their benefit, not ours, is the key. As someone once said, "We shouldn't try to be the best *in* the world. We should try to be the best *for* the world!" When we set aside our religious agendas to make others a success, we have learned the Kingdom mind-set, and have become a part of the transformation movement.

*Jesus, help me to see the practical, felt needs of my family, my city, and
my nation. I want to be Your hands and feet, serving for the purpose of
releasing Your love onto the earth.*

REST: The Church is sometimes known for its willingness to serve, but usually with well-meaning spiritual agendas as the ultimate goal. It almost sounds blasphemous, but serving simply to get people saved is a religious agenda. As pure and noble as it may seem to us as believers, it is manipulative to the world, and is viewed as impure service. The world can smell it a mile away. We put them on the defensive when we carry such reasons for serving into their sphere of responsibility. But, for example, when we volunteer in our local school to help the principal succeed, then we've crossed the line into territory seldom visited by the Church. It is serving for the benefit of another. It's that kind of a servant that the world welcomes.

*Pray for your leaders, whether you agree with them or not. Serve in a
way that shows My excellence and My kindness, and leave the rest up
to Me.*

March 13th

And whatever you do, do it heartily, as to the Lord and not to men.

—Colossians 3:23 NKJV

RISE: Perhaps you've heard it said, "God is number one, the family is number two, and the Church is number three…" That unofficial list is important as it outlines a few of the priorities in a Christian's life that have become confused through the years. I know of many tragedies in pastor's families because they ignored these priorities of Kingdom living. Yet, as good as this list is, it isn't technically accurate. When God is number one, there is no number two.

> *I'm so grateful for the freedom that is found in You, God. Thank You that, because You are my priority, I can pursue the things on my heart as worship to You.*

REST: Out of my love for God, I give myself to my wife and kids. It's not separate from the Lord, but is unto Him. It's not that I can't love my wife without loving God—many unbelievers do that well. But in knowing and loving God, I am released to a measure of supernatural love that is unattainable apart from God. It should be said that anyone who is completely abandoned to God should love others more than they thought possible. It is because of my passion for Jesus that I love the Church the way I do. My love for God is my love for life. They cannot be separated. Loving my family, church, ministry…is an expression of my love for God. God being number one, the only One.

> *I love seeing you play with your children, dance in the kitchen with your spouse, laugh with your friends, and work with integrity at your job. Similarly, it blesses Me to see you serve in your church or share the Gospel with passion. When I have your heart, all that flows from it celebrates our union.*

March 14ᵗʰ

If someone says, "I love God," and hates his brother, he is a liar; for the one who does not love his brother whom he has seen, cannot love God whom he has not seen.

—1 John 4:20 NASB

RISE: Passion for God gives birth to a passion for other things. And it's those other things that are often to be pursued as unto the Lord. We shouldn't experience them as something in competition with, or separate from our devotion to God. If we love God it will be measurable by our love for people. This is such an absolute principle that God says if we don't love others, we don't actually love Him. The point is this: in the wake of our passion for God, passion for other things is created. It is often in giving ourselves to those things that we prove and manifest our love for God.

Help me, God, to love well every person You place before me. Help me to love those closest to me with Your patient consistency.

REST: When we live with genuine passion for God, it creates a passion for other things. While it is possible to value other things above God, it is not possible to value God without valuing other things. This is the key point confronting the religious mindset, which dismisses everything not considered sacred. The effort to accomplish the goal of loving God with no other passions has had to create a monastic lifestyle to survive. And while I admire many of the monastic believers in the past, it is not the model that Jesus gave us. The way we steward the rest of life becomes the litmus test that demonstrates an authentic love for God.

To know Me, to truly share My heart, is to share My love for the world. I've created you to be the salt and the light of the world—engage, participate, share My love with everything you do.

March 15th

Take delight in the Lord, and he will give you your heart's desires.

—Psalm 37:4 NLT

RISE: Most people have a list of things they pray for. They represent the basic desires and needs of our lives and of those we love. If they're not written down on paper, they're at least written in our hearts. On the list are things which have obvious eternal significance—prayer for cities, for the salvation of certain people, healing breakthrough, etc. Following that, there is often a "it would be nice" section of the list. But sometimes God will bypass both of those and go directly to the "I haven't even bothered to ask" part that dwells somewhere deep in our hearts. It is a pleasant and sometimes offensive move.

> *Illuminate the kisses from You, God, that You've sprinkled throughout my day. Help me to not bypass the "unimportant" answered prayers, but to use every opportunity to celebrate Your goodness.*

REST: When God bypasses all of our prayers that have such eternal significance and answers something temporal and seemingly insignificant, it can be confusing. If given the choice, many of us would prefer for God to let us use this trump card for something more important. But He wants to teach us something important: Our requests are important, but our view of Him is more important. If it matters to us, it matters to Him. His bypassing our "urgent" prayer list, my "it would be nice" list, and entering the "secret desires of the heart" list reveals more about our heavenly Father than answering all the other things I had been praying about. .

> *I am revealing My love for you throughout the day. Don't focus so much on your big prayers that you miss these precious moments. I see you. I know you. I love every part of you.*

March 16th

*Yes, feast on all the treasures of the heavenly realm and fill your
thoughts with heavenly realities, and not with the distractions of the
natural realm. Your crucifixion with Christ has severed the tie to this
life, and now your true life is hidden away in God in Christ.*

—Colossians 3:2-3 TPT

RISE: People who see what is unseen have the advantage over everyone else who desire a place of significance. They are the ones who are able to live from Heaven toward earth. When we live conscious of Heaven and eternity, it changes the way we live and radically increases our measure of impact on society. It's really quite amazing that the ones who see Heaven most clearly have little desire for this world, yet they are the ones who have the greatest impact on the world around them

*Holy Spirit, I want the reality of Heaven to be on my mind at all times.
Lead me back to this reality any time I become tangled up in the fears
and pains of this world.*

REST: Awareness of unseen things is a vital aspect of the Christian life. The abundant life that Jesus promised to His disciples is found in this unseen realm. The display of His dominion through miracles and various supernatural expressions are all rooted in this heavenly world. We must access His world to change this one.

*For now, you live in two worlds. But these two realities are not to be
equally prominent. You have been crucified and resurrected with
Christ, seated with Me in Heaven. You live from Heaven to earth, from
provision to lack, from solutions to problems. Heaven is to be your lens,
your homeland, your mother tongue. Earth is to be your target.*

March 17th

I pray that the Father of glory, the God of our Lord Jesus Christ,
would impart to you the riches of the Spirit of wisdom and the Spirit
of revelation to know him through your deepening intimacy with him.

—Ephesians 1:17 TPT

RISE: Changing the course of world history is our assignment. Yet we have gone as far as we can with what we presently know. We need signs to get where we want to go. Signs are realities that point to a greater reality—an exit sign is real, but it points to something greater—the exit. We don't need signs when we travel on familiar roads. But, if we're going to go where we've never gone before, we'll need signs to get there. These signs will restore the wonder.

You promised to be with me always, so I can step out into the unknown,
trusting that You will guide me in every circumstance.

REST: A fundamental lesson for us in this historic fact is that even a church in revival, known for great teaching and citywide impact, needs more revelation. It is not automatic. To say, "The Spirit of God is welcome here, and free to do as He pleases" is not enough. Many of the things we need and long for must be prayed for specifically, and pursued relentlessly. Such is the case with the spirit of wisdom and revelation. Only when wisdom and revelation are passionately pursued do they take the place they deserve in the Christian life. These two elements become the safeguards that keep us from the peril of religion. The foremost apostle prayed this for the foremost church.

Stay hungry for more of My presence. There is no limit to My desire to
share Myself with My Body. The face of Moses shone with My glory, and
you live in a better covenant than he ever did. You will never regret
pursuing more of Me.

March 18th

For the word of God is living and active, sharper than any two-edged
sword, piercing to the division of soul and of spirit, of joints and of
marrow, and discerning the thoughts and intentions of the heart.

—Hebrews 4:12 ESV

RISE: God spoke and the worlds were made. His Word creates. The ability to hear God, especially from His Word, is a mandatory skill if we are to enter divine purpose and true creative expression. It's as necessary as breathing. A yielded heart is impressionable as it studies Scripture and receives God's impressions (fingerprints) easily. Within that sort of tender soil, the Lord plants the seeds of Kingdom perspective that grow into global transformation.

> *Stir up my passion for Your Scriptures, God. Let me encounter Your*
> *Word daily and receive life from it.*

REST: The insights and empowering nature of Scripture provide solutions applicable to every society and culture. The Bible is limitless in scope, timeless, and complete, containing answers to every dilemma of humanity. The study of Scriptures must take us beyond the historical setting, beyond language studies in the Hebrew and Greek, and at times beyond the context and intent of the human authors of Scripture. It's time to hear from God afresh—that His Word would once again become the living Word in our experience.

> *Don't be ashamed if you haven't felt excited about reading My Word.*
> *Instead, pray for the passion. I want to stir up your hunger. My Word is*
> *alive, a place of encounter that I have prepared for you.*

March 19th

*In the beginning was the Word, and the Word
was with God, and the Word was God.*

—John 1:1 KJV

RISE: God is still speaking but everything we hear must be consistent with what He has spoken to us in His Word. In light of these burning convictions, there are standards and traditions instituted by the Church for our protection that practically suck the life and impact out of God's living Word. Though not the original intent, it has been an unintended result.

> *Thank You, Father, that I can practice hearing Your voice without fear because of the gift of Your anointed Word—the standard that I can measure everything I hear against. Help me to internalize Scriptures so well that Your Word is constantly in my heart.*

REST: Being unaware of His presence has cost us dearly, especially as we approach Scripture. King David, who authored and sang songs of His love for God's Word, "set" the Lord before himself daily. He purposed to be regularly conscious of God's nearness and lived from that mindset. The sanctified imagination is a tool in God's hand that enables us to tap into true reality. My approach is this; since I can't imagine a place where He isn't, I might as well imagine Him with me. This is not vain imagination. Rather, it's vain to imagine otherwise.

> *I am here, beside you, within you, closer than your breath. Practice training your senses to become more and more aware of My presence throughout the day. Then, you will begin to realize how present I truly am with you in every moment.*

March 20th

For those who are led by the Spirit of God are the children of God.

—Romans 8:14 NIV

RISE: To value the Scriptures above the Holy Spirit is idolatry. It is not Father, Son, and Holy Bible; it's the Holy Spirit. The Bible reveals God, but is itself not God. It does not contain Him. God is bigger than His book. We are reliant on the Holy Spirit to reveal what is contained on the pages of Scripture, because without Him it is a closed book.

> *Holy Spirit, I need You to guide me through the Scriptures. Open up God's Word, implant it in my heart, help me to encounter Him in new ways.*

REST: Such dependency on the Holy Spirit must be more than a token prayer asking for guidance before a Bible study. It is a relationship with the third person of the Trinity that is continuous, ongoing, and affects every single aspect of life. He is the wind that blows in uncertain directions, from unknown places (see John 3:8). He is the power of Heaven, and cannot be controlled, but must be yielded to. He eagerly reveals His mysteries to all who are hungry— truly hungry. He is so valued in Heaven that He comes with a warning. The Father and Son can be sinned against, but sinning against the Holy Spirit has unforgivable eternal consequences.

> *I've given you the most precious gift I have—My own Spirit—to teach, comfort, empower, and guide you. Even the giants of the faith, like Abraham, Moses, and David, did not have My Spirit living inside of them. Treasure Him. Make your heart supple to His direction.*

March 21st

*I know that you delight to set your truth deep in my spirit. So come
into the hidden places of my heart and teach me wisdom.*

—Psalm 51:6 TPT

RISE: The Word of God is living and active. It contains divine energy, always moving
and accomplishing His purposes. It is the surgeon's knife that cuts in order to heal. It is
balm that brings comfort and healing. But the point I wish to stress is that it is multidi-
mensional and unfolding in nature. For example, when Isaiah spoke a word, it applied
to the people he spoke to—his contemporaries. Yet because it is alive, much of what
he said then has its ultimate fulfillment in another day and time. Living words do that.

> *God, help me to hear what You are saying to me now for this moment
> in time. I want to be like the sons of Issachar, understanding the times
> and hearing You clearly.*

REST: God said we were to choose whom we would serve, yet Jesus said He chose us;
we didn't choose Him. We are predestined from before the foundation of the world, yet
are told that whosoever will may come. Jesus said we had to sell all to follow Him, yet
He instructs the wealthy to be rich in good works. The Holy Spirit knows what truth to
breath on according to the particular season of our life.

> *Don't worry if how I speak to your pastor, your neighbor, or your friend
> is not the same as how I speak to you. I created mankind to hear My
> voice, but I designed each of My children differently. Some see divine
> images, others have inspired thoughts, and some just feel My peace. Let's
> go a journey together to discover our own way of communicating.*

March 22nd

You gave Your good Spirit to instruct them, your manna You did not
withhold from their mouth, and You gave them water for their thirst.

—Nehemiah 9:20 NASB

RISE: Doctrine must be a wineskin kept elastic by the oil of the Spirit. If it is rigid
and unmoving, it will not yield to God's habit of opening up more of His Word to us.
God loves to add to our knowledge things we think we already understand. Too much
rigidity bursts our doctrinal wineskins under the weight of ongoing revelation. The end
result is the Church becomes irrelevant and powerless to the world around them.

> *Father, forgive me for any area in my life where I have grown stiff*
> *against the move of Your Spirit. I want more of You at any cost, so I*
> *yield every structure, assumption, and design of my own at Your feet.*

REST: The Holy Spirit has to be free to speak to us about the things that are on His
heart; especially to those things we have a natural resistance. We must be open to truth
when it has a biblical basis and is accompanied by the breath of God making it come
alive for a specific purpose. The error is building a theological monument around a particular point of view that conveniently excludes certain portions of Scripture to help us
feel secure in a doctrinal bent.

> *Too often the structures built by man become rigid, excluding the move*
> *of My Spirit. The wineskin is crucial. Without it, the new wine of My*
> *Spirit would be poured out and lost. But if the wineskin becomes old,*
> *brittle, and inflexible, it will become irrelevant. Stay connected to My*
> *presence, stay flexible to My Spirit, and stay rooted in My Word.*

March 23rd

Then Jesus exclaimed, "Father, thank you, for you are Lord, the
Supreme Ruler over heaven and earth! And you have hidden the great
revelation of your authority from those who are proud and wise in
their own eyes. Instead, you have shared it
with these who humble themselves."

—Matthew 11:25 TPT

RISE: The desire for rigid doctrine is in direct proportion to our inability to actually hear His voice. It's essential to be able to recognize His voice so we can embrace His revelation, even when it contradicts our traditional upbringing.

I pray that I would remain open to receiving every moment of correction, encouragement, and guidance from Your presence, Lord. Help me to always pursue You above my own thoughts of You.

REST: God is big enough to feed me from a particular verse every day for the rest of my life. The Word of God is infinitely deep. I must come to that which I understand with a childlike heart because what I know can keep me from what I need to know if I don't remain a novice. Becoming an expert in any area of Scripture is the very thing that often closes us off from learning the new things that God is opening up in His Word. Again, it's the childlike heart that attracts revelation from God.

Wonder, that awe-filled curiosity that children carry so naturally, is such a beautiful thing to Me. Fight to maintain your wonder. Fight against cynicism, against disappointment, against assumption. The more you continue to marvel at My Word and at My works, the more you will see.

March 24th

Jesus answered and said to them, "You are mistaken,
not knowing the Scriptures nor the power of God."

—Matthew 22:29 NKJV

REST: The Church has a tendency to create rules in order to protect believers from mistakes or heresy. But sometimes the rules that keep us from error also keep us from our destiny. The appropriate response to dangerous, and intrinsically important ideas is to stay low, stay hungry, take risks, and keep accountable.

> *I come to You hungry and humble, Lord. Help me remain that*
> *way. I want more of You—more of Your presence and more of Your*
> *anointing—at any cost.*

REST: But the answer for many has been to take a more analytical approach to the Christian life, one that is stable in doctrine and disciplines but lives without personal experience, denies the opportunity for risk, and resists emotional expression and passion. Christianity was never to be known by its disciplines. It's to be known by its passion; and those without passion are in far more danger than they know. Demons are attracted to religiously sanitized environments where there is no power.

> *I never wanted to rule a planet of robots, even well-behaved ones. My*
> *heart has always longed for relationship with you. I love discipline when*
> *it emerges from love and vision. It's easy, though, for the rules to replace*
> *the relationship. Stoke up your heart for My presence. Don't be satisfied*
> *with anything else.*

March 25th

So above all, guard the affections of your heart, for they affect all that you are. Pay attention to the welfare of your innermost being, for from there flows the wellspring of life.

—Proverbs 4:23 TPT

RISE: Biblical meditation is a completely different animal than what is encouraged in the New Age culture. Theirs is a counterfeit because it encourages us to empty our minds. True meditation feasts on God's Word. That absolute foundation for thought sets a course of direction that is sure to take one on the journey of a lifetime. It is interaction with the Holy Spirit.

> *I want to set my mind on Your Word, God. Fill me with the Scriptures so I can train my mind to the truth. Let me come to the Bible with a new hunger each time, trusting that Your Spirit will teach me what I need for that moment.*

REST: Whatever my heart is set upon when I come to the Bible, will determine much of what I see in the Bible. That can be good or bad, depending on whether or not I have kept my " heart with all diligence." Those with evil in their hearts can find the confirmation they are looking for through the misreading of Scripture. The problem is not the method or approach to the Bible; it is whether or not we are willing to stay humble, honest, and hungry before the Lord. Our desperation for truth makes us available for things that others seem to continually miss. Keeping a pure heart makes the journey to God's Word a journey where nothing is impossible.

> *I want us to go on a journey of discovering My Word together. Leave behind any fears of inadequacy or boredom. Stay honest with Me and learn to treasure the Scripture. Your spirit will be fed even when you're not aware.*

March 26th

Death and life are in the power of the tongue,
and those who love it will eat its fruit.

—Proverbs 18:21 NASB

RISE: With our speech, we design and alter our environment. Realities are created, ones that didn't exist a moment earlier, through simple proclamations. With this tool, we can build up or tear down, edify or discourage, give life or destroy it.

> *Jesus, every time I say something that I regret, would You help me to honestly search my heart for any lie that has snuck in? I need a new revelation of the power of my words, Holy Spirit. Help me to speak life into my environment every chance that I get.*

REST: The declared word has the capacity to resource earth with Heaven's resources. As reformers we must first pay attention to what we say, realizing that we are actually building the world we have to live in. We have the ability to speak *from* God, revealing His world and His ways.

> *The tongue is not something to be feared. It is a powerful tool, for destruction or creation. Like Me, I have given you the power to impact reality with your words. Spend time with Me, let Me show you the way I see the world, and watch how your declarations begin to release My heart.*

March 27th

*He will glorify and honor Me, because He (the Holy Spirit) will take
from what is Mine and will disclose it to you.*

—John 16:14 AMP

RISE: Jesus describes one of the primary roles of the Holy Spirit. He says this after revealing that all things belong to Him. Jesus is telling us how His inheritance (all things) would be transferred to our account. It would be done through the declaration. Every time God speaks to us, there is a transfer of heavenly resource from His account into ours. Hearing God is essential to the release and the discovery of the vastness of our inheritance in Christ. It is beyond comprehension. It is all things (1 Cor. 3:21).

> *Holy Spirit, You're going to need to help me even begin to grasp that fact that Jesus has given me "all things" as an inheritance. I want to understand more every day what it means for me to be a co-heir with Christ.*

REST: The transfer of "all things," our inheritance, begs this question, "Why would God give us all things?" Because all things will be necessary for us to fulfill the commission that God has given us. Our assignment from God will require the use of "all things" to be under our supervision to accomplish His purposes on earth.

> *Never minimize your call on this earth to mere survival. I created you to thrive and to impact the world for My Kingdom. Don't be shy. Press into your inheritance, pull on My supernatural intervention, because that is how you will begin to release Heaven onto the earth.*

March 28th

And Jesus grew in wisdom and stature,
and in favor with God and man.

—Luke 2:52 NIV

RISE: It's understandable that Jesus would need to increase in favor with man, as it would give Him access and influence within society in ways He wouldn't have without favor. But how is it that the Son of God, who is perfect in every way, needs to increase in favor with God? There is no easy answer, but what is clear is that, if Jesus needed more favor from God to complete His assignment, how much more of an increase do we need!

> *Father, I want to grow in favor with You like Jesus did. I only want to walk through doors to my destiny that You open. Please shut every path other than Yours. I will keep my eyes trained on You.*

REST: As with most everything related to the Kingdom of God, we receive increase through generously giving away what we have. It is no different with favor—grace. Grace is the favor of God; a highly valued heavenly commodity. This is a significant tool because it brings transformation through words of encouragement by attracting the favor of God to the one we choose to serve.

> *I have designed My Kingdom to increase as it is dispersed. There is no lack with Me. Share the grace that I have poured out on your life with others and watch as your favor grows.*

March 29th

You won't be able to say, "Here it is!" or "It's over there!"
For the Kingdom of God is already among you.

—Luke 17:21 NLT

RISE: Contained in the realm of the Kingdom of God are all the answers to life's problems. It doesn't matter if it's the crisis with the ozone layer, frustration in dealing with contentious neighbors, or a problem with a failing marriage or business; the realm of the King's dominion has the answer. That realm of dominion is the realm of the Holy Spirit manifesting the Lordship of Jesus Christ, which is first realized in our hearts.

> *Holy Spirit, help me to turn to You in every situation. You have a solution for everything, no matter how small. Bring people around me who are further along in this journey as both accountability and encouragement.*

REST: Jesus taught us that the *kingdom of God is within* us. All the Kingdom issues are heart issues. Properly dealing with attitudes, ambitions, and agendas is key to enjoying the reign of God displayed in our lives. Our relationship with the Holy Spirit is foundational to the breakthroughs that we all want to see. The secrets of God are our inheritance. We have access to this reality for the sake of those around us. The wonderful things that are to become manifest to the world are to flow from us. God intended that His expression to the world spring from *within* His people.

> *When you make Me Lord over every single area of your heart, so many issues dissolve—disappointment, jealousy, rejection, bitterness. Let Me into every corner of your heart to bring My healing and My righteous reign.*

March 30th

Heal the sick, cleanse the lepers, raise the dead, cast out demons.
Freely you have received, freely give.

—Matthew 10:8 NKJV

RISE: Sometimes we focus on merely changing our words knowing that they carry creative force. Still it's out of the heart that the mouth speaks. Changing the external without dealing with the heart is the way of religion. The push for miracles is the same. Trying to obtain a measure of Kingdom expression on the outside that is not manifest on the inside is the sign that the cruel taskmaster of religion is present.

> *Thank You, Holy Spirit, that You are taking me on the uncomfortable but beautiful journey of healing my heart. Thank You that there is hope and healing for every area of my past and current pains. Guide me on this journey toward inner health.*

REST: We can give away the Kingdom in the measure we experience the *King's dominion* within us. What reigns on the inside rains on the outside. As it was with Peter's shadow, whatever overshadows me will be released through my shadow (see Acts 5:15). The heart is capable of all sorts of evil as well as all sorts of significant spiritual breakthrough. Stewardship of the heart is what determines what is produced there.

> *I know that you've been hurt. I grieve the ways that My representatives injured you and disappointed your heart. Come to Me, let me wrap My arms around you, and we will tackle the work of healing your heart together.*

March 31st

*And I tell you that you are Peter, and on this rock I will build my
church, and the gates of Hades will not overcome it.*

—Matthew 16:18 NIV

RISE: We are first and foremost a people of God's presence. The Church is the eternal dwelling place of God. As such, we are known for our ministry to God, which positions and equips us for more effective ministry to people. For example, evangelism in its purest form is simply an overflow of worship. If the glory of God could be seen on and within the house(s) of God in the Old Testament— though the hands of man built them—how much more is that glory witnessed in this house called the church; for God is building His Church.

*I always want to be known as a worshiper, first and foremost. Help me
to never forget, God, that my first calling is to minister to Your heart.*

REST: We are to display the wisdom of God to be seen by all those in positions of power—including the principalities and powers in heavenly places. The creative expression that comes through wisdom is a reminder to all that exists that this company of believers is commissioned to bring heavenly answers to earthly problems. This will turn heads from the inferior wisdom of this world to the divine wisdom that answers the cry of the human heart.

*I love My Church. She is growing into the Bride that I will be thrilled
to make My own. Spend time with Me, let My glory pour through you,
and then release it to the world. Help to make My Church famous for
love and wisdom.*

April

April 1st

Now the manifold wisdom of God might be made known by the
church to the principalities and powers in the heavenly places,
according to the eternal purpose which He accomplished
in Christ Jesus our Lord.

—Ephesians 3:10-11 NKJV

RISE: To resource the earth with Heaven's resources, our understanding of steward-ship must grow. Many people struggle whenever leaders teach about our simple role stewarding money, and automatically disqualify themselves from the weightier issues—like responsibly managing our gifts, time, relationships, and the world we live in. But the greatest honor bestowed on us as stewards is the responsibility to steward tomorrow, today.

> *Father, expand my understanding of Your authority that I am to steward on the earth. Give me Your vision so that I might pull the promises of tomorrow into today.*

REST: Our role in shaping the world around us through creative expression is never more at the forefront than when we joyfully learn to pull tomorrow into today. God trains us for this role whenever He speaks to us, for in doing so He is working to awaken and establish our affections for His Kingdom. A people whose hearts are anchored in His world are best qualified to serve in this one. He establishes His eternal purpose in us whenever He speaks. His Word comes from eternity into time, giving us a track to ride on. It connects us with eternity, causing us to impact our world through the influence of His world.

> *You are the only one of My creation to whom I have given the power to imagine, speak into, and shape the future with Me. Fix yourself in My presence, see My Kingdom come and My will be done on earth as it is in Heaven.*

April 2nd

Through our union with Christ we too have been claimed by God as
his own inheritance. Before we were even born, he gave us our destiny;
that we would fulfill the plan of God who always accomplishes every
purpose and plan in his heart.

—Ephesians 1:11 TPT

RISE: The believer's inheritance is beyond human comprehension. To put the richness of that gift into the eternal future is to sell short the power of the Cross in the present. He gave us a gift beyond comprehension because we have an assignment beyond reason. Jesus gave us all things because we would need all things to fulfill our call. He intends to fill the earth with His glory, and His glorious Bride will play a role.

I want to be a part of Your Kingdom coming on the earth, Lord. I want
to do all that is in Your heart for me to do. But I need to encounter Your
heart, I need my mind to be renewed, and I need to be filled with Your
power daily.

REST: It is interesting to note that we have already inherited tomorrow—things to come. That makes us stewards of tomorrow in a profound way. God reveals coming events to us, and we steward the timing of those events. This amazing privilege is exemplified in Scripture and gives insight to passages that might otherwise be hard to understand.

Will you trust Me that I have a purpose even when you do not
understand? There are moments in Scripture where I may seem harsh
to you, but do not shy away from them. All of My Word is inspired.
Lean into those verses, bring them to Me, let Me show you My heart
yet again.

April 3rd

*He has blinded their eyes and He hardened their heart, so that they
would not see with their eyes and perceive with their heart,
and be converted and I heal them.*

—John 12:40 NASB

RISE: Many times throughout the Scriptures we are faced with statements and principles that challenge our understanding of God. It's never that He could be perceived as evil or untrustworthy; but He is often mysterious and unpredictable. Such a case is found in the Gospel of John. At first glance it looks as though God has it in for Israel and that He hopes they don't repent because He doesn't want to heal them. Yet the whole of Scripture gives us a different picture. We know God never hardens a tender heart. It's the tender heart that receives what God is saying and doing. Wherever people have truly sought God, He has welcomed them with much mercy and grace, as He is the restorer of broken lives. But a hard heart is a different story completely, as God will harden a hard heart.

Keep my heart tender toward you, God, even when I don't understand.

REST: If Israel would have seen what God had purposed for them within His Kingdom in the last days and asked for it, God would have had to give it to them. He would have answered them even though it was not His correct time for that promise to be fulfilled. So He used their hardness of heart as the basis for blinding them to insure that His purposes would be accomplished on His timetable. Instead of just saying "No," He responded by hardening their already hard hearts so they would lose their ability to perceive Kingdom possibilities. The implication of the story is this: If God lets you see future promises, it's because He's hoping they will hook you and cause you to hunger for those things. It is through a desperate heart that you are able to bring the fulfillment of those promises into your day.

*I am always searching the earth, longing to respond to a heart filled
with hunger for My Word and My presence, to those who are pulling on
My promises with faith.*

April 4th

In the last days...Many nations will come and say, "Come, let us go up
to the mountain of the Lord, to the temple of the God of Jacob. He will
teach us his ways, so that we may walk in his paths."

—Micah 4:1-2 NIV

RISE: We have a bad habit of taking most of the good promises of the Bible and sweeping them under the mysterious rug we call "the millennium." It is a great inconsistency to say the last days began with the day of Pentecost with Acts 2, and then take the wonderful promises of the prophets about the last days, like this verse in Micah, and say they refer to the millennium. The error of our ways is clearly realized in the fact that what is believed actually requires little or no faith to get what most of the Church is waiting for—the world to get worse and the Church to get rescued. This is an irresponsible way to respond to great promises.

> *If You have promises for me—for my generation, for this moment*
> *in time—I want access to them, Father! Help my faith grow in the*
> *expectation of Your fulfilled promises.*

REST: Had David lived with such a mindset, he would have had to live under the restraint of Old Testament law and not provide us the testimony of a life of celebration and joy. He illustrated the New Testament believer before there ever was such a thing. If ever there was a line to cross where it should have been impossible to bring something from a future era into a given time, it should have been during David's day. Yet the desperation of a hungry heart brought about the impossible. David had daily access to the glory of God's presence! This would be something that only the blood of Jesus could make possible.

> *David's hunger stirred My heart. He trusted in My nature because of*
> *the time he had spent communing with Me. He pursued My heart, and*
> *I long to have that with each of My children.*

April 5th

"And they will not need to teach their neighbors, nor will they need to
teach their relatives, saying, 'You should know the Lord.' For everyone,
from the least to the greatest, will know me already," says the Lord.
"And I will forgive their wickedness, and I will never
again remember their sins."

—Jeremiah 31:34 NLT

RISE: If it's true that the promises of restored cities and healed nations are actually millennium promises...and if the promise of God's glory being manifest all over the earth is far off into the future...and if in fact the people of God will not reach a place of true maturity, living like one mature man—then I must ask these questions: Is there anyone hungry enough for what He has shown us in the Scriptures that we will pull into our day something that is reserved for another? Is there anyone willing to lay themselves down to bring more of God's promises across another great divide? Or how about the promise that says everyone will know the Lord? Isn't that one worth pursuing for our cities?

I am hungry for more of You, God. Increase my hunger!

REST: If what I have shared is true, then no one can hide behind their eschatology. No one is exempt because of the doctrinal interpretation of the last days. No one is excused. If you can see the coming future promises and He hasn't blinded your eyes to His intent, then He is hoping to hook you into the role of calling *"into being that which does not exist"* (Rom. 4:17 NASB). It is the role of the desperate heart of faith. We have the opportunity to affect the direction and flow of history through our prayers and intercessions. This is when we take hold of the future. This is why He wants to show us, *"things to come"* (John 16:13). The future is now, and it belongs to us.

My heart is that you would know Me so well that you would grab ahold
of My promises and never let go until you see them fulfilled on the earth!

April 6th

"Behold, the days are coming," says the Lord, "when the plowman
shall overtake the reaper, and the treader of grapes him who sows seed."
—Amos 9:13 NKJV

RISE: God's Kingdom only knows increase and acceleration. It is the hunger of His people that helps accelerate the process of development and growth and actually speeds up time. It is my conviction that God is trying to get rid of our excuse concerning "seasons." The metaphor of the seasons has become an excuse for moodiness, unbelief, depression, inactivity, and the like. It must end. As the technological development has increased exponentially, so the development and maturity of this generation will increase.

Lord, I want to be a part of Your increase. Fill me with the revelation of
Your faithfulness so that I may step into my authority with all boldness.

REST: Trees planted by God's river bear fruit 12 months of the year. They are the prophetic prototype of the last days' generation that has experienced the acceleration prophesied. How else do you think it's possible for the plowman to overtake the reaper? This is an amazing prophetic picture of a time when planting and harvesting are done in one motion. There's a message for us in the cursed fig tree. Jesus cursed it for not bearing fruit out of season. He has the right to expect the fruit of the impossible from those He has created for the impossible. The Spirit of the resurrected Christ living in me has disqualified me from the mundane and ordinary. I am qualified for the impossible, because I'm a believing believer.

Nothing that you have done or have failed to accomplish is involved in
your qualification to do My works upon the earth. It's only faith in Me
that qualifies you for the impossible.

April 7th

As for us, we have all of these great witnesses who encircle us like
clouds. So we must let go of every wound that has pierced us and the
sin we so easily fall into. Then we will be able to run life's marathon
race with passion and determination, for the path has
been already marked out before us.

—Hebrews 12:1 TPT

RISE: We are in a race. It's a race between what is and what could be. We are uniquely positioned with the richest inheritance of all time. It has been accumulating through several thousand years of humanity encountering God and God encountering humanity. The righteous dead are watching. They fill the heavenly stands and have been given the name "cloud of witnesses." They realize that in a relay race, each runner receives a prize according to how the last runner finishes. They invested in us for this final leg of the race, and are now waiting to see what we will do with what we've been given.

Thank You, God, that it is You who equips me to run this race well. I
come to Your presence hungry for whatever You have for me today.

REST: We've been given the capacity to dream and, more importantly, to dream with God. His language continues to be unveiled, His heart is being imparted, and permission has been given to try to exaggerate His goodness. We have been given the right to surpass the accomplishments of previous generations using creativity through wisdom to solve the issues facing us. Their ceiling is our floor. This is our time to run.

I long to pour out My love onto you and, through you, to the whole
world. Come to Me, and let Me show you what I want to do on the
earth. Connect with My heart and release my plans onto the earth. This
is the heart of intercession.

April 8th

Believe in me so that rivers of living water will burst out from within you, flowing from your innermost being, just like the Scripture says!

—John 7:38 TPT

RISE: When any of us go into God's presence and tap into the realm of Heaven, we position ourselves to receive great breakthrough. One of the things that we need to be careful about is going before God with our own agendas. Sometimes I think we go before God and already have an idea of what we want God to do, so we close ourselves off from receiving from and partnering with God and what He may want to do in the moment. In fact, God may want to do something completely different. It is almost as if we say, "Here God, here is my idea; now do it my way." When we do that, we handcuff God. We are no longer partnering with Him.

Father, I want to be a conduit for Your heart on the earth. Draw me into Your perspective and let my prayers birth the dreams of Heaven.

REST: Intercession is just the fruit of being with Him. It was birthed in my own heart because of spending time with Him. I go into His presence to love Him, to experience "Spirit to spirit"—His Spirit with my spirit. When I experienced this for the first time, I remember just being with Him and feeling our hearts connecting. It felt like my heart was picking up the same heartbeat as His—pouring upon me "liquid love" from His heart. His heart was broken for humanity. Our two hearts are intertwined. When you feel that, when you see His heart broken and His amazing love, your only response can be to pray with burning passion—with compassion for a lost generation.

Everything I've designed is for the purpose of intimacy. Prayer was never meant to be a request made from a distance. I want to share My heart with you, to hear your "amen," so that I can heal the world with My love.

April 9th

Blessed be the Lord, who has given rest to His people Israel, according to all that He promised; not one word has failed of all His good promise, which He promised through Moses His servant.

—1 Kings 8:56 NASB

RISE: God's yes together with our yes is what brings about breakthrough in prayer. I'm continually amazed that God would choose to partner with us. But, at the same time, it makes all the sense in the world that He would want us to join with Him in making history. We are, after all, His children. He is a great and all-powerful God and also a loving and caring Father who, I believe, wants to be involved in our lives. Incredibly, He also wants us to be involved in His Kingdom. He wants us to help build His Kingdom here on earth. Some of the prophetic acts that we do come from the Lord, but I think that some of the things that we do are good ideas that the Father says, "Yeah, that's good."

Father, help me understand the secure place I have in Your heart. I want to only pray from that place of confident love and trust.

REST: I am convinced that God likes my ideas. So, when I pray, I pray from a place of security. I go into prayer believing that God is on my side. I feel like our lives can be so intertwined with God's that our thoughts, feelings, and even what we do are melted together with His. When God made us just the way we are, He liked what He made. He likes everything about us. I believe He enjoys our ideas, and we in turn like His ideas. God chooses us.

I love how your mind works. Guard your creativity against the voice of criticism. Sometimes, you are crushing ideas that would bring Me great joy.

April 10th

Then we will no longer be infants, tossed back and forth by the waves,
and blown here and there by every wind of teaching and by the
cunning and craftiness of people in their deceitful scheming.

—Ephesians 4:14 NIV

RISE: We are the offensive team. If you don't understand that, if you are not praying from a place of victory, then you will be an intercessor whose prayer life is marked with defeat. You will be one who is always trying to protect what God has given you from the devil's plans or, worse yet, running after the devil and trying to figure out what he is doing. How wrong is that? If you do not understand that God has already given you the ball, you will live in fear and pray from a place of lack.

Sometimes I come to You praying from a place of anxiety, overwhelmed
by the darkness that surrounds me. Forgive me for losing sight of Your
ever-present victory, God. Bring me back to my rightful, offensive
position as Your child.

REST: On an offensive team, the entire team knows where the ball will go and who will catch it. The entire team knows where to run. They have one focus—to get the touchdown. As intercessors, we must listen for the plays that the Lord is calling and pray them in so that the team can catch the ball and make the touchdown. Our job is not to spend all of our time worrying about the enemy's strategies. We are to make the plays that God calls. A lot of intercessors spend all of their time worrying about what the enemy will do next, but their job is to focus on God and to partner with His plans.

Victory is your inheritance in Me. I have rigged the game. I have written
the end of the story. My light wins every time over darkness.

April 11th

*You will not be subject to terror, for it will not terrify you. Nor will the
disrespectful be able to push you aside, because God is your confidence
in times of crisis, keeping your heart at rest in every situation.*

—Proverbs 3:25-26 TPT

RISE: Fear has a way of coming up and biting you. Everything seems to be going great
in your life and you are walking in peace. All of a sudden, there fear is, trying to enve-
lope you, trying to destroy your peace. We as believers have to make a choice to resist
fear. We as a family have had to make a choice that we would not partner with fear. The
devil has legal rights only if we agree with him. The tool he uses to get us is fear. He does
not play fair with us. He will go right for our soft spots.

*I have been afraid many times. Forgive me, Jesus. Your blood is enough.
The battle between light and darkness has finished, and fear has no
authority over me anymore.*

REST: When I look at the world, I can recognize the devil's plan. The root is fear. It
really is a simple plan. All the devil has to do is make sure that we walk in fear; then all
of our responses will be out of that place of fear. The most repeated command in the
Bible is "Do not fear." From Genesis to Revelation, God has repeatedly told us not to
fear. God knows our humanness.

*"Do not fear" is not a suggestion; it is My command to you. I deserve
every part of your trust. Fear is misplaced trust, and I am jealous for
every part of your heart.*

April 12th

He covers His hands with lightning, and commands it to strike.

—Job 36:32 NKJV

RISE: In hunting, the hunter doesn't simply get a gun and go out and shoot something. They want to make sure that, when they do shoot an animal, their scope—the lens that allows them to aim—is on target. If the scope is off even a fraction of an inch, the bullet will accentuate that difference, potentially missing or—even worse—wounding the animal. At the target range, the hunter makes sure that all of their practice shots line up with the bullet hitting the intended mark. When we intercede, we are "striking the mark" revealed by God's heart. This phrase derives from the Hebrew word *paga*. *Paga* means "to meet"; it is the violent part of intercession. Job tells us of this forceful, *paga* meeting.

> *Keep my eye trained on You, Lord. I don't want to be off even a fraction. Teach me how to meet Your mark in prayer.*

REST: If we are going to be a people who pray with an offensive purpose, "hitting the mark" in our prayers, we must be on a quest to search the heart of God. How can we do that? Where do we go to find God's heart? We go to His Word to find His heart. I find it interesting that the word *Torah* comes from the root word *yarah*, which means "to shoot straight" or "to hit the mark." God has given us the Bible to show us His heart.

> *I have not hidden My heart or My character from you. I share Myself willingly and with great joy. Just take a step toward Me, and I will reveal even more.*

April 13th

Jonathan said to his young armor-bearer, "Come, let's go over to the outpost of those uncircumcised men. Perhaps the Lord will act in our behalf. Nothing can hinder the Lord from saving, whether by many or by few."

—1 Samuel 14:6 NIV

RISE: God is looking for intercessors who are passionate for Him and for His Kingdom to come. Whether by one or two is no matter to Him; it took one man who walked this planet over two thousand years ago to change the world forever. One man! Jesus. Jonathan's attitude is the one we need in our spirits when we carry out our intercessions. Numbers have nothing to do with what God wants to do in the spirit realm. What matters is just passion and courage.

> *Holy Spirit, infuse me with the same courage that Jonathan had. I want the faith to know that nothing can hinder the will of God.*

REST: Jonathan's passion to see justice bore immediate fruit. The Hebrews and those who were in hiding, who were not a part of Saul's army—renegades—came to Saul's side to fight. The courage of one became the courage of many. When you look at Jonathan in this story, you can see how an offensive life is lived. You can see how nothing is impossible with God. As we carry out those seemingly crazy prophetic acts, choosing to live an offensive life before God, God will fight for us.

> *The longing to see My Kingdom come is stirring within every aspect of creation. Will you be My catalyst, inspiring others to pursue even more of My presence?*

April 14th

*And God has made all things new, and reconciled us to himself, and
given us the ministry of reconciling others to God.*

—2 Corinthians 5:18 TPT

RISE: I consider Redding, California my home. Not only is it my home, it's my land. I believe that what I pray and speak over my city will make a difference. The same is true for you; where you live is yours. We are spiritual leaders in our land. As intercessors, we need to take that seriously. Several years ago, there was a brutal murder in our city. I woke up that next morning, read the paper, and was deeply saddened by the news. I went up to our prayer house and wept before God. I asked for forgiveness for the murders that we had committed in our city. I cried for mercy, that God would heal our land from the bloodshed.

> *Forgive me, Father, for the moments when I've passed judgment on my
> city instead of crying out for Your mercy. Show me what it looks like to
> take true ownership over my land.*

REST: As an intercessor, it is my job to take ownership over what takes place in this area. You might say, "Wait a minute—you obviously didn't commit the crime, so why are you taking the blame?" Because I have taken spiritual possession over my land. I take it personally when something takes place in this area that is sinful and wrong. If something has gone wrong, I see it as my responsibility to make it right through confession and repentance. That's ownership—taking your place as an owner who bears responsibility. In a business, the owner does whatever he or she must do to keep that business in favor with the community. As intercessors, we do the same. We do whatever we need to do to keep our region in favor with God. We take ownership and repent on the behalf of the wrongdoers.

> *I long to heal every aspect of the land. Take hold of the reins over your
> city, your region, your nation. Declare My goodness and pull on My
> heart of mercy.*

April 15th

*We do this by keeping our eyes on Jesus, the champion who initiates
and perfects our faith. Because of the joy awaiting him, he endured the
cross, disregarding its shame. Now he is seated in
the place of honor beside God's throne.*

—Hebrews 12:2 NLT

RISE: Intercessors should be the happiest people on the planet because they know the plans of God. God is in a good mood, and He wants to give good gifts to His children. As intercessors, our job is to look ahead to the good gifts that God wants to give to us and to agree with those plans. As a people of God's power, we are to bring Heaven to earth. Joy is a very big part of Heaven. Heaven is filled with joy. It is our responsibility to bring that here on earth.

> *Jesus, I want to be as joyful as You were as You spread the Good News
> of the Kingdom! Help me to constantly refresh my mind in the endless
> well of Your joy and delight.*

REST: As intercessors, we have to be OK with the fact that God is OK with motivating us with gifts. We can see this in the Scriptures. Jesus endured so much while He was here on earth, and He endured it for the promise of joy that was set before Him. Jesus is into joy! We see here that the King of kings and Lord of lords became a man, which was His choosing. And He endured it all for joy. That, in itself, was enough to give Him all of the endurance He needed—enduring the suffering of just being in a man's body after living in the heavenly realm full of light, power, and joy! In my opinion, the joy is what kept Him enduring the earthly living and the dying.

> *I am a good Father who loves giving rewards to His children. It is not
> spiritually mature to think that you don't care about My rewards. True
> wisdom is keeping My promise of reward before you at all times to
> motivate and encourage.*

April 16th

You have loved righteousness and hated wickedness; therefore God,
your God, has set you above your companions by
anointing you with the oil of joy.

—Hebrews 1:9 NIV

RISE: God is speaking about His Son, Jesus, and because He loved righteousness and hated lawlessness, God has given Him the oil of gladness. He had more joy than all of His brethren. He even endured the Cross because of the joy set before Him. This tells us that joy is one of Heaven's greatest treasures. God has anointed Jesus with gladness. That word *gladness* is "exuberant joy." That is what our Jesus is anointed with—exuberant joy. We know that Jesus is our example. Therefore, we should carry that same anointing. *Anointing* means, in the Hebrew Dictionary, "to smear." In the New World Dictionary, the word *anoint* means to rub oil or ointment on. Anointing, that exuberant joy that was poured over Jesus, is what He carried upon Himself.

> *Jesus, I want to have a new revelation of Your joy. I want to see Your*
> *smile and hear Your laugh over me. Help me to value joy the way that*
> *Heaven does.*

REST: When we hang around in the presence of Jesus, we will come into contact with that joy. Have you noticed that a couple who has been married a long time begins to look like each other? And they can even act like each other. The more we spend time with Jesus, the more we will become like Him. You want more joy? Do what that psalmist did in Psalm 73. He went before God. He poured out his heart to God; he found God's presence. We need to go before God and stay there until we feel Him and are changed.

> *My heart is that you would perpetually live in the life-giving strength of*
> *My joy. No matter what you face, it is always available to you. Run into*
> *My arms; I will gladly trade My joy for your worries.*

April 17th

But He answered and said, "It is written, 'Man shall not live by bread alone, but by every word that proceeds from the mouth of God.'"

—Matthew 4:4 NKJV

RISE: In the first temptation, when the devil says, "If you are the son of God, command this stone to become bread," he was trying to get Jesus to fight on his terms (see Matt. 4:3). Because Jesus was just finishing up a 40-day fast, it would have been really easy to do just that—turn the stone into bread to prove to the devil who He was. That would have been agreement with the devil. Jesus had no time for this realm of thinking. Jesus didn't even address the identity part of this question. Jesus knew who He was. He brought the situation right into a heavenly perspective.

> *I never want to get bogged down in the heaviness of the devil's works, God. Give me the perspective of Heaven. I'm holding out to You today that problem that is weighing on my heart. How do You see it?*

REST: The devil will be more than happy to let us in on his schemes and strategies if it will distract us from what Heaven is doing. Jesus was the ultimate intercessor, and He saw right though the devil's tricks. The devil kept trying to bring Him into a dialogue about His identity. Jesus never went there. The devil was looking for just a little agreement. Don't you get the feeling that Jesus was in complete control of the conversation? He never once gave the devil fuel for his madness.

> *There is no corner of the world where My Kingdom is not actively advancing. This is not a level playing ground with competing sides; I have already won. Stay connected to Me and watch the victory unfold.*

April 18th

Make a joyful shout to the Lord, all you lands! Serve the Lord with
gladness; come before His presence with singing. Know that the Lord,
He is God; it is He who has made us, and not we ourselves; we
are His people and the sheep of His pasture.

—Psalm 100:1-3 NKJV

RISE: The Greek word for worship is *proskuneo*; it means "to kiss." It is a feeling or attitude within us that keeps us close to God. It is not just about coming to church on Sunday and singing songs during the worship service. Even though that is an important thing that we do together, it is not the most important thing. Worship comes from within us and goes with us throughout our day. When we adore God, we are kissing Him.

I adore You, God! I lift up a shout of praise to You because of who You
are. All of my attention is set on You.

REST: Warfare worship is coming in on God's terms, not the devil's. We are focused on God, which ushers His power and presence into our intercessions. I was in one of our worship services one Sunday morning, and I kept getting distracted in my spirit. I felt like there were some witches in the room. I found myself completely out of worship. I remember, I kept turning around to look to see if I could figure out what was going on. I did this a few times. Then I heard Holy Spirit whisper, "You are being distracted from Me; just worship Me." It was a little nudge from the Spirit, but I got it. I realized that what I needed to do was just be with God and worship. He would take care of the spiritual matters in the room. My weapon of warfare that morning was to worship Him.

Warfare is not difficult or complicated; set your gaze on Me, let
everything else fade away. I will take care of the rest.

April 19th

One hand full of rest and patience is better than
two fists full of labor and chasing after the wind.

—Ecclesiastes 4:6 AMP

RISE: There is a mindset of performance that can grab hold of us and push us to do things for God that He is not asking us to do. When that happens, it takes us right out of rest. We can feel like we need to do for God so that He will approve of us. We think by doing this God will accept us more and maybe love us more. I'm telling you, you don't have to do a thing for God, and He will love you no less. So many of us have believed that we need to labor and perform for God so that we can gain an identity, so that we might be accepted. But in the Kingdom, we start off accepted. From there our identity is formed.

> *Thank You, Father, that I have already been accepted. As I start my day, will You remind me what You love about me?*

REST: As intercessors, we need to pray out of that new identity, that core belief that says, "I am already accepted! I am already loved! I already have favor with God!" You see, we are already accepted. Unfortunately, many of our life experiences do not teach us this. In life, you get rewarded or receive approval if you do this or that. The Kingdom of God doesn't work that way. God is not sitting up in Heaven waiting to love you if you will do something for Him. He is a lot more interested in our entering into His love and rest.

> *Rest is not the absence of activity just as peace is not merely the absence of war. Both rest and peace are powerful positions in My presence. Release the idea that any achievement would change My love for you, leave the heaviness of the world in My hands, and actively choose to rest in My presence.*

April 20th

And a woman who had been suffering from a hemorrhage for twelve years, came up behind Him and touched the fringe of His cloak; for she was saying to herself, "If I only touch His garment, I will get well."

—Matthew 9:20-21 NASB

RISE: Jesus was known for healing people with and without prayer. In fact, there were times when it looked as though He was not involved at all in the miracle that happened through Him. From the Gospel records, it seemed to have started when one very sick woman saw the potential of a moment and thought if she could just touch His garment, she would be well. She sensed something was available through a touch that was completely unseen. It had not been done before. Neither was there a record of this process ever being included in Jesus' instructions for "how to get your miracle." He never even implied it was possible. She watched Him work and came to the conclusion that He carried something on His person that could be accessed through touch.

> *Lord, I want to learn to rest in Your presence so much that other people see Your power and love flowing out of me as they did with Jesus.*

REST: There's no question that faith was at work in her heart. But rarely, if ever, does a person in her condition become aware of their faith. The focus was not on herself. It was on Him. As a result, faith was her normal expression. Faith sees and responds to unseen realities.

> *You don't need to force yourself to drum up faith; you only need to lock your eyes on Me. Faith is the byproduct of fixing your gaze on the One who is faithful.*

April 21ˢᵗ

God kept releasing a flow of extraordinary miracles
through the hands of Paul.

—Acts 19:11 TPT

RISE: The unseen realities of the Kingdom can be accessed through simple faith and obedience. Faith doesn't come from the mind; it comes from the heart. Yet a renewed mind enhances our faith through an understanding of the unseen. It finds its fuel in knowing the ways of the Holy Spirit—how He moves. Their unique perspectives on reality, from which they drew their miracle, were not the results of years of study and prayer (which obviously have great value in our lives, but serve another purpose). They were responses to the grace made available in the manifested presence of God through the Holy Spirit that rested upon people.

> *I want to know You, Holy Spirit. I invite You into every area of my life today. Teach me how to carry God's presence well. Open my heart to the unseen realities of His Kingdom.*

REST: It's time for extraordinary miracles to no longer be the exception. It's time for them to become the rule—the new norm. The apostles learned from Jesus' example that the greatest treasure was the presence of the Holy Spirit resting upon Him. Learning to host the presence of God is the biggest challenge of the Christian life.

> *You are the chosen recipients of My greatest gift—My Holy Spirit. All of the authority of Heaven is available to you through Him. Treasure this gift and learn all that you can.*

April 22nd

*The kingdoms of this world have become the kingdoms of our Lord
and of His Christ, and He shall reign forever and ever!*

—Revelation 11:15 NKJV

RISE: There is no greater privilege than being a host to God Himself. Neither is there a greater responsibility. Everything about Him is extreme. He is overwhelmingly good, awe-inspiring to the max, and frighteningly wonderful in every possible way. He is powerful yet gentle, both aggressive and subtle, and perfect while embracing us in the midst of our imperfections. Yet few are aware of the assignment to host Him. Fewer yet have said yes. The idea of hosting God may sound strange. He owns everything, including our own bodies. And He certainly doesn't need our permission to go somewhere or do anything. He is God. But He made the earth for humanity and put it under our charge.

Teach me how to host You well, God. It is the greatest longing of my heart.

REST: God planted us here with a purpose. Yet it's a purpose we can't accomplish without Him. Our true nature and personality will never come to fullness apart from His manifest presence. Learning to host Him is at the center of our assignment, and it must become our focus so that we can have the success He desires before Jesus returns. Hosting God is filled with honor and pleasure, cost and mystery. He is subtle, and even sometimes silent. He can also be extremely obvious, aggressive, and overtly purposeful. He is a guest with an agenda—Father to Son. Heaven to earth. It is still His world—His purposes will be accomplished. This leaves us with a question that has yet to be answered: What generation will host Him until the kingdom of this world becomes the Kingdom of our Lord and Christ?

Bringing Heaven to earth is not merely a nice daydream; rather, it is My will for My Body. Will you join Me in this bold and exciting journey?

April 23rd

*Then God blessed them and said, "Be fruitful and multiply. Fill the
earth and govern it. Reign over the fish in the sea, the birds in the sky,
and all the animals that scurry along the ground."*

—Genesis 1:28 NLT

RISE: All that God created was perfect in every way. Not even God could improve its design, function, or purpose. The Garden itself demonstrated Heaven on earth. And the reason for the placement of such an extraordinary place of peace and divine order was extreme—the rebellion of satan brought a scar into what was otherwise a perfect creation. And now peace, the substance of Heaven's atmosphere, was to take on a military function. Disorder had tarnished God's creation. It was now light against darkness, order versus chaos, and glory against that which is inferior, lacking, and hollow.

> *Father, give me a new revelation of the multi-faceted nature of
> Your peace. If it is "the substance of Heaven's atmosphere," I need to
> understand it so that I can release it.*

REST: Adam's immediate responsibility was to tend the Garden. His ultimate responsibility was to bring the same order to the rest of the planet. The implication was that outside of the Garden there was not the same order as existed on the inside. That makes a lot of sense when we remember that the serpent came into the Garden to tempt Adam and Eve. He was already on the planet. The realm of darkness already existed on earth before God made Adam, Eve, and the Garden of Eden. He created order in the midst of disorder so that those made in His image might represent Him well by extending the borders of the Garden until the whole planet would be covered by God's rule through His delegated ones.

> *My order is so much more than just a set of rules—it is aligning every
> aspect of creation with My presence. It means bringing excellence,
> creativity, joy, beauty, and holiness to the earth.*

April 24th

You become my delicious feast even when my enemies dare to fight. You anoint me with the fragrance of your Holy Spirit; you give me all I can drink of you until my heart overflows.

—Psalm 23:5 TPT

RISE: God didn't give Adam and Eve any instructions on spiritual warfare. There is no known teaching on the power of the name Jesus, no instruction on the power of their praise for God, nor is there any known emphasis on the power of His Word. These tools would be a great benefit later in the story. But right now, their entire life was focused on maintaining divine order through relationship with God and spreading it through representing Him well. They were to live responsibly and be productive, have children who would have children who would have children, etc., and expand the borders of the Garden until the planet was covered by their rule. All of this flowed from their fellowship with God. Satan was never the focus. He didn't need to be, as he had no authority. As yet there was no agreement with the devil.

> *Fill me with Your love, God. Drive out any fear that is hiding in my heart. I want to show off our love in front of the enemy as I become more and more like You every day.*

REST: Adam and Eve, the ones who saw God the clearest, had no instructions on warfare, as their dominion repulsed the enemy in the same way that light drives away darkness without a fight. I can't afford to live in reaction to darkness. If I do, darkness has had a role in setting the agenda for my life. The devil is not worthy of such influence, even in the negative. Jesus lived in response to the Father. I must learn to do the same. That is the only example worth following.

> *Intimacy with Me is the place of true warfare. Don't let fear distract you from your righteous purpose on the earth. The enemy has to watch our relationship and experience its influence.*

April 25th

And I will put enmity (open hostility) between you and the woman,
and between your seed (offspring) and her Seed; He shall [fatally]
bruise your head, and you shall [only] bruise His heel.

—Genesis 3:15 AMP

RISE: The whole issue of placing man in the Garden was to create the context in which satan would be defeated by man. God in His sovereignty allowed the devil to set up his rule on planet earth because His intention was to bring eternal judgment to the devil through humankind. In particular, this would happen through the fruitfulness that comes from the intimate co-laboring of God and man.

I want to be reminded, Father, of the true weight and importance of
our connection—both for me individually and for the fate of the world.

REST: After Adam and Eve sinned, defeating the devil became an impossibility, humanly speaking. For this reason, it was necessary for Jesus not only to die in our place, but also to live life as a man, with our same restrictions, limitations, temptations, feelings, etc., so that His victorious life was also as a human. There's no contest in a conflict between God and satan. It has always been about the devil and man—those made in the image of God. Jesus—on earth as entirely God and entirely man—had to live as a man, yet not yield to sin. His death was valuable only if He was sinless, for the sinner deserves to die. He had to be the spotless Lamb.

I want to show off our love. I want the intimacy between you and I to
be so deep that you pick up every aspect of Jesus' life as a model and run
with it in your own!

April 26th

The God of peace will soon crush Satan under your feet.
The grace of our Lord Jesus be with you.

—Romans 16:20 NASB

RISE: Think about it—Jesus not only died for us, He died as us. He became sin, our sin, so that we might become the righteousness of Christ (see 2 Cor. 5:21). With that being the case, His victory is our victory. As we receive the work of Christ on the Cross for salvation by faith, we become grafted into Jesus' personal victory over sin, the devil, death, and the grave. Jesus defeated the devil with His sinless life, defeated him in His death by paying for our sins with His blood, and again, in the resurrection, by rising triumphant with the keys of authority over death and hell, as well as everything else that God originally intended for man that will be revealed in the ages to come.

Thank You, Jesus, for Your incredible sacrifice, for dying for me so that I could enter into Your righteousness and be restored to my original design!

REST: Jesus fulfilled the promise He gave to His disciples when He said, "*I will give you the keys of the kingdom of heaven*" (Matt. 16:19). God never cancelled the original plan. It could only be fully realized once and for all after the resurrection and ascension of Jesus. Another thing to take note of: If Jesus has all authority, then the devil has none! We have then been completely restored to the original assignment of ruling as a people made in His image, people who would learn how to enforce the victory obtained at Calvary. His people are to manifest the beauty of His rule to a world in unbelief. We have been chosen for this purpose. Not because we're better, but because we're the ones who signed up for the ultimate quest. He enlists everyone who is available to learn to carry His presence until all is changed.

Let's go on this journey together. The keys to My Kingdom are yours now, through Christ. Come into My presence and unlock all that I have been saving for you.

April 27th

Jesus said to him, "What do you mean 'if'? If you are able to believe,
all things are possible to the believer."

—Mark 9:23 TPT

RISE: Everything God created was made for His pleasure. He is a God of extravagant joy. He enjoys everything He made. Humanity has a unique place in His creation, though, in that we are the only part of His creation actually made like God. Likeness was made for the purpose of fellowship—intimate communion. Through relationship with God, the finite ones would be grafted into His eternal perfect past and obtain through promise an eternal perfect future. Even the realm of impossibilities could be breached by those created to be like Him.

> *Let me never forget, God, that You created me for Your joy. I am so grateful for how passionately You pursue connection with me.*

REST: No other part of creation has been given access to the realm of impossibilities. We have been invited into a "place" known only by God. The heart of God must be celebrated at this point: He longs for partnership. He risked everything to have that one treasure—those who would worship Him, not as robots, not merely out of command, but out of relationship.

> *You did not just happen. You did not emerge by chance into a cold and random universe. You were designed with delight and attention to every detail. There is nothing that will be impossible for you when you put your trust in Me.*

April 28th

Then Jesus came to them and said, "All authority in heaven and on earth has been given to me. Therefore go and make disciples of all nations, baptizing them in the name of the Father and of the Son and of the Holy Spirit."

—Matthew 28:18-19 NIV

RISE: We were designed to rule like God rules—in generosity and kindness, not self-serving, but always for the higher good of others. We are to rule over creation, over darkness—that we might plunder the powers of darkness and establish the rule of Jesus wherever we go by preaching the Gospel of the Kingdom. *Kingdom* means "King's domain." In the original purpose of God, humankind was to rule over creation. Because of sin, creation has been infected by darkness—disease, sickness, afflicting spirits, poverty, natural disasters, demonic influence, etc. While our rule is still over creation, it has become focused on exposing and undoing the works of the devil. That is the ministry of Jesus that we inherited in His commission. That is the intended fruit of the Christian life. If I have a power encounter with God, which we are required to pursue, then I am equipped to give it away to others.

> *I need to encounter You, Father. Fill me with Your holy fire so that I can give it away.*

REST: The heart of God is for partnership with His created likeness. He's the ultimate King who loves to empower. His heart from day one was to have a people who lived like Him, loved like Him, created and ruled like Him. From day one, God's desire has been to be with His creation as the invited Landlord to look over their increased capacity to rule, making this world like His. In His world, His glory is the center. The more people carry His presence into all the earth as joyful servants of the Most High, the more we will be positioned to see one of Heaven's major mile markers—the earth covered with the glory of the Lord.

> *Become aware of My presence. I long to be with you, working with you to see My glory fill the earth.*

April 29th

*"I'll be with you," God said. "And this will be the proof that I am the
one who sent you: When you have brought my people out of Egypt, you
will worship God right here at this very mountain."*

—Exodus 3:12 MSG

RISE: After God gave Moses a most impossible assignment, Moses asked God the question, *"Who am I?"* (Exod. 3:11). The same question has been asked countless times since. Any time we look to ourselves, we will buy into the lie of insignificance. Moses knew he lacked all the necessary qualifications that one should have to be used by God for something so significant as leading God's own people out of slavery into freedom. When God chooses any of us for something like this, the same question should come to mind. It will if we see the call of God correctly. But God, knowing Moses intimately, was neither troubled nor impressed with who Moses was or wasn't. It was a non-essential. God would go with him.

> *There are many times that I've asked, "Who am I?" Thank You, God,
> that I don't ever need to rely on my own strength. Thank You that I
> never have to worry about measuring up on my own, because You are
> with Me.*

REST: Initially it looks like God ignored Moses' "Who am I?" question. But perhaps He didn't. It seems that he was letting Moses know that his whole identity was not to be in his skills, training, or popularity. It wasn't his gifts or even his anointing. It boiled down to one thing: "You're the one I want to be with." Who was Moses? The guy God liked to hang around. Moses may not have known who he was. But God knew whose he was.

> *When I call you, I will equip you. Quit looking inside yourself for the
> strength and significance needed for your journey. Instead, open the
> weakness in your heart to Me. I am drawn to your reliance on Me.*

April 30th

And John tried to prevent Him, saying,
"I need to be baptized by You, and are You coming to me?"

—Matthew 3:14 NKJV

RISE: Both qualifications and significance appear different here on earth than from Heaven's perspective. Just as humility welcomes exaltation, so weakness qualifies us for strength. And striving for significance will actually undermine our significance. When Jesus wanted to be baptized in water by John, John knew he wasn't qualified. But when you're willing to do what you're unqualified to do, that's what qualifies you.

> *I don't want to take a step in any direction You're not going, Lord. I*
> *know I'm not qualified on my own. I lay all of my weaknesses before*
> *You. I am so grateful for Your grace and empowering presence.*

REST: God often chooses people knowing that they are the key to touching other people's lives. Everyone reading this book was chosen first because of God's love for you. But make no mistake. You are uniquely positioned in this world because of the cry of other people. His favor is upon you so you can be a part of His plan of distributing that same favor to others.

> *You can see, now, that that moment was so much bigger than John the*
> *Baptist. Trust Me, trust Me, trust Me that I know what I'm doing, that*
> *I can see the bigger picture, that—as you abide in Me—we will change*
> *the world.*

May

May 1st

My deep need calls out to the deep kindness of your love. Your waterfall
of weeping sent waves of sorrow over my soul, carrying me away,
cascading over me like a thundering cataract.

—Psalm 42:7 TPT

RISE: The devil is very afraid of a worshiping people. He actually doesn't mind complacent worship, as it seems to work opposite to the real thing—it deadens our sensitivities to the Holy Spirit of God. It works completely opposite to the effects of sold-out, passionate worship. Complacent worship is an oxymoron. Convenience and sacrifice cannot coexist. The enemy knows there's power in the offering and will do whatever he can to distract us from giving it. Sometimes we fail to reach our destiny because we insist on it happening where we are—within reason, with little effort involved on our end. We often cannot get to a new place in worship until we get to a new place in God. I've heard so many people say through the years, "If it is God's will to move powerfully in my life (or church), He knows we're hungry, and He knows where we are." Foolishness! He's not a cosmic bellhop, bouncing around the universe to fulfill our every wish. He has a plan. And we must move into His plan. Wise men still travel, both in the natural and figuratively speaking.

> *Help me to never grow complacent about worshiping You, God. I want*
> *to run after You no matter what it takes.*

REST: The fear of fanaticism has kept many believers from their destiny. The only way to follow the One who died on the Cross in our place is to mirror His devotion! The Extreme One is calling out to extreme ones to come and follow Him. It is with that group He will change the world. Deep still calls to deep—the deep of God is still looking for people who have a similar depth in their hearts to respond equally to Him.

> *My love for you is wide and deep; it stretches farther than you can*
> *imagine. I love to see the depth of your genuine love poured out in its*
> *entirety.*

May 2nd

That the generation to come might know them, the children who would be born, that they may arise and declare them to their children, that they may set their hope in God, and not forget the works of God, but keep His commandments.

—Psalm 78:6-7 NKJV

RISE: Nothing is as fierce an opponent to the powers of darkness as the unified offering to God from multiple generations. This is one of the places where we see the mystery of compound interest in effect in the things of the Spirit. The fact that the devil puts so much effort into dividing the family unit and splintering the generations should testify to us of its importance. It has become all too common for one member of the family to stand out as the spiritual one, while the rest of the family is known for complacency. Tragically, the spiritual one often gets exalted in pride, which brings division, or they lower the standard of their passion to fit the lowest common denominator in the family. Neither route is effective.

I declare over my family today: We will see unbroken generations serving God together. My family's hunger for God will be passed down to my children and my children's children.

REST: Burn with passion no matter what, but maintain humility, being the servant of all. The momentum gained through the generations working together creates a spiritual wealth that truly makes nothing impossible for those who believe. When we add the supernatural power of the resurrected Christ to a people unified to His purpose and one another, nothing they purpose to do will be impossible for them.

I will fight for your family. The enemy has set his sights on bringing division, because he knows that My power pours out on unity. But do not be afraid. Know that you fight against principalities, not one another.

May 3rd

The Lord replied, "My Presence will go with you,
and I will give you rest."

—Exodus 33:14 NIV

RISE: How do you want people to remember you? People work so hard to create an image and form a reputation for themselves. For some it's their beauty or their skills. For others it's their significance or their place in society. And still others work hard to create an image from the spiritual gifts they operate in. The Bible even teaches us the value of a good name (see Prov. 22:1). It is obviously important if it's done correctly. But if you could choose one thing to be known for, one thing that would distinguish you from everyone else, what would it be?

> *Strip away every leftover part of me that still carries the fear of man,*
> *God. Unwrap those lies from my heart in Your tender way, and let me*
> *focus on the thing that truly matters to Your heart—that I would be*
> *known as a person who carries Your presence.*

REST: God chose Israel's reputation for them. At least He chose what He wanted it to be. They were the least of all, the most insignificant of all, the weakest of all nations. There was nothing about their natural qualities that made them stand out from any other people group. But there was this one thing that was to set them apart. It would actually be the glory of God—His manifested presence—that would be their distinguishing mark.

> *I will always finish what I've begun in you. You are never on this journey*
> *alone, if you don't want to be. I have made a promise to be with you.*
> *Join yourself to Me, and I will bring you into the land of My promise.*

May 4th

This means that God is transforming each one of you into the Holy of Holies,
his dwelling place, through the power of the Holy Spirit living in you!
—Ephesians 2:22 TPT

RISE: Moses' life stands today as an invitation for all to enter a deeper place with God. The amazing part is that all that Moses experienced happened under an inferior covenant. His accomplishments and experiences should be held in high esteem by the Church. It would be foolish to do otherwise. But it would be equally foolish to ignore the fact that the high-water mark of the Old Testament was not to remain the high-water mark for the New. It is improper to expect superior blessings from an inferior covenant. Our New Testament heroes of the faith understood this. It gave them permission to press in for more.

> *Jesus, open the eyes of my heart to the astonishing reality of the New Covenant. I want to be called Your friend, like Moses, but I want to pursue everything that has been made available to me by Your death and resurrection.*

REST: The death of Christ satisfied the requirements of the Old Covenant while igniting the fires of the New. When Jesus died, He paved the way for people to come directly into the presence of God daily. This was unheard of in Moses' day. Only the high priest could do that, and it happened only one day a year—the Day of Atonement. The blood made it possible to be a people of His presence. Certainly, this possibility is much more available to us than it was to Israel under the Old Covenant. But the life-altering factor is this: Jesus' death made it possible to not only come into the presence of God daily, but for the presence of God to come into us permanently. We have become the eternal dwelling place of God. Incomprehensible!

> *I have traded a cold, stone temple for the warmth of your heart. I have traded ritual for relationship, precautions for permanent access to Me. Let the magnitude of these changes fill you with the enormity of My love for you and My desire to be with you.*

May 5th

*But without faith it is impossible to please Him, for he who comes to
God must believe that He is, and that He is a rewarder of
those who diligently seek Him.*

—Hebrews 11:6 NKJV

RISE: Many question God's existence, and His nature is questioned by most everyone else. Confidence in His existence and His nature are the essentials to active faith. Faith thrives when we get those two issues settled. And it's not just a knowing He exists, somewhere out there. It's a knowing He is present, here and now. This kind of knowing is revealed by our response—diligently seeking Him. It's that kind of confidence in God. Understanding His nature sets the parameters for our faith. And those parameters are good and broad.

> *I don't want to only ever learn about Your nature from others, God. I want to know who You are because I have experienced You, because You have intervened in my life in ways that reveal who You are to me.*

REST: Moses had a series of life-altering encounters with God. The most notable was when he saw the fullness of God's goodness. There is no greater vacuum in the hearts and minds of humankind than understanding God's nature, especially as it pertains to the goodness of God. It seems that you can't even talk about the extreme kindness of God without someone voicing the concern for "sloppy agape" as they used to say, or an anything goes kind of Christianity. Unfortunately, the fear of exaggerating His goodness has kept many a heart from the liberty that He purchased on their behalf. It's not a rumor; He really is good, always good. And discovering His goodness gives me the grace to serve Him with reckless abandon.

> *If you somehow take advantage of My grace, know that I will correct you like a good Father. But it would be so sad if, merely because you were scared you might go too far, you never actually explored the depths of My goodness.*

May 6th

"And I will shake all nations, and they shall come to the Desire of All Nations, and I will fill this temple with glory," says the Lord of hosts.

—Haggai 2:7 NKJV

RISE: It's hard to imagine that anyone would not want to surrender to this God of perfect goodness. Considering that even the Church struggles with this picture, it shouldn't surprise us that the unbeliever does. They'll need more than words. This one will have to come with presence.

> *Father, help me to be a walking example of Your goodness wherever I go. I will constantly replay the ways that Your goodness has intervened in my life so that Your nature will be constantly on my mind.*

REST: God is referred to as "the Desire of All Nations." That tells me that everyone wants a king like Jesus. He is what everyone longs for yet has come to doubt even exists. The Church represents Jesus, which basically means to represent Him. If we can host Him, and in the process become like Him, then perhaps the world will actually experience "it's My kindness that leads you to repentance" (see Rom. 2:4). They will be able to say, "I've tasted and seen that the Lord is good!" (See Psalm 34:8.)

> *People are scared to give up control over their lives, but that is because they don't truly understand what it means to submit to Love. Giving your life to Me means that everything in your life comes into alignment with how I've created you to be. It's not a limitation, it's freedom and shalom—everything in its right order.*

May 7th

"The glory of this present house will be greater than the glory of the former house," says the Lord Almighty. "And in this place I will grant peace," declares the Lord Almighty.

—Haggai 2:9 NIV

RISE: The most feared and respected people in the Old Testament were the prophets. When they spoke, things happened. Their interactions with God produced a very healthy fear of God that often had a great impact on how people thought and lived. There was one thing that separated them from the rest of the crowd. It was that the Spirit of the Lord came upon them. Everything changed in that moment. They went from a respected citizen of a city to a feared citizen of Heaven. There's no doubt they had a gift from God that was unusual. They could see. Yet it was the Spirit of God upon them that had the most overwhelming influence. God spoke through them, backing His word with signs and wonders. These unusual people brought about some of history's most bizarre moments. And we are richer because of them.

Holy Spirit, I invite You to move in my life in any way that You want. Mark my life in ways that can only point to Heaven.

REST: The prophets were the most feared because the Spirit of the Lord came upon them. That's it. The Spirit of God—the One who, Himself, saturates Heaven with His presence—rests upon people. And when He does, things happen. These early prophets carried the presence of God in a way that was rare, especially for their day. Their role is still often misunderstood in ours. They played a vital role in the increasing revelation of the interaction of God's abiding presence and the purpose of man on earth. If we can see their history clearly and recognize the momentum created by these great men and women of God, we will be positioned to more readily embrace the assignment for our day. Ours is to be a greater day just as God has promised.

I have such wild, beautiful, creative, life-changing things in store for you, My child, the carrier of My presence.

May 8th

But the path of the just (righteous) is like the light of dawn, that shines brighter and brighter until [it reaches its full strength and glory in] the perfect day.

—Proverbs 4:18 AMP

RISE: So many of these stories give us prophetic glimpses into a coming day—a day when what was bizarre and odd would become normal. Even now there are things we live with in the Church that were once thought rare or impossible. Believe it or not, things are moving forward, progressing. There is an obvious progression in the revelation of God for His people and an increase in His manifest presence and glory. He meant it when He said, "*Of the increase of His government and of peace there will be no end*" (Isa. 9:7).

Thank You, Lord, that there is no going backward in Your Kingdom. Your domain is advancing every day!

REST: There has only been increase since those words were spoken. We have to adjust how we think and see to not only realize it but cooperate with what God is doing. We should and must expect progress. Expecting anything less than progression is to think against the true impact of the increasing manifestation of God's righteousness on the earth through His people.

Your grandchildren will witness aspects of My Kingdom that You can only dream about today, just as you are experiencing things of Me that would astound the previous generations. My Kingdom is one of expansion, so stay flexible, partner with Me, and watch as the world becomes more and more like Heaven.

May 9th

For those who have received a greater revelation from their master are required a greater obedience. And those who have been entrusted with great responsibility will be held more responsible to their master.

—Luke 12:48 TPT

RISE: We must steward the life that God gives us. King Solomon experienced disaster in his own life because he failed at this one thing. God gave him more than anyone to ever live. The one verse about him that pierces my heart more than any other is, *"Now the Lord was angry with Solomon because his heart was turned away from the Lord, the God of Israel, who had appeared to him twice"* (1 Kings 11:9 NASB). God gave Solomon the most unusual encounters with Him, twice, but their effect didn't last. We are accountable for what we've been given. It is up to us to keep the impact of an old experience current.

I want to be a good steward, God. Help me to see the empowering presence of grace that You've poured out over my life.

REST: I've seen people receive a dramatic touch from the Lord. And when they don't steward that touch, things go sour in their lives. Critics of revival tend to want to discount the touch of God and say, "See, I told you, that wasn't really God's touch on his life in the first place." Should God be questioned because of man? Jesus talked about healing ten lepers. Only one returned to give thanks (see Luke 17:15-18). Does that mean that the other nine didn't really receive a touch from God? Of course not. The validity of God's work is never determined by man's response, good or bad. His work is measured by this: They had leprosy, and now they don't. Or, "I once was blind, but now I see" (see John 9:25). Or the person touched by God was healed of cancer. The doctor verified it. We give God all the praise.

It is My will to bring Heaven to earth in every way possible. I am at work in the middle of every scenario in your day. Look for Me there.

May 10th

"Sir," Gideon replied, "if the Lord is with us, why has all this happened
to us? And where are all the miracles our ancestors told us about?
Didn't they say, 'The Lord brought us up out of Egypt'? But now the
Lord has abandoned us and handed us over to the Midianites."

—Judges 6:13 NLT

RISE: If there was any verse in the Bible that seemed to describe the heart of people who often miss out on what God is doing, it's this one. If God is with us, why has all this bad stuff happened? And where are the miracles we have always heard about? To this day most don't seem to realize that He doesn't cause the bad stuff but instead equips us with the authority, power, and assignment to deal with the devil and his works. It is up to us to learn how to use the tools God gives us. If we don't, the devil continues to steal. To Gideon's credit, he responds to the word of the Lord and offers a sacrifice to God.

Father, even when I'm scared and hiding, help me to see who You are
and who You have made me to be.

REST: Here is the picture: The presence of God is hosted by a person so significantly that He actually lives through them. It's not cancelling out who they are. It's capturing it to the fullest, immersed in divine influence. It is as though their personality, their gifts, and their demeanor are all being expressed through God living in them. Most importantly, here is another grace moment. Gideon had received favor that brought the enabling presence of God into His life to empower him to do what was impossible for him to do.

I want you to become the fullest version of yourself, the one I had in
mind when I knit you together in your mother's womb. Let My presence
fill you so that your true identity shines forth.

May 11th

But someone might object and say, "One person has faith and another
person has works." Go ahead then and prove to me that you have
faith without works and I will show you faith by my works
as proof that I believe.

—James 2:18 TPT

RISE: Because of the Master's design, everyone lives to make life better. Some serve the betterment of humankind, and others merely serve themselves. But as people, we carry a sense of hope that things can and must be better than they presently are. This affects all areas of life—science, technology, entertainment, etc. Everything lives under the influence of this inner desire. It is in the nature of humans, the result of being made in the image of God. This is the way creative people function. We draw upon God-given abilities to come up with solutions to solve problems and answer whatever issue is in the way of progress.

Thank You, God, for instilling in me the desire for progress and
betterment. Help me to see solutions through Your eyes only.

REST: God works with this instinct and draws us into our potential through promise and the wonder of possibility. Because of this, we live in the tension between what is and what is to come. God has given every human being a sense of hope for a better future. Some drown out that inner conviction through sarcasm, the defense mechanism of disappointment, while others silence that voice by a theology of unbelief. Still others have it stolen from them through abusive treatment by others. But it was planted there in the beginning and can be restored.

Let Me restore the tenderness of hope into your heart. I'm so sorry
for the things that have tried to crush your ability to hope. But I am
trustworthy, and I won't forget My promises to you.

May 12th

*Now hope does not disappoint, because the love of God has been
poured out in our hearts by the Holy Spirit who was given to us.*

—Romans 5:5 NKJV

RISE: Have you ever gone to see a movie because the advertisement made it look
so funny, but when you saw it you noticed all the funny moments in the movie were
already in the trailer? It's a great disappointment. The movie never got any better than
that 60-second spot. God is not like that. He entices and draws us into faith for the
impossible and then completely outdoes Himself. It's just the way He is. He gives a
glimpse of something to come, knowing that even those who saw it coming would be
surprised when it actually did. His coming works are represented in words and pictures
but can never be fully contained in them. He surpasses all description and everyone's
anticipation of good. He is extreme in all the right ways.

Thank You, Father, that my hope in You will never be disappointed.

REST: We have been given one of the greatest privileges of all time—to abound with
hope in a time of hopelessness. Even so, many who have been given the honor to steward hope have allowed the pressures of this life to derail them from their purpose. We
are meant to be a fountain of hope, not mirroring the hopelessness of those without
Christ. This is especially true as it pertains to the last days. When some believers consider the future, they only feel happy that Heaven is near. And they should. That is to
be the great hope for every believer. But our assignment should concern us more than
our destination. We must be known for hope for the day we live in, as the purposes of
God are always great. He will do everything needed, according to His promises for His
victorious bride. When Jesus said there would be wars and rumors of wars, He wasn't
giving us a promise (see Matt. 24:6). He was describing the conditions into which He
was releasing His last-days army of transformational people.

*I am bringing the earth from glory to glory, anticipating My radiant
Bride.*

May 13th

*Abraham was confidently looking forward to a city with eternal
foundations, a city designed and built by God.*

—Hebrews 11:10 NLT

RISE: I believe it was written in the hearts every person that there was more, much more than had ever been considered possible. It's the nature of humanity to crave, dream, and desire. You can't crave for something sweet if something sweet doesn't exist. In the same way, the hunger for more in God testifies that more actually exists and is available. That's what drove Abraham to look for the unseen. It was the inner conviction that something substantial, more real, eternal, and built by God Himself is available for all.

> *I am so grateful to have the scent of Your eternal Kingdom planted
> into every strand of my DNA, God. I want to become more aware of
> Heaven's reality than anything that surrounds me.*

REST: Jesus is the Light that enlightens everyone who comes into the world. Everyone has received this enlightenment. But busyness, shame, and pride keep us from being in touch with the understanding of the unseen that God has put into the consciousness of every person born on this earth. What we do with this insight is up to us.

> *Unwrap your heart from its defenses and run into My arms. You were
> made for more than this, and you can feel it. But don't let that tension
> drive you into disappointment. Instead, let it drive you deeper into My
> heart.*

May 14th

*So you must remain in life-union with me, for I remain in life-union
with you. For as a branch severed from the vine will not bear fruit, so
your life will be fruitless unless you live your life
intimately joined to mine.*

—John 15:4 TPT

RISE: Every believer has an open Heaven. For the believer, most closed heavens are between the ears. Living as though the heavens were brass over us actually plays into the devil's hands as it puts us in a defensive posture. This violates what Jesus accomplished. He put us on offense with His commission, "Go!" Remember, believing a lie empowers the liar.

Holy Spirit, help me to never forget that Heaven has been permanently opened for me. I can charge ahead, bringing the Kingdom with confidence in the finished work of the Cross.

REST: This certainly doesn't mean that darkness isn't able to cast a long shadow over a person, or even a city or a nation. We often find ourselves in spiritually dark environments. I can take you places where just being there could cause you to tremble, as the realm of darkness is so prevalent, destructive, and dominant. Even so, it is an inferior power, one I cannot afford to be impressed with. My attention must be on the provisions and promises of Christ and the open Heaven over me. I believe that keeping my focus on those things describes at least in part what it means to abide in Christ. Plus, our refusal to fear reminds the devil that he is finished!

There is no power stronger than My love for you and for My creation. That love is fierce and mighty, righteous and holy. There is no power of darkness that doesn't scurry away in the face of My love.

May 15th

When He had been baptized, Jesus came up immediately from the water; and behold, the heavens were opened to Him, and He saw the Spirit of God descending like a dove and alighting upon Him.

—Matthew 3:16 NKJV

RISE: We cannot let darkness shape our awareness of the heavenly atmosphere that dwells upon us. The size of the open Heaven over us is affected in some measure by our maturity and yieldedness to the Holy Spirit. Think of the open Heaven as a big oak tree. The bigger and more stable the tree is, the more people can stand under its shade. Mature believers carry Heaven's atmosphere in such a way that others are able to stand under their shade and receive protection. To use another analogy, others can draft on our breakthroughs and become changed.

Father, expand my awareness of Your goodness, of Your power, and of Your tender love so that I can be the tree that others find comfort under.

REST: If we are unaware of the open heavens over us, we will always see what hasn't happened instead of living from what God is doing. We owe it to God to live from the Kingdom reality He has made available. Not doing so costs us dearly. The heavens were torn open, and there is no demonic power that is able to sew them back together. The Father longs for the Spirit who lives in us. What power of darkness exists that could block their fellowship? But when we live with a primary awareness of the enemy and his plans, we instinctively live in reaction to darkness. My life must be lived in response to what the Father is doing. That is the life Jesus modeled for us. Heaven is filled with perfect confidence and peace, while this world is filled with chaos and mistrust in God. We always reflect the nature of the world we are most aware of.

Fill your spirit with My strength, beauty, and grace. Receive the magnitude of My love for you—every single day—so that you can remain connected to the true reality of your authority on the earth.

May 16th

In the year of King Uzziah's death I saw the Lord sitting on a throne,
lofty and exalted, with the train of His robe filling the temple.

—Isaiah 6:1 NASB

RISE: Some are bothered when we talk about God coming into a situation, His Spirit falling upon us, or the Holy Spirit moving in a meeting, etc. Often, as we get ready to minister to people, we will invite the Holy Spirit to come, in the John Wimber fashion. The question is, "Why invite God to come when He is already here?" It's a good question.

> *I know that You are omnipresent—always here—but I also know*
> *that there are aspects of Your nature, realms of Your glory, and*
> *manifestations of Your power that I have yet to see. Lord, fill and keep*
> *filling Your temple.*

REST: It makes no sense whatsoever to pray that way unless we understand that there are different measures and dimensions of God's presence. When He is here, there is always more to come. It's important to hunger for and invite that increase. Isaiah had a perception of this reality when he wrote about the *"train of His robe filling the temple."* The word *filling* implies that His robe filled the temple, but then continued to fill it. He came, but He kept coming. There is always more!

> *There is always more to be had in My presence. I respond to your hunger,*
> *so don't be shy about crying out for more. It's not greedy; it's actually*
> *wisdom to keep seeking more of Me.*

May 17th

*Here's the one thing I crave from God, the one thing I seek above
all else: I want the privilege of living with him every moment in
his house, finding the sweet loveliness of his face, filled with awe,
delighting in his glory and grace. I want to live my life so close to him
that he takes pleasure in my every prayer.*

—Psalm 27:4 TPT

RISE: It's easy to get so preoccupied with the vision for our lives that we miss the process entirely. We are here to grow into the maturity of Jesus, bring as many converts to Him as possible, and transform everywhere we have authority and influence. What we sometimes fail to realize is that all of those assignments are impossible. Every one of them. But strangely, they are possible if they are the fruit of something else. And this is something we can actually do.

*Father, I need Your presence to empower my life. I can't do any of the
things You've called me to do without Your grace, and I don't want to.*

REST: We are called into fellowship with God. In this process, He has made it possible for us not only to come to know Him, but also to have Him live inside of us and even rest upon us. Everything we could ever want out of life flows from that one privilege. King David understood this concept better than most New Testament believers. He referred to it as the "one thing." All of life gets reduced to one thing—how we steward the presence of God. Stewarding the presence of God, hosting the presence, is the only way these impossible dreams can be accomplished.

*However much I want to see the world transformed to look like Heaven,
I want our intimacy to reveal My Kingdom even more. Come and walk
with Me; together is the only way I long to be.*

May 18th

For the kingdom of God is not a matter of eating and drinking, but of righteousness, peace and joy in the Holy Spirit.

—Romans 14:17 NIV

RISE: The fulfillment of these dreams is actually the byproduct of hosting Him well. Jesus affirmed this principle for life when He taught, "*But seek first His kingdom and His righteousness, and all these things will be added to you*" (Matt. 6:33 NASB). The Kingdom of God is not something separate from His actual presence. The Kingdom has a King. In reality, the Kingdom of God is within the presence of the Spirit of God. "*For the kingdom of God is...in the Holy Spirit*" (Rom. 14:17). This command by Jesus is to prioritize our lives down to the one thing, which is eventually evidenced by righteous living.

> *Help me to keep my eyes set on You and You alone, God. Thank You that You've invited me into a Kingdom built on relationship with Your presence.*

REST: When we discuss our responsibilities in life, many good things come to our minds. But for me now it always boils down to the one thing—His presence. What do I do with His presence? What place does the manifest presence of God have with how I think and live? Does the presence of God affect the vision and focus of my life? What is the impact of the one thing on my behavior?

> *Every other aspect—every gift I've given you, every call on your life—is second in line to My desire to establish My Spirit in you. There is no higher calling for My children.*

May 19th

And suddenly there came a sound from heaven, as of a rushing mighty
wind, and it filled the whole house where they were sitting.

—Acts 2:2 NKJV

RISE: The sound that came upon the disciples' prayer meeting after Jesus' death did in fact carry a reality from that world into this one. This heavenly sound transformed the atmosphere over the city of Jerusalem. In one moment, it was changed from the city that crucified Jesus to a city that wanted to know what to do to be saved. How did that happen? Through sound—a sound from Heaven. Both sound and light are vibrations. And on this day, it was the vibration of Heaven that introduced a different drumbeat to a city that was unaware of whose drumbeat they were marching to. For the first time they could see.

> *Holy Spirit, open my ears to hear the sounds of Heaven. I want to know*
> *the songs, melodies, and harmonies that surround Your Kingdom.*

REST: The house of God is the gate of Heaven. Remember, it's the house built on the edge of two worlds. And right here we see the effect on its surroundings when they became open to what God is doing. There was a literal release of something from that world, through the gate into this one. And a city was positioned to experience unfathomable change. The heavenly sound was heard and experienced on earth. The roar of Heaven summoned this city to its purpose and call. In this moment, two worlds collided, and the inferior realm of darkness gave way to the superior nature of His Kingdom. We have the unique privilege of carrying His presence. In doing so, we cause this kind of conflict so that these two realities, called Heaven and earth, could dance together in perfect harmony.

> *My light will always chase away darkness. I long to release this light*
> *through you to the world!*

May 20th

All the while praising God and enjoying the goodwill of all the people.
And each day the Lord added to their fellowship those
who were being saved.

—Acts 2:47 NLT

RISE: When that mysterious sound was released at Pentecost, thousands of people began to gather to the one hundred and twenty at the upper room. It was nine o'clock in the morning. People were still preparing for the day. But they dropped everything. Men laid down their tools; women had their children put down their toys. A sound filled the air that also filled their hearts. Imagine an atmospheric shift over an entire city. A sound was released over them that cleared the air for the first time in their lives. Their thoughts were clear. They could reason. They sensed divine purpose. It seemed as though God was summoning people. And that's exactly what happened.

Do it again, God! Change the heart of an entire city in one moment.
Let me see the atmosphere over my city shift supernaturally.

REST: A gifted musician can get an almost magical sound out of the saxophone as they skillfully breathe across the reed properly placed in the mouthpiece of the instrument. Now in the same way, consider the breath of God blowing across the reed of the hearts of one hundred and twenty people releasing a sound over a city that changed its atmosphere. When you change an atmosphere, you change a destiny. That's what people heard. A harmonic sound that came because one hundred and twenty were together in unity, not only with each other but with the Spirit of the resurrected Christ. It was a sound that initiated the ushering in of 3,000 people in one day. A momentum was created through this open Heaven that made it so people were added to their numbers daily.

Creation sprang forth from My Word, and your heart was intricately designed to respond to My presence. Imagine if My love, My power were released over your city today.

May 21st

I will no longer hide my face from them, for I will pour out my Spirit
on the people of Israel, declares the Sovereign Lord.

—Ezekiel 39:29 NIV

RISE: It is so easy to assume that something like the baptism in the Holy Spirit is primarily to make us more useful in ministry. That makes us top heavy in the sense that we become professionals in areas of life that were really reserved for romantics. There are parts of our walk with Christ that should never be reduced to a list of goals and accomplishments. Instead, this unimaginable privilege of carrying His presence should never reduce me to a laborer for God. The decision of being a servant or a friend is still being chosen by people around us every day. While it is one of my highest privileges to serve Him completely, my labor is the byproduct of my love. This baptism introduces us to intimacy at the highest possible level.

> *I love You, Jesus. I'm so eternally grateful that You came and turned the world upside down by sacrificing Your life so that we could live in union with God forever.*

REST: The heart of God in this matter is clearly seen in this amazing prophecy from Ezekiel. In the outpouring of the Holy Spirit is the revelation of the face of God. There is nothing greater. *"In the light of the king's face is life, and his favor is like a cloud with the spring rain"* (Prov. 16:15 NASB). Rain is a biblical metaphor for the move of the Holy Spirit, thus the term *outpouring*. This verse also links God's face, His favor, with the outpouring of His Spirit. The revelation of the face of God through the outpouring of the Spirit is made available to everyone. The outpouring in Acts 2 was the beginning. The outpouring of the Spirit is the fulfillment of the quest for God's face. This means that wherever we go in revival, we can't go past the face. The only direction to go is to cry out for a greater measure of His presence.

> *There is nothing more worthy of your life's devotion than receiving My love, pursuing My Spirit, and hosting My presence.*

May 22nd

God's word reigned supreme and kept spreading. The number of Jesus'
followers in Jerusalem quickly grew and increased by the day.

—Acts 6:7 TPT

RISE: When you add to the mix a great number of converts, things really get exciting. New believers are known to bring all kinds of issues to the surface. My uncle used to say, "Every household needs a two-year-old." He was speaking naturally. But the same is true spiritually. Priorities get refined automatically when children are around. Chuck Smith of Calvary Chapel in Costa Mesa made such a choice when confronted by this problem at the beginning of the Jesus People Movement. The members were concerned about their new carpet being soiled by the barefoot hippies. Pastor Chuck told them that he would tear out the carpet then. Priorities. Simple but profound.

> *Keep my heart soft and humble, Father. Help me to always welcome*
> *Your new disciples with open arms.*

REST: Of course, when you have a need to justify criticism, you have to find a spiritual term to make it OK. Holiness or discernment is often used for such moments. It amazes me how many people, who have prayed for revival for years, will leave a church once they get it. Great moves of God upset everything. Nothing is left untouched. As fishers of men, our job is to catch the new believers and let Him clean them.

> *I am never offended by a heart truly seeking after me, even if it gets*
> *messy. Messy doesn't scare Me—not your mess or anyone else's. Trust the*
> *process of My Holy Spirit and leave all judgment to Me.*

May 23rd

God, who knows the heart, showed that he accepted them by giving the
Holy Spirit to them, just as he did to us.

—Acts 15:8 NIV

RISE: The apostles had many concerns. Most of them dealt with issues of holiness, which is a very legitimate issue. They had to settle on what salvation by grace really looked like. The first leaders' conference was called to discuss what to do about the Gentiles. As they met, they presented the issues. But the way they came to a conclusion is quite fascinating. They shared testimonies. They each had stories to tell pertaining to God's outpouring among the Gentiles. As they heard the stories, they began to recognize a theme: God poured out His Spirit upon Gentiles before they knew enough to get themselves acquainted with Jewish traditions. In fact, He seemed to move among them with little regard for their own readiness for an authentic Holy Spirit outpouring.

I lay down my right to judge from my own understanding, Lord. I want
to follow the guidance of Your Spirit in all things.

REST: The apostles actually developed their theology around what they saw God do. They didn't approach the issue with an exegetical study of Jesus' sermons to find out what to do. That kind of study is noble and good. But you usually need the move of God to be happening before you get insight about what it is that is happening. I've never heard of anyone studying their way into a revival. At least in part, we limit God to our present understanding of how God moves, all while praying that God would do a new thing among us. What we know can keep us from what we need to know if we don't remain a novice. When we become experts, we have chosen where we level off in our maturity. He still requires that primary advancements in the Kingdom be made through childlikeness.

Children approach Me in wonder, their eyes locked on Mine to see what
I will do next. Don't let the strength of your mind or your desire for
control overwhelm the gift of your openhearted wonder.

May 24th

David retorted to Michal, "I was dancing before the Lord, who chose
me above your father and all his family! He appointed me as the
leader of Israel, the people of the Lord, so I celebrate before the Lord.
Yes, and I am willing to look even more foolish than this, even to be
humiliated in my own eyes!"

—2 Samuel 6:21-22 NLT

RISE: When the day came to bring the Ark back into Jerusalem, King David stripped himself of his kingly garments and put on basically a priest's undergarment. This was not something a king would be seen in normally. But then David was not a normal king. He would become known as the man after God's heart—the man of God's presence. King David danced in an undignified fashion. It might surprise us to find out what is attractive to Him.

God, I give You my right to dignity. I want more of Your presence at
any cost.

REST: Michal was appalled at David's lack of regard for how people perceived his passion, his humility in attire, and his complete lack of public decorum. Instead of greeting him with honor, she tried to shame him. Her disregard for the presence of God revealed that she carried some of the same lack of value for the presence that her father Saul had lived by during his reign. Dumbing down our emphasis on the presence should never be to accommodate the Michals in the house. He followed that comment stating that she basically hadn't seen anything yet. In other words, if that embarrassed her, her future was not too bright. David was just getting warmed up.

I am delighted by your worship. My heart is moved when you release it
all before Me—even your fear of man—and focus on who I am.

May 25th

*"Sing, O barren, you who have not borne! Break forth into singing,
and cry aloud, you who have not labored with child! For more are
the children of the desolate than the children of the married
woman," says the Lord.*

—Isaiah 54:1 NKJV

RISE: Whenever someone despises extravagant worship, they put themselves in an extremely dangerous position. Barrenness is the natural result of despising worship. In doing so they are rejecting the reason why we're alive. Barrenness and the absence of worship go hand in hand. This scene happened again during Jesus' ministry. It was when the costly ointment was poured over Jesus. All the disciples were upset (see Matt. 26:8). The devil actually doesn't mind worship that is tame. Extreme worship exposes religion in everyone. There is a wonderful verse that speaks to the effect of extreme worship on barrenness itself.

*Let my life be an offering of extravagant worship to You, Father. You are
so worthy. I lay all that I am at Your feet.*

REST: In Isaiah 54, we find a barren woman who is exhorted to shout for joy before she becomes pregnant. The end result is that she will have more children than the one who has been having children all along. This provides quite the prophetic picture. The people who are people of worship, regardless of circumstances, will become fruitful in ways beyond reason. Anyone can get happy after the miracle has come. Show me someone who celebrates before the answer, and I'll show you someone who is about to experience the answer. This is the nature of faith—it looks ahead and lives accordingly.

*Shout for joy over the desert places in your life. Offer up worship in the
areas of pain and discouragement. It brings Me joy, and it realigns
your heart to the reality of My Kingdom. Worship your way into
breakthrough.*

May 26th

*God's Law and the Prophets climaxed in John; now it's all kingdom of
God—the glad news and compelling invitation to
every man and woman.*

—Luke 16:16 MSG

RISE: Jesus Christ is perfect theology. What you think you know about God that cannot be found in the person of Jesus, you have reason to question. He is the standard—the only standard given for us to follow. As simple as that thought is, I never cease to be amazed at how many people try to improve on the example Jesus gave us and create a new standard—one that is more relevant. There seem to be two extremes in this regard. One is the Old Testament prophet-type ministry, whose view of God and man are accurate for their time, but very incomplete in regard to this hour that we live in. It is missing one significant ingredient—Jesus, the reconciler. He fulfilled the demands of the Law and made reconciliation with God possible. He would not allow James and John to minister under that anointing when they asked for permission (see Luke 9:54). That season is over!

*Thank You, Father, that I don't have to live under the Old Covenant,
that You sent Your Son to reconcile all of creation to Your heart.*

REST: Then there are the ones who take great efforts not to offend anyone with the Gospel. Honestly, that did not seem to be a value that Jesus carried. The heart is good in the sense they want everyone included in the family. But if we water down Jesus' message and get converts, whose converts are they? If they did not hear the same Gospel of abandonment of all to Jesus, then whose message did they hear? Do we honestly think that the people who were unwilling to sell all in Jesus' day would be any more converted in ours?

The walk of those who belong to Me consists, firstly, in laying down their lives. I am the rewarder, the Father who loves to shower My children with blessings, but your submission to My will is at the heart of our relationship.

May 27th

Jesus, the Anointed One, is always the same—yesterday,
today, and forever.

—Hebrews 13:8 TPT

RISE: There has been a struggle in the Church for millennia about two contrasting challenges—maintaining the standards that Jesus set without going backward. So many want the Old Time Religion so much that they try to preserve a day that no longer exists in the heart of God. The other is the challenge to stay relevant with the current culture. The challenge is difficult as many forsake the moorings of the simple Gospel to become contemporary. Jesus is always contemporary, current, and relevant, more so than anything going on anywhere around us. The Father, Son, and Holy Spirit are ageless. They are relevance at its best.

> *Let me experience the awe of Your holiness, the wonder of Your goodness,*
> *and the weight of Your mercy, Lord. Thank You that the Truth of who*
> *You are never changes.*

REST: Bible schools and seminaries prioritize teaching instead of doing. Greek and Hebrew are important, but not more important than learning to recognize His voice and release the miracle of healing to someone. Leadership courses are important, but not more important than being able to lead someone to Christ or through deliverance. Management of finances is a big emphasis, and should be, considering how many failures there are. But Jesus taught the importance of managing our tongues and our families as well as our money. These are only hard classes to teach when the professors have no experience. Therein lies the problem. People with theories are raising up a generation who are satisfied with theories. Many stop short of a divine encounter because they are satisfied with good theology. One is to lead us to the other.

> *I love your mind, but the conclusions you draw about Me were never*
> *meant to replace your experience of Me. Intimacy is always My goal,*
> *and whatever stands in the way of that needs to come down.*

May 28th

Blessed are the poor in spirit, for theirs is the kingdom of heaven.

—Matthew 5:3 NIV

RISE: I heard a great message from a dear friend, Lou Engle. He leads one of the most important prayer movements in all of history. He preached a masterful message from the Sermon on the Mount. Lou asserted that the words of Jesus, the life of Jesus, the ministry of Jesus, the example of Jesus, and the commission of Jesus are what our lives are to be patterned after. There is no Plan B in the Kingdom of God. God is quite confident in His ability to accomplish Plan A just fine.

> *I have full confidence in You, Jesus. Thank You for giving me a model for every aspect of my life. Thank You that Your sacrifice was enough for all eternity.*

REST: Of all the things that Jesus taught that challenge me to my inner core, I am even more stunned by the things unsaid. He carried the person of the Holy Spirit into the earth. He illustrated a lifestyle that is within reach but must be reached for. It will not come to us. Much of what we need in life will be brought to us, but most of what we want we will have to go get. It's just the way of the Kingdom.

> *I never designed you to live a stagnant life. You were made for purposeful work, for a righteous pursuit. And, there is no other pursuit more righteous than that of My Holy Spirit.*

May 29th

Then, as John baptized Jesus he spoke these words: "I see the Spirit of
God appear like a dove descending from the heavenly realm
and landing upon him—and it rested upon him
from that moment forward!"

—John 1:32 TPT

RISE: Jesus sets the stage for a whole new season. The Old Testament prophets modeled the possibility of living with God's presence amazingly, especially for their day. They showed the impact of the presence of God upon a person for a specific task. But it was Jesus who revealed this as a lifestyle. The Holy Spirit remained upon Him.

Thank You, Father, that You don't pick and choose between Your kids
who will receive Your Spirit. You have poured out Your Spirit on all
of us so that we would be empowered to follow the model of Your Son,
living in complete intimacy with You.

REST: Now I realize that we are not to live by feelings. Emotions are wonderful, but not reliable indicators of God's presence and moving. But there is a feeling that goes beyond emotions, and quite frankly can work regardless of our emotional state. It is the mood of the Holy Spirit Himself that we can become so in tune with that we move as He moves.

It's like a dance, you and I moving together to impact the world. You're
never alone, always in synch with My gentle guidance.

May 30ᵗʰ

But you shall receive power when the Holy Spirit has come upon you; and you shall be witnesses to Me in Jerusalem, and in all Judea and Samaria, and to the end of the earth.

—Acts 1:8 NKJV

RISE: We know that the Holy Spirit lives in us as born-again believers. The amazing promise that accompanies this reality is that He will never leave us. What a promise. What a comfort this is. But the sad reality is that the Holy Spirit doesn't rest upon every believer. He is in me for my sake, but He is upon me for yours. When the Holy Spirit rests upon a person without withdrawing, it is because He has been made welcome in a most honorable way.

I need You to rest upon me like You did Jesus, Holy Spirit. I cannot do the things I've been called to do without Your tangible presence.

REST: I often ask people what they would do if an actual dove landed on their shoulders. How would they walk around a room, or even go about their day, if they didn't want the dove to fly away? The most common answer is "carefully." It's a good answer. But it's not enough. It is this—every step must be with the dove in mind. This is what I believe to be the key to the Spirit that remains. He is the single greatest reference point, not only for direction and power in ministry, but actually for life itself. We've been chosen to carry the presence of God. Amazing.

I am not fickle, but I am tender. What better way to honor My presence than to give the gift of your focus to Me.

May 31st

And do not grieve the Holy Sprit of God.

—Ephesians 4:30 NKJV

Do not quench the Spirit.

—1 Thessalonians 5:19 NKJV

RISE: The more I walk with the Holy Spirit, the more my priorities shift to contribute to this relationship. This opens up new realms in walking with God that I had not considered. To not grieve the Holy Spirit is a command focused on the issue of sin—in thought, attitude, or action. *Grieve* is a word that means "to cause sorrow or distress." It describes the pain the heart of the Holy Spirit can feel because of something we would do or allow in our lives. It is character centered. This is a boundary that must have the attention of anyone who is interested in hosting His Presence more powerfully.

> *Holy Spirit, is there any part of my life—anything that I have grown accustomed to—that grieves You? Please, bring it to mind now. I never want to grieve Your heart.*

REST: To not quench the Holy Spirit is a command that zeroes in on the co-laboring aspect of our relationship. The word *quench* means to stop the flow of. The original language defines it as "to extinguish or put out." This word brilliantly uses two metaphors to illustrate this connection with God. "To stop the flow" could be illustrated by bending a garden hose in half until water no longer flows from it, while "extinguish" portrays the passion part of our walk with God. To lose passion for God always affects our ability to allow the Holy Spirit to flow from us to change circumstances around us. This verse is power centered.

> *I am El Shaddai—all powerful and ever able—but I have given you the ability to affect My Spirit. Stay connected to Me, stay tender toward My Spirit. My desire is for our connection to never be reduced.*

June

June 1st

As you yield freely and fully to the dynamic life and power of the Holy Spirit, you will abandon the cravings of your self-life.

—Galatians 5:16 TPT

RISE: It is true that power is not more important than character. But it is equally true that character is not more important than power. Whenever we make that mistake, the gifts of the Spirit become rewards and are no longer gifts. This emphasis has actually damaged our effectiveness in the gifts of the Spirit. In fact, this approach has caused as much damage in the area of supernatural gifting as flawed character has damaged our witness to the world. Both are essential. Character and power are the two legs we stand on, equal in importance.

Help to develop both aspects of my walk with You, Holy Spirit. I want to meet every situation both with God's power and His purity of character.

REST: For every gifted person without character, I can show you many people with character who have little power. That has been the focus of the Church in my generation in most parts of the world. A lifestyle without power has been considered normal. As a result, they are making little difference in the world around them. We must stop grading on the curve, where our approval comes from fitting in to the accepted standard. We must return to Jesus Christ—perfect theology, the ultimate example of the gifts of the Spirit working in the context of the fruits of the Spirit—character and power.

I will work out this balance in you if you let Me. Open your heart to Me, show Me the weak places in your inner world. I won't leave you as you are; I will always bring you higher.

June 2nd

Jesus gave them this answer: "Very truly I tell you, the Son can do nothing by himself; he can do only what he sees his Father doing, because whatever the Father does the Son also does."

—John 5:19 NIV

RISE: The secret of the ministry of Jesus is in the relationship He has with His Father. His primary mission was to reveal Him by displaying His nature and His will. Jesus is the will of God. In doing so, He made startling statements like, "*I speak to the world those things which I heard from Him*" (John 8:26). Jesus put Heaven on a collision course with the orphaned planet called earth. His dependence upon the Father brought forth the reality of His world into this one. This is how He could say, "The Kingdom of Heaven is at hand!"

> *I want to know what You are saying and doing so well, Father, that I can repeat the words of Jesus with confidence: I only do what my Father is doing.*

REST: All the acts of Jesus were expressions of His Father for all humanity to see. Previous to this all humankind saw the devastating nature of sin and the consequences for such actions. But Jesus came and furnished the one missing element—the Father. The writer of Hebrews called Jesus the exact representation of His Father's nature (see Heb. 1:3). The life of Jesus is the most complete and accurate revelation of the Father ever seen in this world. Jesus said, "If you've seen Me you've seen My Father" (see John 14:9). It is still true. It is the heart of this perfect Father to give life to humankind (see John 10:10) and destroy all the works of the destroyer (see 1 John 3:8). The Holy Spirit is the one who reveals the heart of the Father to and through us (see John 16:12-15).

> *There is no "good cop/bad cop" in My Kingdom. I sent My Son to earth because I wanted the whole world to know My heart. I came to restore, to love, and to welcome you home.*

June 3ʳᵈ

Show me Your ways, O Lord; teach me Your paths.

—Psalm 25:4 NKJV

RISE: Jesus doesn't always tell us what to pursue. Some things only become a part of our lives because we see the ways of God and pursue accordingly. Jesus didn't teach people to touch His clothing to get well. They observed the nature of God working through Him and responded to what they saw was available through that example. We can now use the same principle to see what Jesus carried continuously that really set the precedent for how each of us is to live.

> *Thank You, Lord, that You have given us the ability and the hunger to pursue You. Thank You that connection with You is possible and that You desire it even more that I do!*

REST: We do well to pursue according to His commands. But romance is no longer romance when it is commanded. Some things must be pursued only because they are there. Moses was able to distill the cry of his heart in this simple prayer: "Let me know Your ways that I may know You" (see Exod. 33:13). Discovering His ways is the invitation to come to Him and know Him. Revelations of His nature are invitations to experience Him. As He reveals His nature to us through the moving of the Holy Spirit, He will often leave us without command. Instead, He longs to discover what is actually in our hearts, as it is in the nature of the heart in love to always respond to the open door for encounter.

> *I don't want fear of rejection to drive you into performance, but I long for your love to draw you near. I want you to share your secrets with Me, let Me into the hidden places in your heart.*

June 4th

Once you enter a house, speak to the people there and say, "God's blessing of peace be upon this house!" If a lover of peace resides there, your peace will rest upon that household. But if you are rejected, your blessing of peace will come back upon you.

—Luke 10:5-6 TPT

RISE: The world thinks of peace as the absence of something—a time without war, a time without noise, or a time without conflict. For a believer, Peace is a person—the presence of someone. Our ability to respond to this command of Jesus to release peace over a household is central in His instruction for ministry. It is tied directly to our ability to recognize the presence of the Holy Spirit. It's hard to release with any consistency what you're not aware of. Consciousness of presence will always increase our impact when it comes to influencing the world around us. So much of what we do is done out of ministry principles instead of out of the presence. When we reduce the joy of knowing God to the principles that bring breakthrough, we cheapen the journey. Those who desire principles above presence seek a kingdom without a king.

> *You are my King and my Lord. Increase my awareness of Your presence so that I can move with utter sensitivity to the Prince of Peace.*

REST: Jesus is called the Prince of Peace in Scripture. The Holy Spirit is the Spirit of Christ, the person of peace. And that Peace who is a person is the actual atmosphere of Heaven. That is why peace is like a double-edged sword—it is calming and wonderful for the believer, but highly destructive and invasive for the powers of darkness. Jesus gives His followers quite an assignment: release the person of peace when you enter a home, for in doing so you will release the presence that is the actual atmosphere of Heaven to yielded hearts while at the same time undermining the powers of darkness that are at work in that home. For that atmosphere is expressed through the person of the Holy Spirit. For Jesus, this was Ministry 101.

> *Learning to release My peace means that you need to first know what it feels like to be filled with the presence of Heaven. It's not simply a responsibility for you; it's the best gift I could've given to you.*

June 5th

Go your way; behold, I send you out as lambs among wolves.
Carry neither money bag, knapsack, nor sandals;
and greet no one along the road.

—Luke 10:3-4 NKJV

RISE: For God, miracles are as simple as breathing. No effort is required. Because the Spirit of the resurrected Christ lives within us, miracles are expected. But that is not where His desires are focused for us. He wants our hearts. And while there are many expressions of a surrendered heart, He looks for those who will trust Him. Remember, without faith it is impossible to please Him (see Heb. 11:6). Trust is the issue.

> *I want my trust in You, Father, to be the bedrock that my entire life is built upon. Help me to see areas where I am holding back my trust from Your capable hands.*

REST: To honor Him fully, we have to live in such a way that unless God shows up, what we are attempting to do is bound to fail. This kind of abandonment was the nature of Jesus' life on earth and is now the nature of the believing believer. He said, "Go into a city. Find a place to stay. Don't bring any money. Don't take enough clothing that you can take care of yourself for extended periods of time. Make yourself vulnerable in your abandonment to My purposes so that unless I show up to provide and direct, it will not work." Just as we are exalted by humbling ourselves and we live by dying, so in this Kingdom we are the safest when we are the most vulnerable to danger because of our "yes" to His assignment. The frontlines of battle are really the safest place to be.

> *Your dependency on Me is the greatest strategy in My Kingdom. Learn who I am, trust in Me, choose dependency over autonomy, and I will reveal Myself in your weakness.*

June 6th

*So above all, constantly chase after the realm of God's kingdom and
the righteousness that proceeds from him. Then all these less important
things will be given to you abundantly.*

—Matthew 6:33 TPT

RISE: My idea of protection is quite a bit different from God's. If I had been the one
sending out the disciples, I would've made sure all the needed arrangements for the trip
were taken care of—the contacts, the meeting places, the finances, and sufficient training. I would have also sent about ten or so people to each city to make sure they could
minister more effectively. I am constantly amazed at how differently Jesus thinks. He
sent them on a journey that was fully prepared, but not in the ways that often matter to
me. It was fully prepared because God would go with them.

> *Thank You, Jesus, that You have prepared me for the journey that I am
> facing right now. I am prepared because You will be with me, and You
> don't miss a thing.*

REST: Jesus provided the direction and the presence as seen in the power and authority given to them. What He gave them ensures the natural provisions will be there
because the Holy Spirit is at work. This is the concept that Jesus taught the multitudes
in Matthew. His Kingdom works entirely on the first-things-first principle. The provision of the Lord is not just food on the table. The supernatural provision of the Lord
is divine protection and full impact in our assignment. That is the whole issue: giving
up the reins of being in control of my life to become truly Holy Spirit empowered and
directed. His commission was to go learn how the Holy Spirit moves. Go learn His
ways.

> *Don't think that I didn't care about where My disciples slept or what
> they were going to eat. I cared deeply about each of those things. I just
> knew that if they focused on My presence, the things they needed would
> fall into place.*

June 7th

*Therefore I say to you, her sins, which are many, are forgiven, for she
loved much; but he who is forgiven little, loves little.*

—Luke 7:47 AMP

RISE: Great sinners have lost their innocence in so many areas of their lives. But for
most of them, there remains deep in their hearts an innocence as it pertains to the
Holy Spirit Himself. For most caught in deep sin, this part of the heart is still virgin
territory. I've seen it so many times. The most corrupt, the most immoral and decep-
tive are changed in a moment when the Holy Spirit comes upon them. Under all the
callousness caused by sin was a place of deep tenderness. It is a place that none of us can
see without help from the Holy Spirit. Amazingly, their hearts responded to God when
He showed up. And it's that response that declares that they are worthy of the dove.

> *Help me to never assume I know someone's heart toward You, Lord.
> I will surrender it all to You daily so that I can maintain my heart's
> tenderness to You.*

REST: Conversely, it is often those who have been overexposed to the things of God
that actually build a resistance to Him. Overexposure often happens when a person
hears much teaching from the Word but doesn't come to a place of total surrender.
This was the issue with the Pharisees. The ones who were the most trained to recognize the Messiah when He came, missed Him altogether. Total surrender draws us into
encounters with God that keep us tender. Without that element, we become hardened
to the very word that was given to transform us. A vaccination works the same way. We
are exposed to small portions of a particular disease, which in turn causes our body to
build a resistance. Jesus is not to be tried in small portions. He is to be surrendered to
completely and wholeheartedly.

> *My Spirit is searching the earth constantly to find softness toward Me,
> tenderness to My voice. Sometimes, where I find this openness would
> surprise the Church. But it delights Me.*

June 8th

Because you are close to me and always available, my confidence will
never be shaken, for I experience your wrap-around
presence every moment.

—Psalm 16:8 TPT

RISE: In Heaven there are no thoughts void of God. He is the light, the life, and the heart of His world. Heaven is filled with perfect confidence and trust in God. On the other hand, this world is filled with mistrust and chaos. We will always release the reality of the world we are most aware of. Living aware of God is an essential part of the command to abide in Him. Brother Lawrence of the 1600s illustrated this theme remarkably well. It is presented in the book *The Practice of the Presence of God*. It was said of him that there was no difference between his times of prayer and his times working in the kitchen. His awareness of God and his communion with Him were the same in either role.

God, I come to You desiring that my awareness of You would never dim.
Help me to turn every moment of my day into communion with You.

REST: Living with a continual awareness of Him has got to be a supreme goal for anyone who understands the privilege of hosting Him. He is the Holy Spirit, making holiness a huge part of the focus of our lives. Yet He is as good as He is holy. I get concerned when people have the holiness ambition without discovering the cornerstone of our theology: God is good. I have learned that all my ambition, discipline, and deeply felt repentance had little effect on my life as it pertains to holiness. A holy lifestyle has become the natural result of delighting in the One who is holy—the One who accepts me as I am. All the sweaty efforts have not changed anything in my life worth mentioning, except to make me prideful and miserable. I wish I had discovered this aspect of the Christian life much earlier in my walk with the Lord. It certainly would have saved me years of frustration.

Just come to Me, and let My Spirit do the work inside of you. I am smiling
at you, filled with so much more tender love than you sometimes think.

June 9th

My soul longs, yes, even faints for the courts of the Lord; my heart and my flesh cry out for the living God.

—Psalm 84:2 NKJV

RISE: I'm not sure when it happened, or even how it happened, but somewhere in church history the focus of our corporate gatherings became the sermon. I'm sure the change was subtle and was even justified—it's the high value we have for the Word of God. But to me, it's not a good enough reason. That is not to devalue the Scriptures. It's just that the physical presence of a Bible should never become the replacement for the Spirit of God upon His people. Israel camped around the tabernacle of Moses, which housed the Ark of the Covenant. This is where the presence of God dwelt. This was the absolute center of life for the nation. It was practical for them. Somehow, we must adjust whatever is necessary to rediscover the practical nature of the presence of God being central to all we do and are.

I never want to lose sight of Your presence as my number-one priority, God. I will camp myself around Your presence for the rest of my life.

REST: It's been said of the early Church that 95 percent of their activities would have stopped had the Holy Spirit been removed from them. But it is also stated that 95 percent of the modern Church's activities would continue as normal because there is so little recognition of His presence. Thankfully, these percentages are changing, as God has been retooling us for His last-days thrust of presence and harvest. But we have a ways to go. Being presence centered as a church, a family, and as an individual must be put on the front burner again. It is the heart of God for us, as it helps us mature in that all-important issue of trust.

I love My Church, but the rituals of gathering on Sunday mean nothing apart from My presence. My Bride is meant to be glorious and full of life.

June 10th

Trust God from the bottom of your heart; don't try to figure out
everything on your own. Listen for God's voice in everything you do,
everywhere you go; he's the one who will keep you on track.

—Proverbs 3:5 MSG

RISE: One of the most arrogant thoughts to ever enter the mind is that the presence of God isn't practical. Such a lie keeps us from discovering His nearness. He is the author of the book, the designer of life, and the inspiration for the song. He is the ultimate in practicality. Living conscious of His presence with us is one of the most essential parts to this life. His name is Emmanuel, which means God with us. The "God with us" lifestyle is one we inherited from Jesus. We must live it with the same priority of presence to have the same impact and purpose as He did.

Thank You, God, that there is not one area of my life that You overlook.
I can come to You like a child, sharing every part of my heart.

REST: Trust will take us beyond understanding into realms that only faith can discover. Trust is built on interaction and the resulting discovery of His nature, which is good and perfect in every way. We don't believe because we understand. We understand because we believe. To acknowledge Him is the natural result when we trust Him. The one we trust above our own existence is to be recognized in every aspect and part of life. The word *acknowledge* actually means to know. It is an unusually big word in Scripture with a broad range of meanings. But the thing that stands out to me the most is that this word often points to the realm of personal experience. It is bigger than head knowledge. It is beyond concepts alone. It is a knowing through encounter. In fact, Genesis 4:1 says, "*And Adam knew Eve his wife; and she conceived, and bare Cain*" (KJV). Obviously, a word of this nature is more than an idea. It is deep interaction.

I want you to have a revelation of My nature in every area of your life.
Set your eyes on Me and place your hope in My hands.

June 11th

*Pray passionately in the Spirit, as you constantly intercede with every
form of prayer at all times. Pray the blessings of God upon
all his believers.*

—Ephesians 6:18 TPT

RISE: The presence of God is discovered in prayer. And while that is an obvious truth, many people learn to pray without the presence, thinking their discipline is what God is looking for. Discipline has an important part in walking with Christ, for sure. But Christianity was never to be known for its disciplines; it was to be known by its passions. Prayer is the ultimate expression of partnership with God. It is the adventure of discovering and praying His heart. So many spend their life praying to God when they could be praying with God. This partnership, with its answers and breakthroughs, is supposed to be the source of our fullness of joy.

> *Thank You, Lord, that I can pray with Your heart and from Your perspective. Thank You for the ways I have grown in discipline, but let it never overshadow my adoration of You.*

REST: When we pray anointed prayers, we are praying the heart of God. His heart is being expressed through words, emotion, and decree. Finding the heart of God is a sure way of locking into His presence. And praying in tongues brings us edification and personal strength. While praying this way, the presence of God washes over us to bring great refreshing. I think it's a bit sad when people emphasize that tongues is the least of the gifts, which seems to give them the right to ignore it while they pursue the greater gifts. If one of my children took the birthday or Christmas gift I gave them and refused to open it because they discerned it was one of lesser value than the others, they'd hear a sermon from me they'd not soon forget. Any gift from God is wonderful, glorious, and extremely necessary to live in His full intentions for us. This particular gift is brilliantly useful for living in the presence continually.

> *Use the gift of tongues that I've given you. Let your spirit connect effortlessly to Mine.*

June 12th

For we are His workmanship, created in Christ Jesus for good works,
which God prepared beforehand so that we would walk in them.

—Ephesians 2:10 NASB

RISE: During my prayer times, I carry paper and pen with me because of the ideas I get while I'm praying. I used to think it was the devil distracting me from praying. That's because I measured prayer by how much time I spent doing a one-way conversation. But God measures prayer through time spent in interaction. Time in His Presence will release creative ideas. When I spend time with God, I remember phone calls I need to make, projects I long forgot about, and things I had planned to do with my wife or my children. Ideas flow freely in this environment because that's the way He is. I get ideas in the presence I wouldn't get anywhere else.

Thank You, Jesus, that You have the best ideas, solutions, and strategies
for every area of my life. Nothing slips past Your attention!

REST: When we realize that these interruptions are from God interacting with us, we are able to enjoy the process much more and give Him thanks for having concern for these parts of our lives. If it matters to you, it matters to Him. These ideas are the fruit of our two-way conversation. But in order to keep from leaving the privilege of interaction with God to work on other things, I write these things down so I can return to my worship and fellowship with Him. Because God is resting upon us, we should expect new levels of creative ideas with which to impact our world. I'm not just talking about painting or writing songs, etc. Creativity is the touch of the Creator on every part of life. It's the need of the accountant and the lawyer as much as it is for the musician and actor. It is to be expected when you're the son or daughter of the Creator Himself.

You have creativity in your very bones, even if you're not aware of it yet.
I know, because I put it there.

June 13th

*I have set the Lord always before me; because He is
at my right hand I shall not be moved.*

—Psalm 16:8 NKJV

RISE: There are only two basic emotions in life—love and fear. Turning my attention toward His love for me only increases my love for Him. It's an unending love fest where I delight in Him as He delights in me, which only increases my delight in Him. He is the ultimate pleasure and must be treasured as such. Many of us have been raised thinking there was a lot of work in prayer. Actually, I still value that model, but now only when it comes out of the lifestyle of presence and romance. It is most effective when I'm in love. Discovering His presence daily is the surest way to stay in love.

> *Thank You, Father, that I can feast on Your love every minute of every day. Thank You that Your love overwhelms any and all fear, driving it out of me until all of my focus is on Your goodness.*

REST: David made it a daily practice to place God right in front of him. He turned his attention toward God with him until he became aware of Him. David, the one most honored in Scripture as a person of God's presence, said that this was how he did life. Considering the outcome of David's life, I don't think it's a stretch to say this was a secret to David's success in the presence. He knew that if he didn't turn his attention toward the Lord who was with him, he would live without due north. He would lack the reference point in his compass that put everything else in life in its place.

> *Let all of your efforts emerge from the foundation of a life saturated with My love and intricately intertwined with My presence. There is no other way to live a life with Me.*

June 14th

*Then Jesus came to them and said, "All authority in heaven
and on earth has been given to me. Therefore go."*

—Matthew 28:18-19 NIV

RISE: Jesus brought the disciples into the authority and power He lived in. They functioned under the umbrella of His experience and were deputized as a result. But before He left earth to live at the right hand of the Father, He made sure the disciples knew that the realm they had lived in for three and a half years with Him would never be enough for the days to come. They had to get their own power and authority. Just as authority comes in the commission, so power comes in the encounter. We see it in Jesus' life, and so it is for the disciples. And it's no different for us. There is nothing that training, study, or association with the right people can do to make up for this one thing. There is nothing to replace a divine encounter. Everyone must have their own.

*I need encounters with You, God. I need to receive Your power, because I
can't do what You've called me to do with my own strength.*

REST: Tragically, many stop short of a divine encounter because they're satisfied with good theology. Once a concept is seen in Scripture, it can be shared with others even though there's no personal experience to back it up. True learning comes in the experience, not the concept by itself. Often, we can become guilty of only looking for something to happen to us that is on our list of what constitutes a "biblical" encounter with God. The lists of various experiences discovered in Scripture do not contain God; they reveal Him. In other words, He is bigger than His book and is not limited to doing something for us the exact same way He did for someone else. He continues to be creative, each time revealing the wonder of who He is. We must encounter one who is bigger than we are in every possible way until He leaves a mark. It is wonderful, glorious, and scary.

*You will never be able to reduce Me, box Me in, or fully explain Me.
This is a relationship of trust. You must choose to trust Me, to pursue
encounters with Me, even before you understand.*

June 15th

So Moses said, "I must turn aside now and see this marvelous sight,
why the bush is not burned up." When the Lord saw that he turned
aside to look, God called to him from the midst of the bush and said,
"Moses, Moses!" And he said, "Here I am."

—Exodus 3:3-4 NASB

RISE: There are many interesting encounters that God has had with His people throughout the years. It's a mistake to use one as the standard for all. The two most life-changing encounters I've had with God couldn't be more different from one another. The first was an encounter where I was electrocuted in His presence for hours. The other one was so subtle that it would have been as easy to miss as it was to catch.

> *Anyway You want to show up, Holy Spirit, I want it. Reveal Yourself in*
> *my life in any way You desire. I just need to encounter You.*

REST: It's not how extreme an encounter is with God. It's how much of us He apprehends in the experience—and how much of His presence He can entrust to us. Jesus manifested a lifestyle, as a man, that is intensely practical and can no longer be avoided or considered unattainable. It is possible to carry the presence of the Holy Spirit so well that the Father is revealed to this orphaned planet. That satisfies the quest for divine purpose quite well. Doing exactly as He did is what Jesus had in mind when He commissioned us in John 20:21.

> *I have given you an example to follow and I have given you the means*
> *to get there through My Holy Spirit. You have never been left alone with*
> *this assignment. All of Heaven is cheering you on.*

June 16th

Be still before the Lord and wait patiently for him.

—Psalm 37:7 NIV

RISE: Waiting is not sitting still. It is more clearly seen in setting up an ambush for the one who promised, "*I will be found by you*" (Jer. 29:14). He wants to be found by us, but we must seek Him where He may be found. This is a place of rest that comes out of the conviction of who He is in us and who we are in Him. For that reason, waiting makes sense. Before we were saved, we performed to get an identity so we'd be accepted. After we're saved, we find out we're accepted and that's our identity, and from that reality comes our performance. Resting is a beautiful picture of people who no longer feel the pressure to strive to prove themselves. They are comfortable in their own skin.

> *Thank You, Jesus, for saving me from every aspect of sin and allowing me to rest in God, fully embracing my new identity and confidently waiting on You.*

REST: *Patiently* has two meanings: "pain in childbirth" or "whirling in the air in dance." Both of these activities require incredible focus and strength. We are to wait on God with an unflinching resolve and focus, much like what Jacob had when he wrestled the angel. The same can be said of Elisha when he contended for Elijah's mantle.

> *I have not created you to be passive. You were born to take authority, to pursue My presence, to connect with My heart in prayer and release that upon the earth.*

June 17th

You will keep in perfect and constant peace the one whose mind is steadfast [that is, committed and focused on You—in both inclination and character], because he trusts and takes refuge in You [with hope and confident expectation].

—Isaiah 26:3 AMP

RISE: There are seasons in life when being involved in many diverse activities is not only acceptable, it's good. But there are also seasons when it is deadly. Intense focus restricts what you are willing and able to see. And while this approach will keep you from seeing many things, it will also open your eyes to see more of what you hunger for. Self-control is not the ability to say no to a thousand other voices. It's the ability to say yes to the one thing so completely that there's nothing left to give to the other options.

Holy Spirit, help me understand what season I'm in right now. Is it a season to be full and active in many different spheres, or is this a season to pare down the things that compete for my attention?

REST: The Holy Spirit is our greatest gift and must become our single focus. God targets each of us for a specific encounter that will redefine our purpose on planet earth—the baptism of fire. We were born to burn. And while the danger of turning our attention from the person to the experience exists, it's worth the risk. No amount of miracles, insight, or personal success will ever satisfy the cry of the heart for this baptism. And while many would like to just get it over with, often times there is a deep process involved. For the 120, it was ten days of continuous prayer. Such a singleness of focus is rewarded. I don't think that these encounters are supposed to be one-time events. We must have frequent encounters with God that continuously recalibrate our hearts that we might be entrusted with more and more of God. What a person values they will protect. God will give us the measure of His presence that we are willing to jealously guard.

Don't settle for a life less than what I've promised you. Pursue My presence with a fierce focus, and I will pour out My Spirit on you.

June 18th

*Then taking the cup of wine and giving praises to the Father, he
entered into covenant with them, saying, "This is my blood. Each of
you must drink it in fulfillment of the covenant. For this is the blood
that seals the new covenant. It will be poured out for many for the
complete forgiveness of sins."*

—Matthew 26:27-28 TPT

RISE: Communion is the reminder that Jesus Himself gave to us the ultimate covenant. It is the body and the blood of Jesus shed for us. Blue Letter Bible tells us that the Hebrew word for covenant, *beriyth*, is rooted in a word that means "to cut" or "to eat." Within the expression "cutting a covenant" itself is the graphic depiction of how a covenant was made. When two individuals were cutting a covenant, the ritual included taking a sacrificial animal and dividing the animal into pieces. The two parties would then walk through the scattered carcass, swearing an oath of allegiance in the midst of a path of blood. Essentially, the two parties were making a public declaration that it would be preferable to be like the dismembered animal beneath their feet than to break this promise.

*Jesus, the covenant made by Your blood is permanent and life-changing.
I want to spend my days focused on the gift that is my new reality in You.*

REST: Each blood covenant was a promise of connection, protection, and provision. Like a marriage covenant, where two people are joined into one, the blood covenant created a bond that superseded all other realities. And this was done through the shedding of blood, a public expression that involved the most intimate aspect of life—the blood flowing through our veins. Blood carries and sustains life. Each blood covenant offered a promise that would enhance life, but it came with the potential cost of life.

*The promise I have made to you is no small thing. I will never waiver
or weaken My vow of forgiveness and complete restoration when you
walk with Me.*

June 19th

The cup of blessing which we bless, is it not the communion of the blood of Christ? The bread which we break, is it not the communion of the body of Christ?

—1 Corinthians 10:16 NKJV

RISE: We never need to be distracted by the activity of the enemy. But we can be aware of the battle that is going on all around us for our minds, for our authority, for our health, and for our peace. We have the winning hand every time! Every time we take Communion, we remind ourselves that the devil has been defeated. The Cross had the final word.

> *Thank You, Father, that the battle has already been won, that the end of the story has already been written, and that now I get to explore the fullness of the reality of my victory in You.*

REST: When I'm taking the bread and the wine in a moment like that, I am in a spiritual battle for my health—spirit, soul, and body. Especially when there's something going on in my world that is threatening my wholeness, it's important for me to take Communion more than once a month. It allows me to continually remind myself of who I am, who Jesus is, and what He did. Through Communion, I am brought back to the realization of reality: His world is my true reality, not this one.

> *You are seated with Me in the reality of Heaven. From that place of authority and harmony, you can look at the broken aspects of the world with compassion and hope for a different future. Keep your perspective with Me, and you will begin to see My grace woven throughout every situation.*

June 20th

Take a bunch of hyssop, dip it into the blood in the basin and put some
of the blood on the top and on both sides of the doorframe. None of you
shall go out of the door of your house until morning.

—Exodus 12:22 NIV

RISE: When I take Communion, I take it as a prophetic act, applying it to any situation that is weighing on my heart. A prophetic act is a Holy Spirit-inspired physical action that disrupts the atmosphere. In completing the prophetic act, we are releasing something into the atmosphere that aids in the breakthrough. In Exodus, God had the Israelites kill a lamb and put the blood over their doors. The physical lamb's blood didn't save them; the will of God saved them. But the families that participated in this prophetic act were revealing a heart submitted to God. The lamb's blood was a prophetic act that each family did in order to align themselves with God's will and alert the spirit realm as to whom they belonged.

> *You have given us powerful weapons in the Spirit. Show me, Lord, if*
> *there is a prophetic act that You would have me do over my current*
> *situation.*

REST: When Jesus led the disciples through Communion during their Passover meal together, He was creating and modeling a prophetic act that believers could continue implementing. He was giving us a way to align ourselves with Heaven and bring Heaven's reality to earth. Often when I take Communion, I prophesy to myself. There is something powerful in the spirit realm about the declaration of truth, so I talk to myself out loud. I remind myself who I am, that I'm a child of the King and that I'm strong in Him. I pull on the promises of the Bible as they come to mind. I let the reality of the New Covenant wash over me, changing any mindset within me that needs to be changed.

> *There is a battle for control of your perspective, but I long to show you*
> *how I see you, how I am daily fighting for your heart and for your*
> *destiny to be fulfilled.*

June 21st

*That's right. The time is coming when I will make a brand-new
covenant with Israel and Judah. It won't be a repeat of the covenant I
made with their ancestors when I took their hand to lead them out of
the land of Egypt. They broke that covenant even though
I did my part as their Master.*

—Jeremiah 31:31 MSG

RISE: Jesus Christ shed His blood to cut a New Covenant with His creation. To forever bridge the divide of sin that had put a chasm between man and God, He initiated a New Covenant that was prophesied by Jeremiah. This New Covenant at once echoed and fulfilled the promises made to Abram. Instead of coming to earth as smoke and fire, God sent His Son to come to earth in human flesh to walk with us. Instead of a sacrificial animal torn into two to signify the covenant, God offered His own Son—the spotless Lamb—whose body would be broken as the greatest sacrifice.

*I owed the sacrifice, but You took it on Your own shoulders to set me
free from the debt of sin. The reality of Your love for me brings me to
my knees.*

REST: We are Abraham's promise fulfilled. Scripture says that through our faith we have become Abraham's descendants—as numerous as the stars in the sky and blessed by the Lord. *"And if you belong to Christ [are in Him Who is Abraham's Seed], then you are Abraham's offspring and [spiritual] heirs according to promise"* (Gal. 3:29 AMPC). We are "heirs according to promise." We are the ones God was telling him about thousands of years ago, the ones who would inherit the promises and blessings of the Lord. We are the ones for whom God is a shield and a great rewarder (see Gen. 15:1). The Lord changed Abram's name to Abraham, the father of a multitude, but He also changed our names from slaves to friends (see John 15:15). We have access to God in a way that Abraham, the man who was called the friend of God, had only dreamed about.

*I saw you when I made that promise to Abraham. I was filled with My
love for you when I made you his reward.*

June 22nd

And in the same way He took the cup after they had eaten, saying,
"This cup which is poured out for you is the
new covenant in My blood."

—Luke 22:20 NASB

RISE: After Jesus' blood was spilled for the New Covenant, we became not only heirs of Abraham, but also co-heirs with Christ. We share in the inheritance of Jesus. What Jesus did for all of mankind on the Cross was unconditional. He will never go back or change His mind. Accessing the fullness of the blessing of this covenant, though, is our choice entirely.

> *I want to receive every last part of the inheritance You paid for, Jesus. I*
> *don't want to let any aspect of Your covenant with me go unexplored.*

REST: When we take Communion, we are reminding ourselves of His sacrifice and the personal, unprecedented ways this New Covenant affects every area of our lives. The blood that was shed was a covenant promise for all of eternity. Nothing would be the same. The blood of Jesus paid for everything. It washed us white as snow, so we could enter the presence of the Lord without an intermediary and without fear. The blood of Jesus gave us freedom and authority. Hell has been defeated for all eternity. And now we get to boldly release Heaven on earth.

> *Run into My arms without fear or hesitation. Come into My presence,*
> *easily experiencing My focused delight over you. I gave My most precious*
> *gift so that freedom could be our reality.*

June 23rd

For the "law" of the Spirit of life flowing through the anointing of Jesus
has liberated us from the "law" of sin and death.

—Romans 8:2 TPT

RISE: The blood of Jesus wiped out the power of sin and the judgment that leads to death. Forever. God took back dominion over the earth and kicked out everything that was once ruled by darkness. As heirs with Christ, we have that same authority through Jesus. And when I take Communion, I am not only aligning myself back up with my true identity as a child of God, I am also reminding the devil that he lost. The devil has to watch as I celebrate the resurrection power of Jesus.

> *Disconnection, sin, illness—these have no power over me. I will take*
> *Communion, reveling in Your love, God, and laughing in the face of*
> *the devil's paltry attempts to undermine my confidence.*

REST: The New Covenant has been cut, once and forever. Never again would we have to slice a cow on a hill to walk through it as a sacrifice. Never again would the priest have to go into the Holy of Holies, not sure if he would come out alive, in order to rectify the sins of the people for another year. There was a shift in the atmosphere with the death and resurrection of Jesus Christ. It changed everything forever. We take His blood, represented in the wine, as a beautiful memorial of what Jesus did. By His blood, we can be saved, healed, and delivered.

> *There is no corner of your life that My blood does not cover with healing,*
> *restoration, redemption, peace, and love. Hold up the tender parts of*
> *your heart to Me and let My presence wrap around you.*

June 24th

Surely He has borne our griefs and carried our sorrows...the chastisement for our peace was upon Him, and by His stripes we are healed.

—Isaiah 53:4-5 NKJV

RISE: Jesus died for our sins and for our sicknesses—anything that threatens to steal, kill, or destroy our life in Him is not of Him. When He went to the Cross, He carried with Him every dark thing of the enemy and was the eternal sacrifice on our behalf. This passage of Scripture prophesies the crucifixion and the only moment that God had to turn His face from Jesus. When Jesus took the weight of sin upon Himself, there was no way for God to be a part of that. Can you imagine the sorrow that Christ would have experienced? He had known what it was like to live in total union with the Father. I imagine that it would have been crushing for Him to be without God's presence.

Thank You, thank You, thank You for being willing to take on the isolating burden of my sin so that I could live forever in communion with You.

REST: Isaiah 53 verse 3, directly prior to the passage above, describes Jesus' rejection by humanity, saying that He was *"a Man of sorrows and acquainted with grief."* That word *grief* is the Hebrew word *choliy*, meaning sickness, disease, or sadness. It comes from a root word that literally means "to be worn down." Jesus carried all of our sorrows, our anxieties, our illnesses to the Cross and died. He took the *choliy* of the world onto His shoulders so that we could be *sozo*—healed in spirit, soul, and body.

I know the moments of grief that you have experienced. I have felt them all. But I have come to offer you an exchange—your burdens for My freedom, your sickness for My strength, your sorrow for My joy.

June 25th

Jesus said to them, "I am the bread of life; he who comes to Me will not hunger, and he who believes in Me will never thirst."

—John 6:35 NASB

RISE: When Jesus gives the disciples this imagery as a way for them to think about Him, He does something that He does often throughout the Gospels. He is taking a natural reality that they would be very familiar with and using that to explain a Kingdom truth. Our food pyramid has undergone some dramatic shifts recently, but for many cultures bread is a staple food in the normal diet. Jesus had come from the throne room of Heaven. He is the King of all kings. But He doesn't say, "I am the caviar at your dinner party" or "I am the filet mignon of your life." Instead, He says, "I am the bread of life." Bread would have been foundational to the culture at the time. By equating Himself to bread, Jesus relates Himself to something familiar, but not trivial. Bread was intertwined with daily survival.

Thank You, Lord, that Your presence is not reserved for special occasions, but for daily consumption!

REST: Earlier in John chapter 6, Jesus had fed 5,000 from a few loaves and fishes. The disciples had just witnessed the value of bread for the survival of a whole crowd. Bread is life-sustaining. When Jesus shares a meal with His disciples on that last Passover, He again offers Himself to His disciples as bread. Jesus breaks the bread, saying, *"this is My body"* (Mark 14:22). He offers us the chance to align our bodies with His body, broken and resurrected for us. He is our "bread of life." Our survival depends on Jesus. He is life, hope, and healing.

In Me, you will find life that you could never have imagined when removed from My presence. Align yourself daily with the reality of Heaven and watch as My life-giving presence flows into you.

June 26th

And when He had given thanks, He broke it and said, "Take, eat; this is My body which is broken for you; do this in remembrance of Me."

—1 Corinthians 11:24 NKJV

RISE: As soon as I wake up, there are a thousand things competing for my attention. Before my feet hit the ground, I can read news from all over the world, find a recipe for dinner, scroll through photos on Instagram, listen to a worship song, and text a friend. If the mind is a battlefield, then a big part of the current battle is a fight for space. It's a battle for time, for quiet, and for focus. Now, I'm not saying that everyone needs to have hours each day set aside for time with the Lord. That's wonderful if you can do that, but not every season of life is conducive to that kind of time. Young mothers, for example, must learn how to turn their hearts toward Him for a few minutes while doing the dishes or putting the baby to bed. What we can all do, though, is to create a meditative space—a space for remembering—during our time of Communion with God.

> *Holy Spirit, help me recognize the meditative spaces open in my life that I fill with other things besides You. I value Your presence above all else, so help me to manifest that truth in the reality of my day.*

REST: There are some days that, because of my schedule, I take Communion quickly. But most days, I love to take the time to meditate on who God is and what He's done. The Lord wants to reveal different aspects of Himself to us, so every time I take Communion, I ask Him, "What does this mean today? What aspect of You do I need to have at the forefront of my mind today in order to keep myself aligned with You?" He is my daily bread. As I connect with Him, I meditate on His goodness and all that He's done. I take the time to remember.

> *It is My presence that brings life to ritual and tradition. There are so many things I want to show you, so many new aspects of My love and power that I long to release into your life.*

June 27th

Love the Lord your God and keep his requirements,
his decrees, his laws and his commands always.

—Deuteronomy 11:1 NIV

RISE: Throughout the Bible, the Lord speaks to His people about the power of memory. In Deuteronomy, the Israelites are about to enter into the Promised Land. They've wandered the desert for 40 years, being sustained and guided supernaturally the whole way. Almost an entire generation has passed away, and the children of those who fled from Egypt are about to walk into the *"land flowing with milk and honey"* (Deut. 11:9). Moses gives them some instructions from the Lord, but then he qualifies this commandment. Moses says that the people who have seen the miracles of the Lord, the ones who lived through the parting of the Red Sea and the provision of manna, are the ones with the responsibility to heed God's commandments.

I have a responsibility to steward the testimonies of Your goodness in my
life. Help me to think of practical ways that I can do this!

REST: When we take Communion "in remembrance" of what Jesus did on the Cross, we are stewarding the greatest testimony in history. The Israelites escaped Egypt after ten supernatural plagues rained down on their captors. They walked through the Red Sea on dry land. They were led by pillars of cloud and fire. They were fed supernaturally, never got sick, and wore the same clothes for 40 years. Yet they didn't have Jesus. They didn't have the Cross or the resurrection. Matthew 11:11 makes it clear the kind of gift we have received. *"Truly I say to you, among those born of women there has not arisen anyone greater than John the Baptist! Yet the one who is least in the kingdom of heaven is greater than he"* (NASB). John the Baptist knew Jesus as family, followed God faithfully, yet he was never born again. He didn't know life with the resurrected Christ living inside of him. You and I, we get that honor. We have that responsibility.

You have been born into a generation that has unprecedented access to
My presence. That was not a mistake; you have been born into a specific
time for My purpose.

June 28th

Set your mind and keep focused habitually on the things above [the heavenly things], not on things that are on the earth [which have only temporal value]. For you died [to this world], and your [new, real] life is hidden with Christ in God.

—Colossians 3:2-3 AMP

RISE: Memory is a powerful tool. It shapes our present by creating expectation for repetition. The brain is literally creating pathways from your thought patterns. Scientists who study the brain are confirming what the Bible says: What you allow your mind to dwell on shapes your expectations and, ultimately, your perception of the world. The neurons in the brain strengthen and change with our thought patterns. The more you make certain connections, the more likely your brain will make that connection in the future. Some describe it similarly to the way a popular hiking trail gets worn down and widened. For example, if you're used to thinking the world is out to get you, that neuropathway will have a strong connection in your brain. Something might happen to you, and you think, "Well, there it goes again. I knew bad things happen to me."

Holy Spirit, help me to see the pathways in my thinking that are not from You. I want to reroute them to mirror Your perspective, but I need Your help.

REST: The grace of the Lord always makes room for transformation. You can change these neuropathways by what you set your mind on. So when Paul writes to advise the Colossians to focus on the things of Heaven, it's not just a nice idea. It's actually advice that will change the "hardwiring" of our brains. We are new creations. We know a reality that is greater than any circumstance we can see. We have "the mind of Christ," and God is inviting us to use it (see 1 Cor. 2:16).

I have a never-ending supply of grace just waiting to be released into areas of transformation in your life. Let My Holy Spirit reveal to you the areas in your thinking that are not filled with My hope, My joyful confidence, and My redemptive perspective.

June 29th

Whenever you eat this bread and drink this cup, you are retelling the
story, proclaiming our Lord's death until he comes.

—1 Corinthians 11:26 TPT

RISE: A beautiful thread weaves between our past, our present, and our future. In our past, we have what God has done—all of the stories of His faithfulness and grace. In our present, we have the command to remember those testimonies, to build our trust in God and align ourselves with Him. From that place, change will come.

> *Thank You, Father, that I don't have to force change into my life. You are the author of every beneficial transformation inside of me. So I will intentionally remember the testimonies of Your goodness, aligning myself with You, and let Your Holy Spirit shift anything within me that needs to be shifted.*

REST: The act of proclaiming is like sharing the testimony. It is releasing the reality of the Cross into the world. When you're remembering God and trusting in Him completely, then you are filled with hope for the future of the world around you. We can take Communion in remembrance of all that He has done for the world and for ourselves personally, and we can look toward the future with hope. Matthew 17:20 says, "*if you have faith the size of a mustard seed, you will say to this mountain, 'Move from here to there,' and it will move; and nothing will be impossible to you*" (NASB). This promise is embedded in the body and blood of Christ.

> *Begin to weave declarations into the daily rhythm of your life. In the face of disappointment, declare fulfillment. In the face of illness, declare health. Proclaiming My death means proclaiming every area of restoration that My death precipitated.*

June 30th

He prayed even more passionately, like one being sacrificed, until he
was in such intense agony of spirit that his sweat became
drops of blood, dripping onto the ground.

—Luke 22:44 TPT

RISE: Often, we don't really want to remember the brutality of what Jesus went through for us. It's gruesome and uncomfortable. But when I remind myself of the details of Christ's death, I find that it keeps my heart in a posture of overwhelming gratitude. It also renews my perspective on whatever challenge I'm going through. For 33 years, Jesus lived on earth—three of those spent serving in a fruitful, but probably exhausting time of public ministry. As He neared the end of His life, Jesus wrestled with what He was about to do.

> *Jesus, I want to let my heart break for the pain, isolation, and suffering*
> *that You went through on my behalf. I never want to forget the price*
> *that You willingly paid for me.*

REST: Jesus was the only one, besides the Father, who was aware of what He was about to go through. The intensity of that anticipation, not only of His own physical death but also of the agony of being separated from the Father because of the sin of the world, must have been so painful that He literally sweat blood. When He was carrying that reality, the betrayal by Judas and the rejection from His closest disciples must have been an added weight on His heart. So when I'm remembering the betrayal of Jesus, I'm not just focusing on the injustice. I'm focusing on Jesus. I'm reminding myself of the way that He walked through betrayal. If Jesus can do that, then He's offering me a model for how to deal with my own hurts and grievances. He's showing me what His love can overcome.

> *I will let your heart break for My pain, but so that My great love for you*
> *can pour into every cracked place. It was for you that I died, and I would*
> *do it all over again. You are worth it.*

July

July 1st

*In this way, every generation will have a living faith in the laws of life
and will never forget the faithful ways of God.*

—Psalm 78:7 TPT

RISE: This verse draws the connection between memory, trust, and obedience. Dwelling on the goodness of God, continually reminding ourselves of His faithfulness and His promises—these are the building blocks of trust. And when we trust God, aligning ourselves with His commandments comes so much more naturally. Without our keeping Him in the forefront of our minds, that confidence crumbles, and fear takes hold.

*I want to be forever building my trust in You, God. Help me to see Your
hand in my life in a way that keeps me aware of Your nature and Your
love for me.*

REST: There are very real consequences to our forgetting who God is. When His goodness and faithfulness are not fresh in our mind, we can become calloused toward God. We can feel hesitant to trust in His goodness. And that can lead to a heart that has not been cultivating gratitude. We can see the results of that within our own lives and the lives of the Israelites. As soon as they started forgetting, they began to fear, and they put their trust in something else. Because the Israelites turned from trusting in God completely, He allowed His presence to be removed from their midst. They were no longer recipients of His strength, and they no longer had access to His glory. We live under the New Covenant. God has promised never to remove His presence from us, but we still have the same choice that the Israelites had.

*Will you trust in My love for you? Will you remember the ways in which
I have smiled upon your life? Turn away from fear and self-reliance; let
yourself be dependent on My love.*

July 2nd

For God so loved the world that He gave His only begotten Son, that whoever believes in Him should not perish but have everlasting life.

—John 3:16 NKJV

RISE: Doubting God's faithfulness can become an all-too-familiar heart issue. Will He take care of me? Will He provide for me? Was His blood enough for what I'm going through? Each time we take Communion, we are testifying to the enormous, radical love of God. We are reminding ourselves that we had a debt that we could never, ever repay and that we were condemned to death; there was nothing we could do about it. But God.

Thank You, Jesus, that Your sacrifice was enough for everything I am going through. Thank You that I am never alone in my struggle. You are with me, and You have a solution.

REST: His love was so extravagant that He sent His Son to die in our place, to suffer indescribable pain so that He could take on the sins of the world. John 3:16 is the first verse many of us learn as a child. It's a powerful one that we can take for granted because it's so familiar. I would encourage you, as you take Communion, to meditate on this verse. Allow your remembrance of Him to take you to a new level of understanding. It was all for love. Love took Him to that Cross, and love kept Him there. When you take Communion, experience the invitation to remember the weighty reality of His absolute and perfect love for you.

Love cannot exist without freedom, so I have woven into the world the potential for My own grief—the option for you to reject My love. But there is never a moment when My heart is not open to you, waiting to embrace you.

July 3rd

Therefore, with minds that are alert and fully sober, set your hope on the grace to be brought to you when Jesus Christ is revealed at his coming.

—1 Peter 1:13 NIV

RISE: Jesus never requires perfection in order to come to Him. That is the scandal of His saving grace. We don't need to be anxious about taking Communion, searching for any potential hidden sin. Fear is never productive; it just gets in the way of love's transforming power. However, when we participate in the body and blood of Christ, we do want to posture our hearts in an intentional way. This intentionality not only brings the respect and honor due the sacrament, but it also helps us to create the space in our hearts for the Spirit of God to move and transform us through Communion.

> *I never want to take Your sacrifice lightly, Lord, or let the ritual of participating in Communion become routine or void of meaning. Help me to slow down, to intentionally focus on the astonishing nature of Your saving grace.*

REST: When we participate in Communion, it is important for there to be a sense of soberness. I don't mean somber, as in "gloomy or depressing." Far from it. But there needs to be a sense of gravity about what we are getting to participate in. We have such a good Father, who is so incredibly full of grace, but I would never want to lose sight of His holiness or His awesome power. On the one hand, we have Jesus inviting the little children to come to Him. And, on the other, we have Jesus returning to earth with eyes that flame like fire. It's not either/or; it's both/and. When we participate in the body and blood of Jesus Christ, sober reverence is a healthy and appropriate reaction.

> *I never want you to fear Me in a way that makes you hide or pull away from My presence, but it is in My nature to awe. I am a good and gentle Father, but I am also the King of kings who reigns in absolute power and righteousness.*

July 4th

Let joy be your continual feast. Make your life a prayer. And in the midst of everything be always giving thanks, for this is God's perfect plan for you in Christ Jesus.

—1 Thessalonians 5:16-18 TPT

RISE: Thankfulness is showing appreciation. I often hear people yearning to know God's will for their lives, but it says it right here. Stay thankful. Stay connected to God. When the Bible tells us to be thankful no matter the circumstance, it is not expecting us to create an emotion out of thin air. Gratitude is a response. There has to be a previous action or reality. When we take Communion, we are responding to all that the Lord has done and continues to do for us. Keeping our hearts postured toward the Lord in gratitude is one of the biggest keys to success we find throughout the Bible.

I am so grateful for all that You've done for me, God. Help me to notice the daily kisses from You so that gratitude will flow from me no matter what the circumstance.

REST: Hebrews 13:15 encourages us to "continually offer up a sacrifice of praise to God." We've all been in the midst of experiences where the phrase "sacrifice of praise" feels very real. When you're exhausted or hurting, sometimes worship and expressing gratitude is the last thing you want to do. But look at the Samaritan leper. Ten leprous men were healed by Jesus, but only one of them fell down to give Him thanks. Jesus wasn't in need of gratitude, but He knew that it would do something for the man. Jesus asked about the other nine men who hadn't returned, and then He told the Samaritan, "*Stand up and go; your faith has made you well*" (Luke 17:19 NASB). The man was already healed. But that word "well" is that Hebrew word *sozo* again. His body had been healed, but there was something about his expression of gratitude that made him whole.

No matter what is swirling around your life, I am worthy of your praise. I am unchanging. My nature is constant and perfect, so let your praise rise up from that place of realization.

July 5th

He who offers a sacrifice of praise and thanksgiving honors Me; and to
him who orders his way rightly [who follows the way that I show him],
I shall show the salvation of God.

—Psalm 50:23 AMP

RISE: First Peter 2:9 says that we have been made "a royal priesthood." As believers under the New Covenant, we now have the privilege of ministering to the Lord. When we offer up a "sacrifice of praise," we are bringing honor to God. Focusing our hearts on gratitude brings Him glory, which alone is enough.

> *I want my every breath to bring You glory, Father. I long to have my*
> *praise bring joy to Your heart. If there are any areas of my life where I*
> *am avoiding the "sacrifice of praise," I invite Your Holy Spirit to show*
> *me right now.*

REST: But the Bible goes on to explain that gratitude also reorients us correctly, inviting the "salvation of God" into our lives. That word *salvation* is the Hebrew word *yesha*, which means "rescue and safety," but it also means "deliverance, prosperity, and victory." The psalmist said to *"enter His gates with thanksgiving and His courts with praise"* (Ps. 100:4 NASB). When we come to the Lord with thankfulness, we have access to His presence and His covering. We get to participate in His victory.

> *The fullness of My presence is attracted to your praise. The sweet*
> *fragrance of your gratitude, acknowledging My goodness, draws you*
> *into My inner sanctuary.*

July 6th

Praise the Lord! Praise God in His sanctuary; praise Him in His
mighty firmament! Praise Him for His mighty acts; praise Him
according to His excellent greatness!

—Psalm 150:1-2 NKJV

RISE: I love the story of the first miracle that Jesus did. I love that Mary pulled Jesus' public ministry into the limelight before it was time. And I love that Jesus created wine for a party. Jesus loves celebration. We can celebrate alone, of course, but more often a celebration is an experience we want to share with the people we love. When we take Communion, it is our chance to celebrate with our brothers and sisters in Christ. Jesus has changed our lives, and that deserves a party. After all, what's a celebration without friends? There is something sacred about corporate Communion—partaking of the body and blood of Christ with the vibrant, diverse Body of Christ. Communion is a vertical realigning of ourselves with Christ, but it is also a horizontal realigning—we are the Body of Christ.

> *Thank You, Jesus, that You care about my relationships with those*
> *around me. Help me to give grace to others often and with ease.*

REST: God loves unity. It was His idea. This is why examining our hearts is such an important part of Communion. Not because we have to prove to God that we're worthy of His blood and body. We already know that's impossible. We examine our hearts because it's a time of reunion, both with the Spirit of God and with our fellow believers. In corporate Communion, we get to stand with others and confess that He took a burden from our shoulders that we could never carry. Experiencing that radical grace means that we now get to access and release that grace to others. We get to offer forgiveness to others, cleansing our hearts from the detrimental effects of bitterness and unforgiveness. Jesus loves His Church. He is coming back for a strong, healthy, and united Bride.

> *When you received the gift of My covenant promise, you became a part*
> *of a family. Some of the things you need, I have placed within your*
> *community. Keep your heart tender to those around you.*

July 7th

My old self has been crucified with Christ.
It is no longer I who live, but Christ lives in me.

—Galatians 2:20 NLT

RISE: The Bible is 100 percent true, so if I'm not experiencing its promises, there must be a reality that is greater and truer than the one that I am experiencing. That we would need reminding of this greater reality comes as no surprise to the Lord. It's as if He said, "Listen, I know some days are going to be hard. I know there are going to be moments when it feels like the reality of Heaven is far away. Your child is sick, or you lost your job, or your best friend died, or you did that thing you swore you would stop doing. I know. I'm leaving you something—My body and My blood—to remind you who you are and where your true home is. I'm leaving you this reminder of My salvation, My healing, the comfort of My presence, and My victorious return."

You are the compass of my life, Father. Help me to be everything You created me to be so that the world can know how good You are.

REST: Human nature is constantly attempting to create rules outside of a relationship. Communion is not a magic pill, and God is not a vending machine. He does not want us to eat a wafer and drink some grape juice every day so that He will grant our wishes. Communion is about lining ourselves up with Him—spirit, soul, and body. It is a chance for us to remember the debt of sin that hung around our necks—too big for us to ever repay on our own—and the way that our Jesus took that debt with Him to the Cross so that you and I could have life, and have it abundantly (see John 10:10). It's a chance for us to come—in all humility and honor—into the presence of the Lord, to praise His name for all that He has done, and to celebrate in union with other believers.

Take this tool of remembrance and let it pull you back into alignment with Heaven's perspective of who you are—protected, loved, provided for, a source of great delight.

July 8th

My beloved ones, just like you've always listened to everything I've taught you in the past, I'm asking you now to keep following my instructions as though I were right there with you. Now you must continue to make this new life fully manifested as you live in the holy awe of God—which brings you trembling into his presence.

—Philippians 2:12 TPT

RISE: Every time we take the bread and the wine in remembrance, it is a prophetic proclamation of what has already happened, as well as what is yet to come. Consider this—Communion declares that Jesus died for us and is returning for us. When people surrender their life to Jesus, they are born again. In other words, they're saved. We know this teaching from God's Word. But the implication of the verse from Philippians is that I am also being saved. This doesn't deny what happened to me when I received Christ. It just emphasizes the daily, ongoing process of personal transformation.

Thank You, Holy Spirit, for every area of my life that is in the process of being transformed by Your gentle guidance. I want to become more like Jesus every day.

REST: So, not only were you once saved, but you are also being saved right now. The crowning touch to this glorious truth of our salvation comes when we die to meet Him or He returns to take us to Heaven. In this coming event, we find that we will be saved. Our salvation will then be complete. Participating in Communion is a wonderful privilege that declares what I call the bookends of our salvation in that it addresses the past and the future. Sharing in the broken body and the shed blood of Jesus helps us with the present.

Living within the tension of "now" and "not yet" is a part of the divine wrestle of the human life. Don't hide from tension or smooth it over, but allow your questions to pull you into an even closer dialogue with Me.

July 9th

For I received from the Lord what I also passed on to you:
The Lord Jesus, on the night he was betrayed, took bread,
and when he had given thanks....

—1 Corinthians 11:23-24 NIV

RISE: Picture something powerful—the very night that Jesus was betrayed, He gave thanks. In the midst of the ultimate betrayal, He gave an offering of thanksgiving. He didn't just tell us to praise Him in hard times; He gave us the ultimate example to follow. In betrayal, He gave thanks. Thankfulness is one of the most vital attributes within the reach of every person alive. If I could prayerfully lay hands on people and impart a thankful heart, without question, I would. And I would make that the single greatest focus of my life. An impartation of thankfulness would have the greatest impact on the hearts and minds of people. It would literally change the world as we know it. Thankful people attract breakthrough.

Help me to see the moments when I could turn to thankfulness, but instead allow frustration or discouragement to seep into my heart. I want to do the work of maturity until I too can give thanks in the midst of betrayal.

REST: Following the major sporting events like the Super Bowl, World Series, World Cup, and the like, it has become common to see athletes thank God for enabling them to win. I love to see them boast in God and testify of Him every chance they get. But let's be honest—it's not that challenging to give thanks when you've won. The real prize is when we give Him thanks in the middle of something difficult or wrong. That's where the pearl is formed, so to speak. Pearls are formed through irritation. Whenever we give thanks in the middle of hard things, we are presenting something to Him that is priceless. Jesus did it at His darkest moment—betrayal.

Gratitude in the midst of pain and loss is a gift you will only be able to give Me on earth. In Heaven, there is no pain, so the stunning beauty of this choice has a limited lifespan, making it all the more precious.

July 10th

Since we are now joined to Christ, we have been given the treasures of redemption by his blood—the total cancellation of our sins—all because of the cascading riches of his grace.

—Ephesians 1:7-8 TPT

RISE: I believe in the power of Communion so much that I love to make confession over my family of how the blood of Jesus sets us free. This confession absolutely terrifies parts of darkness. I know from personal experience that it's the one thing of which they are absolutely terrified. They know that the blood of Jesus is the dividing line that separates someone the demonic can control from someone they can't touch.

I lift up each member in my family to You by name, Lord. I plead Your blood over their lives and over any who are not yet following You.

REST: I love to hold this before the Lord and pray for the people around me. I just plead the blood of Jesus over their lives. It's not just grape juice that we're drinking. I pray that each of us would fully realize the effect of what we're doing during Communion. I believe that the Lord is going to release unusual miracles of healing in the taking of the bread. He is going to release unusual miracles of deliverance to people and family members who are maybe a thousand miles away or more by our taking the juice (representing the blood) and pleading the blood of Jesus over their lives. Prayer while partaking of Communion is possibly one of the most underrated prayers that we could ever pray. Communion is not a magic formula. It's us being convinced that the blood of Jesus sets free. And that expression of faith puts us into a position to influence the destinies of our families, the people around us, and the entire world.

When you unite yourself with My heart and release that reality through your prayers, there is nothing more powerful.

July 11th

God blessed them; and God said to them, "Be fruitful and multiply, and fill the earth, and subdue it; and rule over the fish of the sea and over the birds of the sky and over every living thing that moves on the earth."

—Genesis 1:28 NASB

RISE: The backbone of Kingdom authority and power is found in the commission. Discovering God's original commission and purpose for mankind can help fortify our resolve to a life of history-changing significance. To find that truth we must go back to the beginning. Man was created in the image of God and placed into the Father's ultimate expression of beauty and peace—the Garden of Eden. Outside of that Garden, it was a different story. It was without the order and blessing contained within and was in great need of the touch of God's delegated one—Adam.

You love order, beauty, and life, God. Thank You that You've placed that love and Your creative authority within Me. Help me to steward well all that You've placed in my hands.

REST: Adam and Eve were placed in the Garden with a mission. It was God's intention that, as they bore more children who also lived under God's rule, they would be extending the boundaries of His Garden (His government) through the simplicity of their devotion to Him. The greater the number of people in right relationship to God, the greater the impact of their leadership. This process was to continue until the entire earth was covered with the glorious rule of God through man. But in Genesis chapter 1 we discover it's not a perfect universe. Satan had rebelled and had been cast out of Heaven, and with him a portion of the fallen angels took dominion of the earth. It's obvious why the rest of the planet needed to be subdued—it was under the influence of darkness (see Gen. 1:2). God could have destroyed the devil and his host with a word, but instead He chose to defeat darkness through His delegated authority—those made in His image who were lovers of God by choice.

I long to fill the earth with our manifested love story—your heart submitted to Me, flourishing in every way.

July 12th

*Don't you know that when you offer yourselves to someone as obedient
slaves, you are slaves of the one you obey—whether you are slaves to
sin, which leads to death, or to obedience, which leads to righteousness?*

—Romans 6:16 NIV

RISE: The sovereign one placed us—Adam's children—in charge of planet earth. "*The
heaven, even the heavens, are the Lord's; but the earth He has given to the children of
men*" (Ps. 115:16). This highest of honors was chosen because love always chooses the
best. That is the beginning of the romance of our creation—created in His image, for
intimacy, that dominion might be expressed through love. It is from this revelation that
we are to learn to walk as His ambassadors, thus defeating the "prince of this world."
The stage was set for all of darkness to fall as man exercised his godly influence over
creation. But instead, man fell.

> *Thank You, Jesus, that it is only because of Your sacrifice that I can now
> be restored to my original design as a beloved co-creator with the Father,
> bringing Heaven to earth.*

REST: Satan didn't come into the Garden of Eden violently and take possession of
Adam and Eve. He couldn't! Why? He had no dominion there. Dominion empowers.
And since man was given the keys of dominion over the planet, the devil would have
to get his authority from them. The suggestion to eat the forbidden fruit was simply
the devil's effort to get Adam and Eve to agree with him in opposition to God, thus
empowering him. Through that agreement, he is enabled to kill, steal, and destroy. It's
important to realize that even today satan is empowered through man's agreement.
Man's authority to rule was forfeited when Adam ate the forbidden fruit. In that one
act, mankind became the slave and possession of the evil one.

> *That sneaky worm, satan, has no authority on earth unless he can trick
> you into removing your trust from My hands. Build your trust in Me
> like a fortress; refuse to hand over your keys of authority.*

July 13th

For the Son of Man has come to seek and to save that which was lost.

—Luke 19:10 NASB

RISE: God's plan of rulership for man never ceased. Jesus came to bear man's penalty for sin and recapture what had been lost. Luke 19:10 not only speaks about what mankind lost to sin but about the fact that his dominion over planet earth was also lost. Jesus came to recapture both. Satan tried to ruin that plan at the end of Jesus' 40-day fast. The devil knew he wasn't worthy of Jesus' worship, but he also knew that Jesus had come to reclaim the authority that man had given away.

> *Thank You, Jesus, that everything that was lost to sin has been fully restored through Your death and resurrection!*

REST: The Father wanted satan defeated by man—one made in His image. Jesus, who would shed His blood to redeem mankind, emptied Himself of His rights as God and took upon Himself the limitations of man. Satan was defeated by a man—the Son of Man—who was rightly related to God. Now, as people receive the work of Christ on the Cross for salvation, they become grafted into that victory. Jesus defeated the devil with His sinless life, defeated him in His death by paying for our sins with His blood, and again, in the resurrection, rising triumphant with the keys of death and hell. In redeeming man, Jesus retrieved what man had given away, restoring us completely to those who rule as people made in God's image.

> *I have given back to you that which mankind tossed aside—authority over the earth, intimacy with Me, and a realignment of every part of your being to My presence.*

July 14th

Let this mind be in you which was also in Christ Jesus, who, being in the form of
God, did not consider it robbery to be equal with God, but made Himself of no
reputation, taking the form of a bondservant, and coming in the likeness of men.

—Philippians 2:5-7 NKJV

RISE: Israel expected their Messiah to come as the King who would rule over all other kings. And He did. But their misunderstanding of greatness in His Kingdom made it difficult for them to grasp how He could be born without earthly fanfare and become the servant of all. They expected Him to rule with a rod of iron. In doing so, they would finally have revenge on all those who had oppressed them throughout the ages. Little did they realize that His vengeance would not be aimed so much at the enemies of Israel as it would be toward the enemies of man—sin, the devil and his works, and the self-righteous attitudes fostered by religion.

> *I am often like the Israelites, wanting to exact revenge on those who hurt*
> *me. Teach me, Lord, to shift my focus from battling people to taking*
> *authority over the spiritual realities that are grappling for influence.*

REST: Jesus the Messiah came—full of surprises. Only the contrite in heart could keep up with His constant coloring outside the lines and stay unoffended. His purpose was revealed in His primary message: *"Repent, for the kingdom of heaven is at hand"* (Matt. 4:17). Now, there's something that caught them completely off guard: He brought His world with Him! Repentance means much more than weeping over sin or even turning from those sins to follow God. In fact, turning from sin to God is more the result of true repentance than it is the actual act. Repentance means you change your way of thinking. And it's only in changing the way we think that we can discover the focus of Jesus' ministry—the Kingdom. This is not just a heavenly mandate to have happy thoughts. Obeying this command is possible only for those who surrender to the grace of God. The renewed mind is the result of a surrendered heart.

> *I know you have behavior that you long to change. Focus less on the*
> *actions and more on My face. Turn from self-analysis to hiding yourself*
> *in Me. I will do more than you ever could with a tender heart.*

July 15th

Blessed are the poor in spirit, for theirs is the kingdom of heaven.

—Matthew 5:3 NIV

RISE: How would you describe a group of people who left cities for days at a time, traveling great distances on foot, abandoning all that life involves, only to follow Jesus to some desolate place? The hunger of the crowd, those who had just watched Jesus perform the miraculous, pulled a reality from the heart of God that they didn't even know existed. I call them "poor in spirit." And Jesus gave them the promised manifestation of the Kingdom with healing and deliverance. He then followed the miracles with the sermon, for it was common for Jesus to teach so He could explain what He had just done. In this case, the actual presence of the Spirit of God upon Jesus stirred up a hunger for God in the people. That hunger brought a change in their attitudes without their being told it should change. Their hunger for God, even before they could recognize it as such, had created a new perspective in them. Without an effort to change, they had changed.

> *Keep me poor in spirit, God. I want every encounter with You to stir up even more hunger in my heart.*

REST: The Kingdom comes in the presence of the Spirit of God. It was His presence they detected, and it was His presence they longed for. For them, it didn't matter if He was doing miracles or just giving another sermon; they just had to be where He was. Hunger for God brings about the ultimate humility. The Sermon on the Mount is a treatise on the Kingdom. In it, Jesus reveals the attitudes that help His followers to access His unseen world. As citizens of Heaven, these attitudes are formed in us that we might fully apprehend all that His Kingdom has available. The Beatitudes are actually the "lenses" that the Kingdom is seen through. Repentance involved taking on the mind of Christ revealed in those verses.

> *Come to Me, My child; let My presence shape the way you think. Blessings and joy will be the fruit of our relationship!*

July 16th

*For we walk by faith, not by sight [living our lives in a manner
consistent with our confident belief in God's promises].*

—2 Corinthians 5:7 AMP

RISE: Faith is the mirror of the heart that reflects the realities of an unseen world—
the actual substance of His Kingdom. Through the prayer of faith, we are able to pull
the reality of His world into this one. The Scriptures contrast the life of faith with the
limitations of natural sight. Faith provides eyes for the heart, and Jesus expects people
to see from the heart. He once called a group of religious leaders hypocrites because
they could discern the weather but couldn't discern the times. We often think that the
ability to see into the spiritual realm is a special gift rather than an unused potential of
everyone. But Jesus addressed that charge to the Pharisees and Sadducees. The very fact
that they, of all people, were required to see is evidence that everyone has been given
this ability. They became blind to His dominion because of their own corrupted hearts
and were judged for their unfulfilled potential.

> *Open the eyes of my heart, God, to the unseen realm. I want to live my
> life fully planted in Heaven so that I can see the world as You do.*

REST: We are born again by grace through faith (see Eph. 2:8). The born-again experience enables us to see from the heart (see John 3:3). A heart that doesn't see is a hard
heart (see Mark 8:17-18). Faith was never intended only to get us into the family. Rather,
it is the nature of life in this family. Faith sees. It brings His Kingdom into focus. All of
the Father's resources, all of His benefits, are accessible through faith. The Bible instructs
us to turn our attention toward the invisible. Herein lies the secret to the supernatural
realm that we want restored to the Church. Jesus told us that He only did what He
saw His Father do. Such an insight is vital for those who want more. The power of His
actions—for instance, the mud in the eye of the blind—is rooted in His ability to see.

> *You were born to change the world, but to fulfill that calling you need to
> see like I do. Come close, let Me show you how accessible the supernatural
> is to My children.*

July 17th

From here on, worshiping the Father will not be a matter of the right place but with the right heart. For God is a Spirit, and he longs to have sincere worshipers who worship and adore him in the realm of the Spirit and in truth.

—John 4:23-24 TPT

RISE: God is very committed to teaching us how to see. To make this possible, He gave us the Holy Spirit as a tutor. The curriculum that He uses is quite varied. But the one class we all qualify for is the greatest of all Christian privileges—worship. Learning how to see is not the purpose for our worship, but it is a wonderful byproduct. Those who worship in Spirit and truth learn to follow the Holy Spirit's lead. His realm is called the Kingdom of God. The throne of God, which becomes established upon the praises of His people (see Ps. 22:3), is the center of that Kingdom.

> *Holy Spirit, my heart is wide open to You. Come, teach me and guide me in the nature of the Kingdom. I have pledged my life to worshiping Him who deserves all of my praise.*

REST: It's in the environment of worship that we learn things that go way beyond what our intellect can grasp (see Eph. 3:20)—and the greatest of these lessons is the value of His presence. David was so affected by this that all his other exploits pale in comparison to his abandoned heart for God. We know that he learned to see into God's realm because of statements like, *"I have set the Lord always before me; because He is at my right hand I shall not be moved"* (Ps. 16:8). He saw God daily, not with the natural eyes, but with the eyes of faith. That priceless revelation was given to a worshiper. It's in the wonderful ministry of worship that we can learn to pay attention to this God-given gift—the ability to see with the heart. As we learn to worship with purity of heart, our eyes will continue to open. And we can expect to see what He wants us to see.

> *David kept no part of his heart from Me—the beautiful as well as the ugly. There is so much I want to show you. Open your heart to Me without restraint.*

July 18th

*In this manner, therefore, pray: Our Father in heaven, hallowed be
Your name. Your kingdom come. Your will be done
on earth as it is in heaven.*

—Matthew 6:9-10 NKJV

RISE: We were created for intimacy. From that intimacy comes our commission to rule. He views ruling differently than most of us do. We rule through service. Christ-likeness—excellence with humility—is the real goal. Prayer is the simplest activity of the believer. Child to father, lover to lover—a conversation, sometimes spoken. Prayer is also one of the more complicated issues for us. Formulas don't work in this Kingdom relationship. The honor that we have in being able to pray is beyond all comprehension. We are His representation on earth—ambassadors of His world. Our cries, all of them, touch His heart.

*Would You reveal to me Your value for prayer, God? I want to grow in
my love of conversing with You. I want to know the ways that it touches
Your heart.*

REST: Intimacy is the main purpose of prayer. And it's through relationship that God entrusts to us the secrets of His heart, that we might express them in prayer. That's what He did with Simeon and Anna as He stirred their hearts to pray for the coming of the Messiah long before He was born (see Luke 2:25-38). If these things were going to happen anyway, what would be the purpose of prayer? God has apparently given Himself a self-imposed restriction—to act in the affairs of man in response to prayer. God has chosen to work through us. We are His delegated authority on planet earth, and prayer is the vehicle that gives occasion for His invasion. Those who don't pray allow darkness to continue ruling. The enemy's greatest efforts at deceiving the Church are centered on the purpose and effect of prayer.

*My connection with you is so precious to Me. And, like any best friend,
I long to hear what's on your heart and share with you those things that
are on Mine.*

July 19th

Endless love beyond measurement that transcends our
understanding—this extravagant love pours into you until
you are filled to overflowing with the fullness of God!

—Ephesians 3:19 TPT

RISE: There is a difference between immediate and ultimate goals. Success with an immediate goal makes it possible to reach an ultimate goal. But failure in the immediate prevents us from reaching our final goal. Bowlers know this. Each lane not only has ten pins at the far end, it also has markers on the lane itself. A good bowler will aim at a marker in the lane as an initial target. Yet they receive no points for hitting it. Points are only given when the ultimate target is hit—the pins at the end of the lane. Likewise, salvation was not the ultimate goal of Christ's coming. It was the immediate target. Without accomplishing redemption, there was no hope for the ultimate goal—which was to fill each born-again person with the Holy Spirit. God's desire is for the believer to overflow with Himself.

> *Father, I need to be filled with the Holy Spirit. I don't want it to be a*
> *one-time thing. I need the continual infilling of You to fulfill the destiny*
> *that You have called me to.*

REST: The resulting fullness of the Spirit was different than anyone had ever before experienced. For that reason, the greatest of all Old Testament prophets could confess: "I need to be baptized by You," meaning, "I need Your baptism—the one I was assigned to announce!" The baptism in the Holy Spirit makes a lifestyle available to us that not even John the Baptist had access to. Consider this: We could travel off of this planet in any direction at the speed of light, 186,000 miles a second, for billions of years, and never begin to exhaust what we already know to exist. All of that rests in the palm of His hand. And it's this God who wants to fill us with His fullness.

> *I want to show you the beautiful mystery of My expansiveness. You will*
> *never reach the limits of My presence. There is always more available for*
> *you. Let me pour out My Spirit, filling you time and again.*

July 20th

*Anoint them just as you anointed their father, so they may serve me
as priests. Their anointing will be to a priesthood that will continue
throughout their generations.*

—Exodus 40:15 NIV

RISE: To fulfill His mission, Jesus needed the Holy Spirit; and that mission, with all its objectives, was to finish the Father's work (see John 4:34). If the Son of God was that reliant upon the anointing, His behavior should clarify our need for the Holy Spirit's presence upon us to do what the Father has assigned. It's vital to understand that we must be clothed with the Holy Spirit for supernatural ministry. In the Old Testament, it was the anointing that qualified a priest for ministry. According to Jesus' example, New Testament ministry is the same—anointing brings supernatural results. This anointing is what enabled Jesus to do only what He saw His Father do, and say only what He heard His Father say. It was the Holy Spirit that revealed the Father to Jesus.

*If Jesus needed You, Holy Spirit, how much more do I need to be filled
with the anointing of the Father? I can't do it without You.*

REST: It would seem that with all the significance attached to the name *Jesus*, anyone desiring to undermine His work of redemption might be referred to as "anti-Jesus," not "anti-Christ." But *antichrist* was the name given to this spirit of opposition. The spirits of hell are at war against the anointing, for without the anointing mankind is no threat to their dominion. Jesus' concern for mankind was applauded. His humility was revered, but it was the anointing that released the supernatural. And it was the supernatural invasion of God Himself that was rejected by the religious leaders. This anointing is actually the person of the Holy Spirit upon someone to equip them for supernatural endeavors.

*When you place yourself in a position of dependence on Me and My
Spirit, My heart is delighted. Your places of need for Me are beautiful
in My eyes.*

July 21st

*This man came to Jesus by night and said to Him, "Rabbi, we know
that You are a teacher come from God; for no one can do these signs
that You do unless God is with him."*

—John 3:2 NKJV

RISE: Jesus, the model teacher, never separated teaching from doing. He is the pattern for this gift. God's revealed Word, declared through the lips of an anointed teacher, ought to lead to demonstrations of power. It was understood that God's kind of teachers don't just talk—they do. And the "doing" that is referred to in John's Gospel is the performing of signs and wonders. Jesus established the ultimate example in ministry by combining the proclamation of the Gospel with signs and wonders. He then commanded His disciples to minister with the same focus—the 12 were sent out with, "*And as you go, preach, saying, 'The kingdom of heaven is at hand.' Heal the sick, cleanse the lepers, raise the dead, cast out demons. Freely you have received, freely give*" (Matt. 10:7-8).

*Father, forgive me for all of the ways that I have not put into practice
that which I freely preach. Help me to seize the opportunities to step out
in faith so that I can do ministry like You.*

REST: As men and women of God who teach, we must require from ourselves doing with power! And this doing must include a breaking into the impossible—through signs and wonders. Bible teachers are to instruct in order to explain what they just did or are about to do. Those who restrict themselves to mere words limit their gift and may unintentionally lead believers to pride by increasing knowledge without an increased awareness of God's presence and power. It's in the trenches of Christlike ministry that we learn to become totally dependent upon God. Moving in the impossible through relying on God short-circuits the development of pride.

*It's so much easier to leave My anointing in the comfortable realm of
the theoretical, but I was never meant to be boxed in like that. I came
to invade the world in every practical sense—healing, deliverance,
provision, salvation. My love is tangible.*

July 22nd

If only you could learn the meaning of the words "I want compassion
more than a sacrifice," you wouldn't be condemning my innocent
disciples. For the Son of Man exercises his lordship over the Sabbath.

—Matthew 12:7-8 TPT

RISE: Most of the Pharisees spent their lives serving God without ever discovering the Father's heart! Jesus offended these religious leaders most because He demonstrated what the Father wanted. While the Pharisees thought God was concerned about the Sabbath, Jesus worked to help the ones the Sabbath was created for. These leaders were accustomed to the miracles of the Scriptures remaining in the past. But Jesus broke into their comfort zones by ushering the supernatural into their cities. With every miracle, He showed the entire religious community the Father's business. For them to adapt, everything would have to be overhauled. It was easier to brand Him a liar, declaring His works to be of the devil and eventually killing this One who reminded them of what had to be changed.

> *I never want to forget the true purpose of ministry, Jesus. Fill me with*
> *the Father's compassion so that I can release His love.*

REST: Understanding that the Father's business has to do with signs and wonders is no guarantee that we will truly fulfill God's purpose for our lives. It is much more than doing miracles or even getting conversions. The supernatural interventions of God were done to reveal the extravagant heart of the Father for people. Every miracle is a revelation of His nature. And in that revelation is embedded an invitation for relationship. The Pharisees' error is a very easy one for us to repeat. They had no understanding of the Father's heart. And much Christian activity exists that has no relationship to that supreme value. More than learning how to identify our personal gifts or discover ways to be more successful in ministry, we need the Father Himself. The Gospel is the story of the Father wooing the hearts of mankind through His love. All the other stuff we do overflows from that discovery.

> *I long to give My people favor in every realm of society, but you will not*
> *influence those you do not love. Let My heart fill yours so that you can*
> *see every person through My mercy-filled eyes.*

July 23ʳᵈ

*Go therefore and make disciples of all the nations...teaching
them to observe all that I commanded you.*

—Matthew 28:19-20 NASB

RISE: Many believers have made it their primary goal in life to be well-respected citizens of their communities. Good character enables us to be solid contributors to society, but most of what is recognized as a Christian lifestyle can be accomplished by people who don't even know God. Every believer should be highly respected and more. It's the "and more" part that we're often lacking. While character must be at the heart of our ministries, power revolutionizes the world around us. Until the Church returns to Jesus' model, we will continue to be recognized by the world merely as nice people—while it is overcome with disease and torment, on its way to hell. Some Christians actually have considered it to be more noble to choose character over power, but we must not separate the two. Character is shaped through obedience.

> *Thank You, Father, that as I obey Your command to bring Heaven to
> earth through Your supernatural interventions, my heart and soul will
> be shaped and transformed by Your presence.*

REST: Many consider themselves unworthy of God using them in the miraculous and therefore never pursue that realm. Isn't it ironic that Christians will disobey God by not diligently seeking after spiritual gifts—they won't lay hands on the sick or seek to deliver the demonized—because they realize their need for more character? In none of the commissions of Jesus to His disciples did He deal specifically with character. Is it possible the reason there are so few miracles in North America is because too many before us thought they had to become better Christians before God could use them? Yes! That single lie has kept us in perpetual immaturity because it protects us from the power encounter that transforms us.

> *My discipleship program is not long and arduous. I never wait around
> for perfect people to release My Kingdom. I want to use everyone,
> especially you. Experience My presence and leave the rest up to the
> transformative power of My grace-filled Spirit.*

July 24th

And I will send the fulfillment of the Father's promise to you.
So stay here in the city until the mighty power of heaven
falls upon you and wraps around you.

—Luke 24:49 TPT

RISE: Jesus commanded the most highly trained individuals in the supernatural to ever walk the earth to "wait in Jerusalem for what the Father has promised" (see Acts 1:4). Even though they had been with Him, even though they had experienced His power through their own ministry, they were to wait for *dunamis*—the ability to perform miracles. It is as if they had been working under the umbrella of His anointing. The time had come for them to get an anointing of their own through an encounter with God. The baptism of fire would give them their own ongoing encounter that would help to keep them at the center of God's will when persecution came.

> *Thank You, Jesus, for giving us these examples of how to walk out Your commandments as Spirit-filled humans. Thank You that I can look to Your Word as guidance for every area of my life.*

REST: The baptism of the Holy Spirit is an immersion into the *dunamis* of Heaven. The ability to pray in tongues is a wonderful gift given through this baptism. I pray in tongues constantly and am grateful for such a gift from God. But to think that speaking in tongues is the purpose for such a holy invasion is embarrassingly simplistic. It would be the same as saying that when Israel crossed the Jordan River it was the same as possessing the Promised Land. Yes, they could see it, but they did not possess it! Their river crossing gave them the legal access to the possession. This wonderful Spirit baptism has given us such an access. But to stand on the banks proclaiming it's all mine is foolishness at best. Such ignorance has caused great numbers of people to halt their pursuit once they've received their spiritual language. They have been taught they are now full of the Holy Spirit. But a glass is only full when it overflows. Fullness can only be measured by overflow.

> *For the sake of the world, keep pursuing the infilling of My presence.*
> *There is so much more that I long to pour out on you, and so much more that the world needs to see of Me.*

July 25th

It shall come to pass in that day that his burden will be taken away
from your shoulder, and his yoke from your neck, and the yoke will be
destroyed because of the anointing oil.

—Isaiah 10:27 NKJV

RISE: The presence of God is to be realized in the anointing. Remember, *anointing* means "smeared"—it is God covering us with His power-filled presence. Supernatural things happen when we walk in the anointing! For the most part, the anointing has been hoarded by the Church for the Church. Many have misunderstood why God has covered us with Himself, thinking it is for our enjoyment only. But we must remember, in the Kingdom of God we only get to keep what we give away. This wonderful presence of God is to be taken to the world. If it isn't, our effectiveness decreases. Does He leave us? No. But perhaps this phrase will help to clarify this point: He is in me for my sake, but He's upon me for yours!

> *Jesus, I know that You have placed me strategically in the world to release Your Kingdom. Can You highlight to me, now, the people I am in contact with who are on Your heart?*

REST: I owe the world a Spirit-filled life, for I owe them an encounter with God. Without the fullness of the Holy Spirit in and upon me, I do not give God a surrendered vessel to flow through. The fullness of the Spirit was the goal of God throughout the law and prophets. Salvation was the immediate goal, but the ultimate goal on earth was the fullness of the Spirit in the believer. Getting us to Heaven is not near as great a challenge as it is to get Heaven into us. This is accomplished through the fullness of the Spirit in us.

> *It's only here on earth that you get to partner with Me to bridge the gap, releasing healing and restoration on a broken world. When you are with Me in Heaven, all will be perfect, but I long to be fully with you on earth as well.*

July 26th

*Till we all come to the unity of the faith and of the knowledge of the
Son of God, to a perfect man, to the measure of the stature
of the fullness of Christ.*

—Ephesians 4:13 NKJV

RISE: Jesus was the suffering servant, headed for the Cross. But Jesus is triumphantly resurrected, ascended, and glorified. The "as He is, so are we" declaration is far beyond what any of us could have imagined, especially in light of the glorified description of Jesus in the first chapter of Revelation. Yet the Holy Spirit was sent specifically for this purpose—that we might attain "to the measure of the stature of the fullness of Christ." The Holy Spirit comforts us, gives us gifts, reminds us of what Jesus has said, and clothes us with power. But He does all of this to make us like Jesus. That is His primary mission. So, why didn't the Father send Him until Jesus was glorified? Because, without Jesus in His glorified state, there was no heavenly model of what we were to become!

*I never want to diminish who You are by only focusing on Your suffering,
Jesus. I am so grateful for the Cross and all that You sacrificed, but I am
even more grateful that is not the end of the story!*

REST: The Christian life is not found on the Cross. It is found because of the Cross. It is His resurrection power that energizes the believer. Does this diminish the value of the Cross? No! The shed blood of the spotless Lamb wiped out the power and presence of sin in our lives. We have nothing without the Cross! Yet the Cross is not the end—it is the beginning, the entrance to the Christian life. Even for Jesus the Cross was something to be endured in order to obtain the joy on the other side (see Heb. 12:2).

*The suffering of My Son was never My ultimate goal. Destruction,
pain, death—those are the realms of the enemy. I came to bring life, joy,
peace, health, and love into every area of life. Let the resurrection power
of My Kingdom fill your life.*

July 27th

And then you will never be shaken or intimidated by the opposition
that rises up against us, for your courage will only prove as a sure sign
from God of their coming destruction and that you have
found a new life.

—Philippians 1:28 TPT

RISE: For too long the Church has played defense in the battle for souls. We hear of what some cult or political party is planning to do, and we react by creating strategies to counter the enemies' plans. Committees are formed, boards discuss, and pastors preach against whatever it is the devil is doing or about to do. This may come as a surprise, but I don't care what the devil plans to do. The Great Commission puts me on the offensive. I've got the ball. And, if I carry the ball effectively, his plans won't matter.

Thank You, Lord, that the end has already been written, and we are on
the winning team! Help me to navigate what it looks like to think, act,
and speak from a place of victory in You.

REST: As foolish as it may sound, much of the Church in this hour seems to be distracted by the plans of the opposing team, even though they're sitting on the sidelines. Satan reveals his plans to put us on the defensive. The devil roars, and we act as if we got bit. Let's stop this foolishness and quit praising the devil with endless discussions of what's wrong with the world because of him. We have the ball. The alumni from the ages past watch with excitement as the two-minute offense has been put on the field. The superior potential of this generation has nothing to do with our goodness, but it does have everything to do with the Master's plan of placing us at this point in history. We are to be the devil's worst nightmare.

If you knew that failure was not an option, what would you do? Now,
imagine that freedom, that confidence, and that authority in every
area of your life. This is the victorious mindset of Heaven that I want
to impart to you!

July 28th

Wherever He entered villages, or cities, or countryside, they were
laying the sick in the market places, and imploring Him that they
might just touch the fringe of His cloak; and as many as
touched it were being cured.

—Mark 6:56 NASB

RISE: For massive worldwide revival to reach its dominating potential, it must be taken out of the four walls of the church and launched into the marketplace. We are to quietly, powerfully, decisively influence through service; and when you run into a person with an impossibility, let him know the reality of Heaven is within arm's reach! Infiltrating the system involves both purity and power. Purity is seen in the character of men in the Bible, like Daniel and Joseph, as they demonstrated loyalty and forgiveness beyond reason. Power was released through the use of their gifts.

> *Help me, Holy Spirit, to grow in both purity and power. I never want to*
> *become out of balance in either area, but to continually advance in both*
> *until I look just like Jesus.*

REST: To be effective as leaven in the Babylonian system, we must rethink our understanding of these subjects. God's people must find a heart to see others succeed. Anyone can wish good upon someone who conforms to his or her beliefs and disciplines. But the ability to express loyalty and forgiveness before someone is saved may be the key to touching that individual's heart. Personal integrity is the backbone of all life and ministry, and our credibility is founded on this one thing. We can be gifted beyond measure. But if we can't be trusted, the world will turn a deaf ear to our message. Integrity is holiness, and holiness is the nature of God. Yieldedness to the Holy Spirit is at the heart of the integrity issue.

> *If you treat every person whom I place in your sphere of influence as My*
> *treasure, you cannot go wrong. I have called you to act with integrity no*
> *matter what those around you—even those above you—are doing. In*
> *this way, you are My light to the world.*

July 29th

Surely the Sovereign Lord does nothing without revealing
his plan to his servant the prophets.

—Amos 3:7 NIV

RISE: Understanding what is about to come is important, but not to equip us to plan and strategize more effectively. On the contrary, it's important to understand God's promise and purpose for the Church so that we might become dissatisfied—so that we will become desperate. Intercession from insatiable hunger moves the heart of God as nothing else can. Revival is not for the faint of heart. It brings fear to the complacent because of the risks it requires. The fearful often work against the move of God—sometimes to their death—all the while thinking they are working for Him. Deception says that the changes brought about by revival contradict the faith of their fathers. As a result, the God-given ability to create withers into the laborious task of preserving. The fearful become curators of museums instead of builders of the Kingdom.

> *Father, I never want to get stuck preserving something You once did if*
> *it means missing the current thing You want to do. Open my eyes to see*
> *anything that I need to release into Your hands as I pray for revival.*

REST: Others are ready to risk all. The faith of their fathers is considered a worthy foundation to build upon. They have caught a glimpse of what could be and will settle for nothing less. Change is not a threat, but an adventure. Revelation increases, ideas multiply, and the stretch begins. God's activities on earth begin with a revelation to mankind. The prophet hears and declares. Those with ears to hear respond and are equipped for change. In order to understand who we are and what we are to become, we must see Jesus as He is. We are about to see the difference between the Jesus who walked the streets healing the sick and raising the dead and the Jesus who today reigns over all. As glorious as His life was on earth, it was the before side of the Cross. Christianity is life on the resurrection side of the Cross.

> *The old wineskin cannot hold the weight of the new wine, because it*
> *becomes brittle and fragile as the new wine stretches it out. Keep yourself*
> *supple to My rhema word. I want to guide you with My gentle touch,*
> *taking you from glory to glory.*

July 30th

Be faithful to guard the sweet harmony of the Holy Spirit
among you in the bonds of peace.

—Ephesians 4:3 TPT

RISE: Every follower of Jesus is unique. Our gifts, personalities, backgrounds, and cultures all work to create a beautiful mosaic called the Church, the Body of Christ. How wonderful that the life of Jesus, so perfect and complete, is able to flow through different personalities, giving unique flavors to what others are able to taste and see. The four Gospels illustrate this point quite well. The perspectives, values, callings of each writer are seen as they illustrate what it is to follow Jesus and become like Him. For example, Luke the physician shows a compassion and care that isn't as pronounced in Mark. The efficiency and economy of Mark's Gospel illustrates the most bang for your buck in this life as a disciple. You don't find that valuable trait in Luke. Similar things could be said of each of the four Gospels, not to mention the great diversity in the writers of the epistles. God seems to love and celebrate this theme.

Help me to value diversity in the same way that You do, God. I want to
be known for unity and love, seeing the value in each person.

REST: Each of the writers in the New Testament reveals his individuality in what he wrote. Their personalities are visible without contaminating or distorting their revelation of Jesus. I find this to be so encouraging. I tend to become the weakest in faith when I compare myself to those whose gifts are so much different from mine, excelling in ways that I'll never be able to touch. Comparison is dangerous, and, in fact, it's deadly. The call of God for each believer is equally diverse. The gifts and responsibilities are vast—so vast, in fact, that it will take the entire Church working together to accomplish the assignment given to us to represent Jesus unto the discipling of nations.

To value one person's gifts above another is to devalue the intricate
individuality of My design. I am expressing Myself through each person
on the earth. Don't miss it, in yourself and in others!

July 31st

A thief has only one thing in mind—he wants to steal, slaughter, and destroy. But I have come to give you everything in abundance, more than you expect—life in its fullness until you overflow!

—John 10:10 TPT

RISE: When the surpassing greatness of His world touches this one, there must be ways to measure its effects. By design, Heaven is to influence earth. While we will never see nor understand all of the impact our life of faith has on the world around us, we can see some of it clearly. And we must. We know that the devil came to kill, steal, and destroy. It is reasonable to conclude that the effects of his influence are measured by death, loss, and destruction. Jesus came to give life. And in doing so, He came to destroy the works of the evil one (see 1 John 3:8). We must guard our hearts from the deception that attributes death, loss, and destruction to God.

Forgive me, Father, if I've ever given You authorship over destruction in my life. Thank You that You are always focused on redemption and restoration.

REST: Our assignment becomes horribly weakened when we see God as the author of these things, as it is impossible to successfully believe for freedom when it is against our concept of the will of God. Freedom will only be experienced in the measure to which we see God as being good. Jesus rebuked a storm. If that storm was the will of God the Father, then Jesus is fighting the will of God. The result is we end up with a divided house. We know that is not true as Jesus came to give life. Life shows up best where death once reigned.

I am not ambivalent about My will for the world. I came to earth so that My Kingdom would reign through you, My beloved child. If it is not found in Heaven, it is not found in My will on earth.

August

August 1st

And we know that all things work together for good to those who love God, to those who are the called according to His purpose.

—Romans 8:28 NKJV

RISE: The hardest part of living in a miracle culture is waiting for the miracle. The battle is in the mind. And it can get pretty intense, especially when the miracle doesn't come quickly, or even at all. I have friends who have suffered greatly for the Gospel. They have been beaten, shot at, imprisoned, criticized, betrayed, and more. But before any of these happened at that level, they experienced an extremely powerful baptism in the Holy Spirit. They have said that without that encounter with God, they would have quit and lost heart. That baptism is for the purpose of power, miracle power. And sometimes that power is for the miracle of endurance.

> *There are miracles that I am still waiting for, God. I don't understand why they haven't happened yet, but I give up my right to understand. I trust You and Your timing completely.*

REST: Many tend to get introspective and self-condemning when there's a lack of breakthrough. But power is also needed for endurance. The manifestation of power upon the apostles was certainly for miracles. But perhaps what should stand out the most was their God-given ability to endure hardship without blaming God, themselves, or the people of God. This, in some ways, might be the greater miracle. The promise given to us in Romans 8 wouldn't even be necessary if everything always worked the way we expected.

> *I know it is uncomfortable, but so much glory is being built in you during the waiting. Dig down deep into our history together, let your trust in Me build an even stronger foundation. I see the cry of your heart.*

August 2ⁿᵈ

*He has told you, O man, what is good; and what does the Lord
require of you but to do justice, and to love kindness, and to walk
humbly with your God?*

—Micah 6:8 ESV

RISE: Heaven's culture is first and foremost presence focused. Everything in Heaven is connected to and thrives because of the presence of God. There is nothing in Heaven that exists apart from His presence. He is the beauty of that world. As worshipers, we are exposed to the surpassing greatness of His world. As a result, we are called to implement His values here.

> *Show me the culture of my home, Lord, of my work and of my city.
> Reveal to me how I can affect the culture of each place so that it looks
> more like the culture of Heaven.*

REST: It is safe to say that Heaven has a culture of honor. Under His Lordship, everyone is celebrated for who they are, without anyone stumbling over who they're not. Every feature of every life is a thing of beauty and value. The commands that God gives us about our relationships here only serve to mirror the reality that already exists in His world. It is possible to experience the lifestyle of Heaven now. Our manner of life can be shaped by the lifestyles of those in Heaven. There it is. The measure of Heaven to earth is seen in the importance we place on His presence, His values, and His lifestyle. When the values of His world impact our daily lives, Heaven's culture becomes real and measurable.

> *There isn't one single aspect of your life, your family, your city, your
> nation that I don't want to be intimately involved in shaping. I
> care about it all. Each outpouring of My Spirit is meant to shift the
> atmosphere more and more toward that of Heaven.*

August 3rd

Yet you, Lord, are our Father. We are the clay, you are the potter;
we are all the work of your hand.

—Isaiah 64:8 NIV

RISE: The Netherlands is an amazing country known for many things, not the least of which are its dikes, windmills, wooden shoes, and tulips. My friend and I were there to speak in a pastors' conference in the cold and damp month of November. During a conference break, we visited a series of extremely large greenhouses where tulips were grown. When we entered the greenhouse, I was amazed at the color and the beauty of these flowers, seemingly beyond number. Row after row, section after section demonstrated their ability to grow beautiful flowers any time of year. The tulips that didn't have a chance to survive in the rather hostile weather outside thrived in the atmosphere provided by the greenhouse.

> *I want to help create a culture where Your Kingdom thrives amidst the chaos of the world. Lord, help me to start with the atmosphere of my own mind. I want to be a greenhouse of Your presence.*

REST: When the Church discovers and lives in Heaven's culture while here on earth, we create an atmosphere that is very similar to the greenhouse in its effect over a city. In the right atmosphere (prevailing culture) we are more likely to grow the things we have vision for because the spiritual climate contributes to the vision and mandate of the Lord. It comes down to having absolute trust in Him in the journey. And that is a lot easier to do when I come completely abandoned and surrendered to His purposes, with no hidden agendas of my own. This really is the only way to come to the Lord of all—yielding to His Lordship.

> *Don't limit in your mind how much influence My Kingdom can have on the earth. Cultivate an attitude of thankfulness, but stoke up the flames of your hunger to see more of the culture of Heaven released on the earth.*

August 4th

Have I not commanded you? Be strong and of good courage;
do not be afraid, nor be dismayed, for the Lord your God
is with you wherever you go.

—Joshua 1:9 NKJV

RISE: Establishing His will in the earth seems rather simple on paper, but in real life it requires a willingness to try, fail, and try again. I have learned little in this life of faith apart from the freedom to experiment. Rarely does a child ride a bike successfully on the first attempt. That's why I taught my kids to ride at the park where there was a lot of grass so that when they fell, they fell on the grass. As much as was possible, they fell safely. Many leaders think their job is to discourage people from trying, so then they won't fail. When I speak of failing, I'm not referring to moral or ethical failure or experimenting with lifestyles that are contrary to the teaching of Scripture. I am referring to the God-given desire to learn how to represent Jesus well in purity and power.

Thank You, Father, that You aren't scared of my messes. I will keep
my heart pure toward You, but I release the pressure of being perfect. I
refuse to be so afraid of failure that I don't try.

REST: We become most productive when our hunger for fulfilling His mandate for our lives is greater than our fear of failure. I believe the willingness to fail is a necessity for growth, especially as we hunger for the supernatural. Someone has to get the breakthrough so the others can benefit. While wisdom and loving care for people must always be evident, supernatural breakthroughs are equally necessary for all of us to grow into God's dream for us. After all, He has destined me to be like His Son Jesus in purity and power. The reality is someone else may get the breakthrough before I do. That's wonderful! It's not a race against other believers. It's a race against time. But often the absence of examples to follow in the supernatural parts of our faith is what makes experimenting an even greater part of our lives.

Your bold attempts, made for My Kingdom, bring Me joy even when
they fail. Keep pushing forward past fear, past self-doubt. I am cheering
you on!

August 5th

*The Lord is not slow about His promise, as some count slowness, but
is patient toward you, not wishing for any to perish but for
all to come to repentance.*

—2 Peter 3:9 NASB

RISE: God is good. I consider this to be the cornerstone of our theology. He is as good as He is holy. I don't know anyone in the faith who would disagree with this statement of God's goodness. If we're honest, we have to believe it, as it is in the Scriptures. It's not the statement of faith that needs adjusting as much as it is our definition of His goodness that needs attention. God is credited with many horrible things because of the thought that He is God and in control of everything. It is true that God is in charge, but I wouldn't agree that He is in control.

> *You are good all the time, even when I become overwhelmed with
> difficulties. Father, help me to see examples of Your goodness today and
> to know that I am created to dream big.*

REST: He is God and can force His purposes on all He has made, should He want to. But He has chosen to create something called free will, and in doing so made it possible for things to happen He didn't approve of. God wants all people to come to Him instead of perishing. Is anyone perishing? Yes. Is it His will? No. So we can't afford to come to such careless conclusions just because we haven't seen the breakthrough we've been praying for. Every parent should understand the difference between *in control* and *in charge*. We are in charge of our households, but not always in control of what happens there. God created a world in which our wills would have an effect on the outcome. And in turn we were written into His sovereign plan.

> *My love for every person is unending, but I know that love cannot exist
> without the freedom to choose against it. There are so many things I
> long to see manifested on the earth. My heart is consistently beckoning
> creation back into My embrace.*

August 6th

*For assuredly, I say to you, if you have faith as a mustard seed, you will
say to this mountain, "Move from here to there," and it will move;
and nothing will be impossible for you.*

—Matthew 17:20 NKJV

RISE: Nothing is impossible. Without this important point, we live intimidated and somewhat controlled by the evil circumstances of life. It becomes all too easy to accept things as they are, without carrying the responsibility to address these things in Jesus' name. An assumption is then made that whatever happens was meant to be. We know that God alone lives in the realm where nothing is impossible. He is God. He is infinite, while everything else is finite. There is one beautiful exception to this rule—He made it possible for those who believe Him to experience the same reality He does.

> *Holy Spirit, help me to become even more aware of Your presence living
> within me and resting upon me. I need to understand at a deep level all
> that is possible with You.*

REST: Faith gives us access to a realm known only to God. This is the privilege given to His children, to those who believe. Whenever we become people who truly believe that nothing is impossible with God, we begin to look for problems into which His Kingdom can invade. When I truly believe nothing is impossible for God and nothing is impossible for those who believe, I will respond to that inward conviction of the heart by recognizing I carry solutions for the death, loss, and destruction that plagues humanity. When I find them, I must take the risks necessary to see the situation changed for the glory of God.

> *The same Spirit, carrying resurrection life, that was inside of Jesus on
> the third day now lives inside of you. Let My Spirit flow through you to
> change the world, bringing glory to My name and revealing My heart
> to the lost.*

August 7th

*And He raised us up together with Him [when we believed], and
seated us with Him in the heavenly places, [because we are] in Christ
Jesus, [and He did this] so that in the ages to come He might [clearly]
show the immeasurable and unsurpassed riches of His grace in [His]
kindness toward us in Christ Jesus [by providing for our redemption].*

—Ephesians 2:6-7 AMP

RISE: Jesus' blood paid for everything. When Jesus hung on the Cross, He made one
final statement: "*It is finished*" (John 19:30). His job was completed. Everything that
needed to be done for our eternal destiny was accomplished in that moment. The ram-
ifications of this fact are far-reaching. There is nothing that we will ever need, even 100
billion years from now, that will not have been provided for at the Cross. It was that
complete.

> *I know that I can trust You with all things, Jesus. I repent for the
> moments when I let worry steal my focus from You. Every area of my
> life has been covered by the redemptive power of Your blood.*

REST: It can be said that it will take the ages to come just to scratch the surface of
understanding the richness of His grace. But it all points back to the Cross of Jesus, that
place of great suffering and death. There is nothing that will come up at any time in the
future that would require God to do something in addition to the redemptive work on
the Cross. It truly is finished. Because Jesus took care of everything at Calvary, I owe
Him my trust when things do not look good or according to what I felt was promised
to me. Our lives are comprised of acts of faith as well as an abiding trust. Bold faith
stands on the shoulders of quiet trust.

> *I know that there have been things you haven't understood, areas of
> disappointment. Don't hide those feelings from Me. Kept from the
> healing balm of My love, they will fester into pockets of doubt and
> bitterness. Open them up, let Me heal your heart as you build your faith
> in Me.*

August 8th

*You even formed every bone in my body when you created me in the
secret place, carefully, skillfully shaping me from nothing to something.
You saw who you crated me to be before I became me!*

—Psalm 139:15-16 TPT

RISE: Each person is significant. It is easier to place the title of significance on an individual who has accomplished much. And that would be true, but not the whole truth. Every person is significant in God's eyes, and therefore must become so in ours. There are times when I come upon a person who is behaving in an almost inhuman way, actually more like an animal. Only God knows what brought them to such a place of devastation. And while I've protected myself from looking down at such individuals, it's a challenge to see their significance. I remind myself that when they were born, someone looked at that baby and commented how cute they were. It's not a mental game. It's a reminder that rarely are people born in such a place of disrepair. And if they are, they are still valuable to Jesus and must become valuable to me.

> *Thank You, Father, that You have woven Your value into our very
> DNA. Open my eyes to the precious care that You gave when You
> created me and those around me.*

REST: Sometimes we do better at recognizing the importance of another person, but struggle with our own value. This also is something that must change. We are so resistant to self-centeredness and pride that we often overreact and create habits of self-criticism and self-judgment in its place. We are to love others as we love ourselves. If we have little realization of our value in God's eyes, it will show in how we love others. I cannot find my value in my gift or title, though. I am a child of God. Period. Whenever we build our identity around our title, we turn to a performance mentality in serving the Lord. It's just not healthy. We are stable only when we see ourselves as a child of God.

> *Jesus understood His value and authority, but He did not flaunt
> it. Instead, He washed the disciples' feet. He laid down His life for
> mankind. I am inviting you to receive My love as a child and then to
> serve with the heart of royalty.*

August 9th

*Then they will rebuild the ancient ruins, they will raise up the former
devastations; and they will repair the ruined cities,
the desolations of many generations.*

—Isaiah 61:4 NASB

RISE: When we know who He made us to be, we'll never want to be anyone else. He has wrapped up His significance in the destiny of every person He called to Himself for salvation. One of the most important parts of recognizing a person's significance is that Jesus chooses people long before they could earn such favor. One of my favorite portions of Scripture in this regard is found in Isaiah 61. This is the passage that Jesus quotes when He starts His ministry in Luke 4. This is where the Spirit of the Lord comes upon Him for healing, deliverance, and restoration of broken lives.

> *I am quieting my heart before You this morning, God. Will You show
> me who You made me to be? What is special about me? What do You
> love about me?*

REST: Who are "they" that Isaiah speaks of, the ones who will be rebuilding the cities? It's the afflicted, brokenhearted, captives, prisoners, mourners, burned-out ones, and the fainting ones because of weakness described in the previous verses. Think about this. The most broken in society, the ones the Church often rejects and society certainly rejects, are the ones anointed by God to rebuild our cities that have been destroyed through devastation. They are the builders. Seeing their significance before they have earned it is actually what positions them for their own breakthroughs in ways that are valuable to entire cities. How we treat these disenfranchised, considering their significance in God's eyes, becomes key in seeing our cities restored to God's design and purpose.

> *Your weaknesses do not intimidate Me. And your broken parts will
> never disqualify you from the destiny that I have designed for you. Bring
> your weaknesses to Me and trust that I will make something beautiful.*

August 10th

There will be no end to the increase of His government or of peace,
on the throne of David and over his kingdom, to establish it and to
uphold it with justice and righteousness from then on and forevermore.
The zeal of the Lord of hosts will accomplish this.

—Isaiah 9:7 NASB

RISE: The mere expectation of evil increasing in the earth, without a conviction of God's heart for answers, creates a people without hope. In a strange sense, we then become a people who are encouraged over the increase of evil, as it becomes a sign that we are in the last days spoken of in Scripture. We must never find encouragement in the lack of breakthrough of Kingdom realities. It is time to make a decision not to embrace any theology for the last days that doesn't require faith to see it happen.

> *Lord, show me right now any area of my thinking about the world where I've lost hope for redemption—be it a relationship, a realm of society, or even an aspect of myself. I want to hope for breakthrough everywhere!*

REST: Many believers answer my challenge by saying their hope is in the return of Christ. While His return is more glorious than any of us could possibly imagine, our faith must produce impact on the realities we face now. It is a weak Christian culture that allows and sometimes gives honor to those who have a faith in the return of Jesus but have little to no faith in the power of the Gospel to effect change right now. Once again, faith then becomes untested and unproven without a measurable impact on the world around us. Our expressions of faith must have an effect on the death, loss, and destruction we are confronted with on a daily basis. These tragic realities are the enemy's fingerprints. Our faith must be a "right now" faith that replaces the fingerprints of darkness with the fingerprints of a loving Father who sent His Son to redeem, restore, rebuild, and renew. This is faith touching the now of life.

> *You were never made to be hidden away from the world. I created you with authority to carry My presence, to reveal My light into every nook and cranny.*

August 11th

Wisdom is so priceless that it exceeds the value of any jewel.
Nothing you could wish for can equal her.

—Proverbs 8:11 TPT

RISE: According to Scripture, wisdom is the principal thing and is to be sought after as a priority. Nothing we could desire is better than or equal to the value of wisdom. Interestingly, pursuing wisdom is prioritized much like "seeking first the Kingdom of God" is in the New Testament. Throughout Proverbs, seeking wisdom is what releases the blessing of God in all the other areas of life. Whether health, finances, position and title, or the beauty of meaningful relationships, all are enhanced and enabled through our prioritized pursuit of wisdom. This journey brings us to the wonderful discovery that wisdom is also a person. Jesus is our wisdom (see 1 Cor. 1:30).

> *Jesus, You are the person of wisdom, and You live inside of me. I am so aware of my need for more of You. Help me to tap into Your presence and the wisdom found there.*

REST: Wisdom is a person, so living in wisdom is a relationship where we learn to truly see through His eyes, gaining His perspective. And it is that perspective that enables faith. It could be said that wisdom gives faith a context in which to function. In the same way that the banks of a river give direction to the water, so wisdom gives faith a direction, a target.

> *I created you to dream so big that you'd need to rely on My wisdom, My presence, and My perspective to see your dreams fulfilled. Don't limit yourself to what you can do on your own. I am here, waiting to pour out My presence on you.*

August 12th

For the earth will be filled with the knowledge of the glory
of the Lord as the waters cover the sea.

—Habakkuk 2:14 NIV

RISE: Often, weak theology that looks so good on paper is what becomes the disguise for cowardice as it pertains to our responsibility in invading the impossible. This in turn keeps us from pursuing what is possible in our lifetime. The answer to experiencing more of His Kingdom is found in our relationship with Him. It is the readiness to embrace His design by saying yes to this relational journey. Jesus didn't set a boundary, saying, "Believe for this much, but no more." He set a direction in teaching and action, but never set the boundaries that present-day leaders set for us. In fact, to give us the hope and courage we'd need, He announced that we would to do greater works than He did. We can't do greater until we've done the same. He is inviting us into a profound exploration of what it looks like when His Kingdom becomes more fully manifest now.

> *It's so hard for me to even comprehend doing greater works than You,*
> *Jesus. But I know that Your Word is true, so I need You to expand the*
> *understanding of my heart so that Your Word can be fulfilled through*
> *my life.*

REST: Because Jesus set a seemingly impossible ideal for us in prayer and because He didn't set boundaries, how could we give ourselves to anything less than a full expression of God's dominion realized over the whole earth? None of us have been given a strategy on how that is supposed to happen apart from following the example that Jesus gave us by destroying the works of the evil one (see 1 John 3:8). We were given a direction, a prayer, a commission, and an example to follow. And all of that is given to us without restraints.

> *Don't make it too complicated. When you see the works of the enemy—*
> *pain, sickness, destruction—move toward it in all authority. You have*
> *already been commissioned as a part of My heavenly army.*

August 13th

Now may God, the inspiration and fountain of hope, fill you to overflowing with uncontainable joy and perfect peace as you trust in him. And may the power of the Holy Spirit continually surround your life with his super-abundance until you radiate with hope!

—Romans 15:13 TPT

RISE: When we are pursuing the miraculous, the possibility of giving false hope is very real and painful. When false hope is given, it is usually in the context of hype, which I despise. It promises miracles, breakthroughs, fulfilled dreams, and perhaps even material blessing in the name of faith. But it can't deliver. I do think it is often a carnal attempt at faith and sometimes well intended. Hype is dishonest at its root. Those who live this way lose credibility over time. Yet my concern and focus is more on our not giving people an inferior or weak hope. Both caution and fear are often called wisdom by those unwilling to live with the level of risk necessary to bring about significant advancements in our Kingdom lifestyle and experience. Whenever weakness in faith is given a virtuous name, it has permission to stay.

> *A lack of faith is no less dishonest than pretending that You are a vending machine, God. Forgive me for both. Help me to walk in absolute honesty and boldness as I proclaim who You are.*

REST: Hope is to affect everything! Our approach to the past must be through the blood of Jesus. I am as clean as Jesus, as I stand before the Father washed in the blood of the Lamb. Our approach to the present is to be as sons and daughters who know they are forgiven and now must live responsibly to see His Kingdom come to every part of life. Our approach to the future is to lay down our lives so that what He has intended to happen on the earth will, in fact, happen, and we will have received our assignment in shaping the course of history responsibly. Hope joyfully takes people to breakthroughs otherwise unattainable.

> *I am the Alpha and Omega. I don't need false publicity, but I do want the world to know the truth about who I am. I want you to know, through your experience, the depth of My goodness.*

August 14th

"I will shake all nations, and they shall come to the Desire of All Nations, and I will fill this temple with glory," says the Lord of hosts.

—Haggai 2:7 NKJV

RISE: As a group of believers, we have purposed to live with the idea that the Gospel is perfectly suited for every area of life. It is practical and needed. In His wisdom, He has solutions for every problem and has a heart for every person. Our approach is inspired by the verse that states He is "the Desire of All Nations." In other words, everyone wants a king like Jesus. He is what everyone longs for; they just don't know it. As such, Jesus is perfectly suited to give influence, meaning, and significance for all aspects of life.

> *Forgive me, Father, for any fear I've had about sharing the Gospel with those around me. You are the desire of the nations. Help me to share the truth about Your love in a way that my friends and family can understand.*

REST: The 500-year anniversary of the Reformation was recently celebrated. The leaders of that day were successful in shaping their culture because they believed God had answers for every part of life. It didn't matter if it was banking, or business, or education, or science, and so on. The point is this Gospel is designed to bring the reality of the Kingdom into every part of life. And in doing so, people are fulfilled in purpose. The people of God must embrace the privilege of living in the open, regardless of the field of influence, so that the reality of God's Kingdom is recognizable. Remember, He said, *"Taste and see that the Lord is good"* (Ps. 34:8). Taste is experience. See is perception. Once people experience the reality of the Kingdom, their perception will change. Give them a taste.

> *The universe is bursting with My creativity. There isn't one area that I haven't lovingly focused on, so don't imagine that there is one aspect of your life—My precious child—that I don't care deeply about. Bring it all to Me.*

August 15th

But solid food belongs to those who are of full age, that is, those who by reason of use have their senses exercised to discern both good and evil.

—Hebrews 5:14 NKJV

RISE: Most every believer lives with the knowledge that the Holy Spirit lives in him or her and that He will never leave. That knowledge is a vital biblical truth. But truth is to be known by experience. Religion idolizes concepts but avoids personal experience. Knowing He is my provider is reassuring. But it does me little good if I don't seek Him for provision. The concept of salvation does me no good unless I'm saved. Being born again is the experience we have after receiving the message of salvation. And so, the abiding presence of the Holy Spirit must become a felt reality.

Sometimes I'm scared to share the desires of my heart. I don't know why. But I repent from hiding. I want to show You every area of need, Papa, anticipating Your intervention.

REST: Many will think I mean we are to live by our emotions or that our emotions define what is true. That would certainly lead to another set of problems. While that is true, a felt reality will usually affect my emotions. It had better be real enough to affect part of my life. Everything about us, from our minds to our emotions to our physical bodies, is designed to recognize and dwell in the manifest presence of God. Learning how to live in that reality is called maturity. We must put a demand on our faith and stop allowing complacency to define our life in Christ. The idea of the Holy Spirit abiding with us always must affect how we do life. And that life can be lived with a consciousness of Him that He affects faith, attitudes, conduct, and so much more. He is the pleasure of life. We often speak of using faith for a miracle, which is right and good. But what if we were to also use our faith to discover God with us?

I cannot be the Lord of your life in theory only. Lay your life at My feet, put your dreams in My hand, trust Me with the timing.

August 16th

And He got up and [sternly] rebuked the wind and said to the sea,
"Hush, be still (muzzled)!" And the wind died down [as if
it had grown weary] and there was [at once]
a great calm [a perfect peacefulness].

—Mark 4:39 AMP

RISE: For most people, peace is a time without war, or a time without conflict, or as simple as a time without noise. Take note that it's always the absence of something. In the Kingdom of God, peace is the presence of someone. Peace is a person. Jesus is the Prince of Peace. When the prevailing influence on our hearts and minds is the presence of Jesus, we have peace that conquers. The wonderful reality of this kind of peace is that it is not defined or controlled by its surroundings. This kind of peace changes its surroundings. Jesus slept in a storm and then released peace over that storm, and the storm stopped. What was in Him influenced what happened around Him.

> *Holy Spirit, help me to recognize when I am carrying Your peace today and when I have misplaced it. Keep me sensitive to my internal atmosphere.*

REST: Peace is the atmosphere of Heaven. And that peace is with me constantly. But if I violate that peace through fear, anger, or other such contradictions to His nature, it is no longer a felt reality. I'm not saying the Holy Spirit left me. I'm just saying that peace is no longer something that I draw from and can steward well. Because He will never leave me, peace is in my account, but it's not in my possession. I need to make a withdrawal. I protect my peace at all costs. If I find that I'm without it, I go back to figure out where I left it. It's that simple. At some point, for example—maybe during a phone call or a meeting—I exchanged peace for fear. And that's a bad deal. I traded something eternal for something that works its way into our lives only to steal, kill, and destroy. Wrong thinking doesn't coexist with peace. Repentance, changing the way we think, restores our peace.

> *Make living from My peace a priority. I have made it easily accessible to you. My peace dismantles chaos. It brings the atmosphere of Heaven into your every moment.*

August 17th

*So keep your thoughts continually fixed on all that is authentic and
real, honorable and admirable, beautiful and respectful, pure and
holy, merciful and kind. And fasten your thoughts on every glorious
work of God, praising him always.*

—Philippians 4:8 TPT

RISE: Living in peace is a relational journey with the Holy Spirit. That journey is at its best when we have an absolute trust in God, demonstrated through abiding in Christ. When I embrace fear, I am doubting God. Our entire life on this planet is about learning to trust the One who is perfectly faithful and trustworthy. Our reasoning, apart from divine influence, always wars against this One who is worthy of our trust. And that is the battle. It's a battle in the mind to spoil and infect our hearts. Winning this battle affects every area of life.

*Jesus, You displayed absolute trust in God. I want to live that out in
the same way. Lead me into deeper trust; strengthen my foundation
in You.*

REST: Rejoicing, prayer, supplication, and thanksgiving all help to settle the battle for our minds. Paul gives us insight on what to fill our minds with. The implication is that if it is filled with the things of God, there will be no room for thoughts that violate our view of His nature. And whenever we discover His nature, we also discover our new nature in Christ. We always become like the One we trust.

*Let My Lordship over your life be manifested in your very thoughts. I
want to fill you with My presence, but you must keep your focus on the
source of life, turning from fear to My endless love.*

August 18th

And the peace of God, which surpasses all understanding, will guard
your hearts and minds through Christ Jesus.

—Philippians 4:7 NKJV

RISE: It is important to pray, bringing our needs, fears, and challenges to God. He welcomes us in any state we are in. But the prayers of authority are never prayed in fear. Fear-based prayers are the prayers of servants, not sons and daughters. Again, He welcomes me in whatever condition I am in. In His mercy, He ministers to us and heals us. But He has called us into a lifestyle that is much higher than that. I encourage people to pray until the fear and anxiety are gone. For me this process always involves worship and feeding my heart on the promises of God. As we return to a place of faith, we become useful co-laborers in making the decrees necessary to bring about God's will in a given situation. Giving thanks is what helps to keep us in tune with our Father who never lies and is always worthy of our trust. Thankfulness flows effortlessly from the one who has experienced this internal victory.

> *I am so grateful for who You are, God. I will review Your many*
> *kindnesses to me throughout my day today. Setting my mind on Your*
> *goodness helps me to stand securely in the realm of peace.*

REST: It's interesting that if I protect my peace, His peace will protect me. Perhaps it sounds like a contradiction. But it isn't. If I protect my heart from all the things that violate my trust in Him, He will rise up to protect me from the unseen fiery darts headed in my direction. His peace protects us where we lack understanding. It's beautiful to see that peace goes beyond comprehension, as real faith is always superior to natural reasoning. I like to put it this way: If I give up my right to understand, He will give me the peace that passes understanding.

> *If your own rationale becomes king, you will miss out on so much of My*
> *Kingdom. Submit your right to understand it all into My hands. I can*
> *carry more than you think, and I long for you to receive the blessings*
> *that come from My Lordship.*

August 19th

*But you are a chosen race, a royal priesthood, a holy nation, a people
for God's own possession, so that you may proclaim the excellencies of
Him who has called you out of darkness into His marvelous light.*

—1 Peter 2:9 NASB

RISE: I grew up at a time when those who were pastors, missionaries, and evangelists were considered to be in the ministry. They had sacred assignments because of their obvious responsibility to preach the Gospel. It seemed to escape our notice that every believer living the Gospel in the everyday affairs of life wasn't considered as important as preaching. Nor was there the same value for those with occupations that were not overtly spiritual. The thought that every believer was in ministry regardless of their occupation was foreign to most.

> *Thank You, Lord, that I have been called into Your ministry. Help me
> to keep that awareness at the forefront of my mind as I go about my
> work today.*

REST: In reality, there is no secular job for a believer. In all honesty, I've met people whose approach to their job in business is more holy than some I've known in their approach to pastoring. It's not the task that makes it holy. It is holy entirely based on the One who called us to that task, giving us His commission. His call is always holy. My approach to the call determines my effectiveness. Once we say yes to the responsibility, it is sanctified by the One who gave us the assignment. I would never want to lower the esteem given to the missionary, etc. I simply want to raise the value for all who have said yes to the call of God, whether it is full-time evangelistic work or to be a missionary, or a dentist, or a stay-at-home mom. Saying yes to God is the big deal. It is the daily yes to God that sanctifies the work.

> *I have intentionally placed distinct passions, gifting, and calls within
> the hearts of My people. Everyone has the same commission—to release
> My Kingdom—but diversity is a part of My strategy. Do what I've
> called you to do with excellence and integrity. Release the Kingdom
> wherever I have planted you.*

August 20th

Be careful to follow every command I am giving you today, so that you
may live and increase and may enter and possess the land the Lord
promised on oath to your ancestors.

—Deuteronomy 8:1 NIV

RISE: We sometimes miss how much God values the natural world. When He was leading Israel out of Egypt into the Promised Land, He took them through the wilderness. There, He was manifested among them through the pillar of fire by night and the cloud during the day. They entered the wilderness through two walls of water as the Red Sea split in two. Manna appeared on the ground daily. Water was provided for them out of a rock. On and on these stories go, as God sustained them through miracles. But He was taking them to the Promised Land, where they'd have to work for food. In most of our thinking, the idea of God supernaturally supplying our need is the picture of the Promised Land. But it wasn't to God. He wanted them trained in the supernatural through unusual provision so that they would grow in their trust of Him. In turn, He could then trust them with the abundant supply He intended for them in the Promised Land.

> *Thank You, God, that You bless what I put my hands to. Help me to step*
> *out in faith and total dependence on You.*

REST: God's heart is to have co-laborers—people with whom He can partner to express His heart and nature in the earth. He wanted them to be faithful to their assignment and work hard, and then to let Him breathe on their labors so they would experience supernatural supply through increase and blessing. Their crops would then produce more than what was natural; their cattle would remain healthy and produce great increase. The fact is, the supernatural God worked with their natural labors to illustrate His heart for mingling His efforts with Israel's. Trusting Him with little to nothing, as Israel did in this story, was a school to train them to do a good job in stewarding God's abundance.

> *Your posture of dependence on Me is the starting point. But you were*
> *never created to be merely passive bystanders. Take active steps toward*
> *your dreams, toward your goals, and toward releasing My Kingdom. I*
> *will meet your faith-filled steps.*

August 21ˢᵗ

*Jesus reached out his hand and touched the leper and said,
"Of course I want to heal you—be healed!" And instantly,
all signs of leprosy disappeared!*

—Matthew 8:3 TPT

RISE: Having respect for the world before their conversion is an unusually important value. That is not to say that we treasure ungodliness, carnality, or any such thing. It's just wise to recognize the hand of God at work in environments we have little to no influence in. Honoring the person God honors is always important. Religious bias and arrogance keep us from that at times, but it can become a part of our mode of operation if changes are made in our thinking. Understanding this one concept would have helped me navigate many of the controversial issues in church life through the years. Jesus simply thought differently from us. Differently from all of us.

> *As I go about my day, Holy Spirit, would You show me people whom I can honor in specific ways today? Give me Your eyes to see the gold in them and the courage to speak encouragement into their lives.*

REST: The sanctifying presence and power of God changes the equation for us all in our dealings with the world around us. It used to be that the only safe place for the believer was to be separate from everyone who didn't live righteously. And while there is wisdom in staying away from those whose goal it is to bring you down, there's much to be said about the impact we can have because God's power and presence is a felt reality in and through the life of a believer. When you touched a leper in the Old Testament, you became unclean. But in the New Testament, Jesus touched the leper and the leper became clean. Jesus has now given us the commission to do the same. In the Old Testament, a person is to stay away from angry people. In the New Testament, a believing spouse sanctifies the life of the unbelieving spouse. It's the effect of the presence and power of God in the believer on their surroundings.

> *You have been chosen to host My presence on the earth. Trust in the redemptive power of My Spirit and release it generously into every area of darkness.*

August 22nd

Now I say to you that you are Peter (which means 'rock'),
and upon this rock I will build my church, and all
the powers of hell will not conquer it.

—Matthew 16:18 NLT

RISE: We use the term *church* quite liberally. It describes the buildings we meet in. At times, we use it to describe the people we meet with. But this word is, originally, actually a secular term. And the Holy Spirit chose it above the many Hebrew and Aramaic terms available to describe what He was about to do. He could have chosen a Hebrew word. But He didn't. I personally believe He made this decision because the secular term was the only one that accurately described His intent. The word for *church* is the Greek word *ekklesia.* This is the word the Holy Spirit used to describe His people on the earth. He could have used the word *temple, assembly,* or *tabernacle.* But He didn't because there is something very powerful and uniquely hidden in the word *ekklesia,* revealing a primary assignment.

> *Broaden my understanding of Your Church, Jesus. I don't want to be stuck—even in my thinking—within the four walls of a building. I want to know Your original intent for Your Bride.*

REST: The origins of this word were not religious at all. Not even by implication. Ed Silvoso defines *ekklesia* like this: "It had been used for centuries in both the Greek and Roman empires to refer to a secular institution operating in the marketplace in a governmental capacity." That is stunning. It was secular in nature and was not used to describe religious gatherings. Putting it another way, God was planting His *ekklesia* within the surrounding systems of government and society in order to impregnate them with the DNA of the Kingdom of God.

> *I never meant for My people to hide inside a building. That is not My design for My Church. You were designed to disperse throughout the world, to infiltrate existing systems with My love and perspective.*

August 23rd

RISE: Jesus doesn't rid us of the corporate concepts found in the word *temple* or *assembly* or *gathering*. Those terms reveal the stationary roles we have in our corporate meetings and smaller gatherings. This would well describe the meetings in the temple and from house to house (see Acts 5:42; 20:20). But *ekklesia* is different because it is mobile. It moves. It is wherever the people of God are. And they are governmental representatives, infusing the DNA of God's world into this one. The corporate gatherings are vital. But they are unto something. And that something is the governmental representation of the Kingdom of God found in the lives of two or three people in agreement, impacting the secular institutions in which they are planted.

> *I give You permission, God, to shake me out of my comfort zone. I never want to diminish Your intention for Your Church on the earth. Expand my understanding to stretch my expectation.*

REST: Just the definition of this word is alarming. It's a gathering of two or three people who exist in the marketplace, bringing governmental influence. What government? The Kingdom of God—His government. Once again, I love our corporate gatherings. I think they are more important than most people realize. But the focus that Jesus had was not different. He wasn't destroying the need to gather. Instead, He redefined who we are and what He has given us to do. Being consistent with our new nature we are to bring His government into this world's government by our presence in focused agreement. It is in this setting that we find the Kingdom of God has an effect on its surroundings like leaven does on a lump of dough (see Matt. 13:33).

> *Wake up, My Church. You were designed to represent the realm of Heaven in agreement with one another as you release every aspect of My Kingdom into the world.*

August 24th

The sum total of all your words adds up to absolute truth, and every one of your righteous decrees is everlasting.

—Psalm 119:160 TPT

RISE: Christians don't always fare well in a setting of discussing controversial ideas. One of the reasons is that we tend to use Scripture to prove our point. It makes perfect sense to do so in our world. But it is usually a good indication of how out of touch we are to the world around us. It comes down to this: It rarely works if we're talking to people who have no value for the Bible. It makes the believer feel good because we're using Scripture. We sometimes even feel good about being rejected, which is a normal outcome in those situations. It qualifies as low-grade persecution to some. But we don't get any points when we suffer as a fool.

> *You are so good at reaching people where they are without compromise, Jesus. Help me to translate the truth found in Your Word to a people who don't yet have a value for You.*

REST: The Bible is God's Word. It carries the power of God for the complete transformation of a life, city, and nation. But it is not always the best use of truth to quote Scripture at people who have no value for it. I'm not saying God can't use it. But, in that context, I'd rather speak out of biblical intelligence (applying biblical principles without directly quoting the Bible). His logic will outweigh anyone's brilliance. Speaking with biblical intelligence, we communicate the absolutes of Scripture without requiring the hearer to believe in the Bible. The law of God is written in the heart, and speaking in this manner awakens such a God-given conviction to truth. That means the truth we speak of stands on its own, causing the hearer to rethink their values because of what we've said. Speaking out of biblical intelligence still carries the weight of the Word of God. And both His power and presence back it up. People then often become hungry for what the Bible has to say once they see your use of biblical principles for life.

> *I will reach the hearts of My people in any way possible. That is the strength of My loving pursuit. I am not scared to speak their language to bridge the gap.*

August 25th

*To all who are in Rome, beloved of God, called to be saints: Grace to
you and peace from God our Father and the Lord Jesus Christ.*

—Romans 1:7 NKJV

RISE: In all Paul's letters written to churches, he called all believers saints. Imagine
how different the book of Romans would have been if he had said, "To all the sinners
in the church of Rome." We confess we are saved and are thankful for His forgiveness,
but our self-image is often inconsistent with His work on our behalf. Our beliefs about
ourselves often deny His work of redemption. His work on Calvary was so complete
that He told us to think of ourselves as dead to sin. While positive thinking has a good
effect on people's outlook on life, our nature is never changed through it. This teaching
has got to be more than that. Otherwise, God is nothing more than a cheerleader trying
to get our hopes up.

*Thank You, Jesus, that You call me a saint because of the redemptive
power of Your blood. I can fully own that identity because it is based on
Your power and sacrifice, not my own performance.*

REST: There are many who will take a bullet in defending the death and resurrection
of Christ, and rightly so. But these same individuals question their own new nature in
Christ. In reality, our confidence in His death and resurrection and our new nature are
to be one and the same. These two realities must be joined together as one thought, as
that is how God sees it. My confidence in His death and resurrection is the basis for
confidence in my personal transformation. The word *consider* basically implies "do the
math." Add up the facts: Jesus died + He was raised from the dead + our faith is in
His redemptive work for our salvation = we died with Him and have the nature of the
resurrected Christ as our own.

*Imagine the sadness you'd feel if you gave your child a priceless gift only
to have them reject it because they felt disqualified. I am the one who
qualifies you. I am the one worthy to call you clean, pure, children of
God. Clothe yourself with your new identity in Me.*

August 26th

I in them and you in me—so that they may be brought to complete unity. Then the world will know that you sent me and have loved them even as you have loved me.

—John 17:23 NIV

RISE: One of the strongest ways of illustrating and releasing the culture of His world into ours is by how we do relationships. Jesus said they will know of our faith in Christ by our love for each other. Listen to those words—*they will know*. One of the most profound tools of evangelism ever is this simple truth. Love each other well. Not only does it bring strength to one another and glorify God, it draws people to Christ. Could it be any clearer? I don't think so. The impact we are to have on revealing the culture of Heaven is in part by how we love and serve each other. Relationships done well also attract the presence of God. He said He would be with the two or three gathered in His name. In attracting His presence, we automatically attract the reality of His world into our environment. They are inseparable. This is, in part, a fulfillment of the commission we have to see His Kingdom come.

Holy Spirit, show me three people this week whom I can intentionally love. I want the way that I love to point people to Your goodness, God.

REST: A wonderful African proverb comes to mind in light of this subject: "If you want to go fast, go alone. But if you want to go far, go together." That is so true. It is common to see short spurts of success and breakthrough throughout the Church. These successes are often accomplished by individuals who have good hearts, great faith, and exciting zeal. But the breakthroughs often don't last, because there is no community on board to sustain them. They went fast, but they weren't able to go far. Our successes in life, in many ways, depend on community. People loving people. My approach is this: If the vision for my life doesn't require the help of others, it's too small of a vision. All Kingdom realities are realized and sustained through family.

I have intentionally placed you within your community—for comfort, for shelter, for growth, for a greater revelation of Me. Prioritize family wherever you go.

August 27th

Now may the God who gives perseverance and encouragement grant
you to be of the same mind with one another according to Christ Jesus,
so that with one accord you may with one voice glorify the God and
Father of our Lord Jesus Christ.

—Romans 15:5-6 NASB

RISE: Community is so important, but it is also true that other people can slow down your progress and growth. Joining with the wrong people can inhibit growth and progress, not increase it. There are those who are so driven by their own agenda for life that they can't hear or give time to another person's purpose in life. Bless them and love them. But don't waste your time developing a one-sided relationship without a clear word from God. I've tried to make it a practice to serve everyone in front of me, regardless of whether they seem to be for me or against me. But I only pour my time into those who have that fire in their eyes when I declare our purpose in life.

Father, help me to see those whom You've placed in my life for the
purpose of intentional relationship. I want to love everyone, but I need
Your wisdom to protect and develop those closest relationships.

REST: Find those whose hearts burn for Jesus like your heart. Connect with those who are humble, loving, and servant-hearted. And the more you discover loyalty in them, strengthen the relationship. As you do this, learn to do life together. It's in accountability that we find some of our greatest strength. Live with friends to whom we can give an account for how we are managing our strengths and weaknesses. Accountability is usually thought of as the way we help one another with sins and weaknesses that we may struggle with. And that is true. But it's only part of the story. Accountability needs to become holding each other accountable for fulfilling our dreams and purposes in life. Accountability—give an account for our ability. Loyal friends are treasures.

You are called to love everyone, but you are not called to do life in the
same way with everyone. Find the ones who will hold you accountable—
with grace and love—to My call on your life.

August 28th

*I urge you, my brothers and sisters, for the sake of the name of our
Lord Jesus Christ, to agree to live in unity with one another and put
to rest any division that attempts to tear you apart. Be restored as one
united body living in perfect harmony. Form a consistent choreography
among yourselves, having a common perspective with shared values.*

—1 Corinthians 1:10 TPT

RISE: From what I understand, the atomic bomb was made through the principle of fission. That is where an atom is split, releasing an amazing amount of power. We know the reality of this fact through the bombs that were dropped in World War II. But there is a superior power that is made through the concept of fusion. That is where two atoms are merged together. And in doing so, there is a release of seven times the amount of power than there is through the splitting of an atom. Uniting is exponentially more powerful than dividing. This is a profound truth that applies to all of us. Churches split, and there's a release of new vision and power. What would happen if these churches would unite?

*Thank You, Lord, that unity is such a big part of Your heart and vision
for us. Teach me how to find heart connection and honor even with
those whom I don't see eye to eye.*

REST: Obviously, unity in the Church is big in God's heart. And this concept is very useful in that setting. But I'm talking about unity that is a bit different, perhaps a bit more mature. Unity begins with simple things like respecting one another and giving honor or value to one another. That's a good beginning. But God is looking for people who will actually get to know each other and give their lives for one another. Partnerships in life are essential. Longevity is essential. That's where we learn to help to partner with each other's dreams.

*I long for you to feel the power of the love that sacrifices self, that fights
for one another's dreams, that celebrates every win without jealousy. It
is a love worth fighting for.*

August 29th

Peter spoke up and said, "But Lord, where would we go? No one but you gives us the revelation of eternal life."

—John 6:68 TPT

RISE: Jesus was capable of addressing the secrets of the heart in ways that are almost unknown today. His words were so life-giving. Even when Jesus spoke of things they didn't understand, those words brought them life—if, of course, they listened with their hearts. That is exactly what happened when Jesus gave His most offensive sermon of all—"eat My flesh and drink My blood" (see John 6). At the end of the message, after a mass exodus by the crowd of thousands, Jesus asked His disciples if they were also going. Peter responded, and I'm paraphrasing here, "We don't understand Your message about eating Your flesh or drinking Your blood any more than the crowd that left. But what we do know is that whenever You speak, we come alive inside."

> *Lord, give me ears to hear Your words of life. And help me to extend the kind of grace and trust—always seeing the gold—in others that You modeled.*

REST: Jesus modeled the ultimate culture of confrontation. That culture was matched and surpassed by the honor He gave those around Him. Jesus was known for trusting people long before they deserved it. The examples are so many that it would be rather tiring to list them all. But one very notable example is with the demoniac referred to as the man of the Gadarenes (see Matt. 8:28-34). This man had so many demons that when Jesus cast them out into the pigs, 2,000 pigs committed suicide by drowning in the sea. That is a significant amount of torment. For me, the most amazing part of the story is that when this newly delivered man wanted to follow Jesus, He said no. In my mind, if anyone needed a little extra help and training before being sent home, it was this man. Instead, Jesus sent him back to his hometown to testify of what God had done for him.

> *Trust in the transformative power of My grace. Trust it within yourself and trust it within others. The miracle of becoming a new creation is as supernatural as raising the dead.*

August 30th

But Jesus sent him away, saying, "Return to your own house, and tell
what great things God has done for you." And he went his way and
proclaimed throughout the whole city what great things
Jesus had done for him.

—Luke 8:38-39 NKJV

RISE: The destinies of the cities in this region were placed under the responsibility of the man of the Gadarenes, who had just been set free. How long had he been delivered? An hour? Two? The point is, this man wouldn't be allowed to pick up trash in the church parking lot in many churches around our nation. And he certainly wouldn't be allowed to preach. But Jesus sent him to his hometown as the only evangelist for the region. We tend to overtrain, to compensate for our own lack of faith in a person's conversion. This story reveals the greatest risk in ministry I can find. The reward for this risk was the next time Jesus came back to that region, every person from every city showed up to hear Him speak. The cities that drove Jesus out of town couldn't wait for the privilege of hearing Him again. This is quite a difference. It is the remarkable impact of one untrained man to awaken an entire region to the purposes of God. And it worked.

> *Father, I forgive any leader in my life who ever sent me the message that*
> *I was unqualified. I release my judgment of them and bless them for all*
> *that they did well. Fill me with Your level of faith, Jesus!*

REST: As powerful as the example of the man of the Gadarenes is, it's Jesus' trust in His disciples that astonishes me most. These were men whom He spent time with only to discover, day after day, how completely unqualified they were for the profound and powerful ministry Jesus had in mind. But when you realize what qualifies a person to Jesus, you see they were perfectly chosen and qualified. And so are we.

> *I am not naïve to your weaknesses. I simply see beyond them. Do not*
> *stay small, nervous about My potential pruning—it is for your benefit.*
> *Run large with Me, and I will redirect you as we go.*

August 31st

When the disciples James and John saw this, they asked, "Lord, do you
want us to call fire down from heaven to destroy them?"

—Luke 9:54 NIV

RISE: Let's be honest. Moving in the spirit of murder is a serious offense. And Jesus
didn't treat it lightly, but followed the disciples' request with a stern rebuke and once
again pruned their misconception of the Kingdom. But here's what Jesus didn't do. He
didn't punish His team. He didn't set them on the sidelines of ministry for a season
until they learned the proper treatment of those who disagree. I don't even want to
imply that those kinds of responses don't have merit in certain situations. But for most
of us, this situation was grounds enough for at least a time out. Instead, Jesus refined
their perception of how His Kingdom works.

> *Jesus, thank You for showing me what Kingdom leadership looks like.*
> *Help me to give myself and others the same measure of grace and truth.*

REST: While Jesus corrected them over every issue of the heart that surfaced following
their successful ministry trip, He also empowered them. He didn't just point out what
was wrong. He gave them His perspective in every issue of the heart. It should become
apparent that Jesus is not quite as nervous about messes as most of us are. Instead of
reading into the story that God doesn't care about mistakes or deep issues of flawed
character, look at what moves Him—co-laborers who work to represent Him well by
bringing freedom to captives and healing to those in need. In each case, Jesus pruned
their thinking by redefining values and concepts. All pruning is done by His voice for
more fruitfulness (see John 15:2-3). Pruning by nature acknowledges fruitfulness but
brings adjustments for the purpose of greater increase.

> *I know your heart even more than you do. Nothing that you show me*
> *about yourself could scare Me or make Me turn away from you. You are*
> *my cherished child. I will always be here to gently turn you back to My*
> *ways.*

September

September 1st

*And whatever you do, in word or deed, do everything in the name of
the Lord Jesus, giving thanks to God the Father through him.*

—Colossians 3:17 ESV

RISE: How to balance ministry and family is a great question that plagues most households in the faith, as we long to be faithful in ministry, the home, work, and involvement in our communities. Juggling the everyday affairs of life and managing a healthy home environment is a challenging task, for sure. But, as I began to pastor, the Lord started challenging me about my priorities in ways that were a great surprise. My discovery was quite astonishing to me and started me on a journey that affected my life in ways far beyond the obvious application of God and my family as priorities. My discovery was almost what some would call a rude awakening. It was this: When God is number one, there is no number two.

I want to worship You, God, in all that I do. Help me to see that every area of my life—work, family, hobbies—is to be done as an offering to You.

REST: As long as I had a list of priorities, I'd have to leave my first priority to do the second, and so on. This new insight implied I could only serve God. I guess that's logical. But the implications were life-changing, as I had to learn how all of the aspects of my life could become a part of my service to God. Every area of my life must be part of my worship of God Himself. If there's a part of my life that cannot be an expression of my love for God, it shouldn't be in my life. This change in perspective didn't change my practice as much as it changed my confidence that I was delighting God's heart. I always made family first. But what I didn't realize was how much God was being loved through my love for my wife and children. There is no vacation from God. I don't stop my service to God while I serve people. It's actually quite the opposite. He takes it personally.

Don't imagine a limit to My delight in you. Feel My pleasure as you delight in your family, as you work with excellence, as you play and rest.

September 2nd

Then Jesus spoke up and said, "My food is to be doing the will of him
who sent me and bring it to completion."

—John 4:34 TPT

RISE: So many think ministry is standing behind a pulpit and preaching. Thankfully that is included, as that is a part of my assignment. But in reality, it is a very small part of that vast subject. This is important to understand. If we don't realize what our actions mean to God, we do not receive the strength and encouragement God intended for us out of our own obedience. The moment all of us are waiting for is when He says, *"Well done, good and faithful servant"* (Matt. 25:23). I realize this is speaking of a future event. But He breathes that into our heart every time we know with confidence that we have done the will of God.

Holy Spirit, increase my awareness of You throughout my day. I want
to feel Your pleasure as I give each activity as an offering to the Lord.

REST: Doing what brings Him pleasure—whether it's preaching, praying for the sick, or going on a picnic with my family—delights the heart of our Father who takes it personally. It's the manner in which we do what we do. Laying hands on the sick, or working in the garden, or even going to a Little League game all become spiritual activities because of who they are done for. Worship sanctifies the offering. The will of God nourishes the soul in the same way that healthy food nourishes the body, bringing it great strength. If we are ignorant of what brings Him joy, we live unconscious of the strength and encouragement that He made available for us in the action. Obeying Him releases strength and confidence to us, but it also helps to establish our identity in Christ. These are true spiritual nutrients.

It's your heart I'm after—a heart turned toward Me in praise and
adoration. I want to bring the fruit of that heart posture into every area
of your life, not just those things that have been labeled "spiritual."

September 3rd

We laughed and laughed and overflowed with gladness. We were left
shouting for joy and singing your praise. All the nations saw it and
joined in, saying, "The Lord has done great miracles for them!"

—Psalm 126:2 TPT

RISE: For a culture to influence entire cities and then nations, it has to exhibit health in all aspects of life—family, work, play, rest, etc. Where we truly succeed, people will long for the same. Practical Kingdom success attracts the masses. Picture a city set on a hill that is all lit up at night. Those who need shelter rejoice when they see the city that is so prominent in the landscape. They know exactly where to go. When we have excellence and success in these areas, we have an impact on the world around us.

Father, I need Your wisdom to be at the foundation of every area of
my life. I want my family, my work, even my play to speak of Your
excellence, creativity, and integrity.

REST: Children probably learn more through play than in any other time of life. This is where they learn that learning is fun and that taking risks is a part of life. They are driven to climb higher, run faster, and yell the loudest. Riding bikes is fun. But seldom do they leave it at that. They try to ride up ramps and sail through the air. They lift the front wheel off the ground and see how long they ride on the back wheel. It is all a part of play. It is all a part of learning. Laughter is a huge part of play, which distinguishes them from their adult counterparts. This should concern us, as Jesus said we are to become like children. Learning to enjoy life and celebrate every part is so liberating. It actually releases us into our destiny and purpose.

Don't fall into the trap of taking yourself too seriously. My Kingdom is
*righteousness, peace, and **joy**. There is transformative power in play,*
delight, laughter, and fun.

September 4th

So then, whether you eat or drink or whatever you do,
do all to the glory of [our great] God.

—1 Corinthians 10:31 AMP

RISE: We have to make sure that we require ourselves to think bigger than we find to be comfortable. God has not called us to do what is humanly possible or reasonable. We are children of a King who knows no impossibility. And He longs for His heart to become ours. The American Church spends something like 95 percent of its income on itself. Practically put, our focus is on caring for ourselves. We build buildings, create programs, hire staff and the like to take care of ourselves. While those percentages concern me, I really love the privilege of caring for ourselves. But at the same time, this behavior reveals how little the average believer is aware of our international responsibility.

> *Jesus, thank You for the ways that You modeled for me a kind of self-care and intimacy with the Father that overflowed into a lifestyle of compassion and service for others.*

REST: We want all believers and their households to be healthy and productive. It's a very real need to have entire communities model healthy relationships, productivity, prosperity with purpose, providing a place where children can freely grow up with dreams, with adults who contribute to their destinies. But, once you're healthy and happy, we want you deployed into your world-changing role. It doesn't matter to us if you're a missionary to a foreign field, a dentist or a doctor, a stay-at-home mom, or a pastor—fill in the blanks. Do what's in your heart, and do it as unto the Lord. Dream and obey to find out what might be possible in your lifetime. Work is worship. This is a significant part of the reformation in thought and practice that we are seeing unfold before us. I truly believe that this is part of what will help us bring about the greatest revival the world has ever seen.

> *Don't get trapped in seeking perfection before you step into the things I've called you to do. Pursue healing, but don't wait until everything is in perfect order to bring My Kingdom onto the earth.*

September 7th

*Beloved friend, I pray that you are prospering in every way and that
you continually enjoy good health, just as your soul is prospering.*

—3 John 2 TPT

RISE: At the center of God's own heart is a love for beauty and pleasure. He created all things for Himself to enjoy and for His creation to delight in Him. There is no delight, beauty, or pleasure outside of Him that can satisfy the cry of our hearts. He designed the sunrise and the sunset. The stars shine at His command, revealing His delight in the sons and daughters of God. He created the baby's smile and the elderly's laughter. He is the God of beauty and design and has called us into the co-laboring role to put our mark on what He has made. Just as Adam gave names to all the animals, so God has invited us into a relational role of creativity, enhancing the beauty of His creation. This truly represents the joy of the journey and an abundance of heart.

> *Holy Spirit, give me the eyes to see God's hand in every moment of
> beauty. I want to experience His pleasure in all that I do.*

REST: This verse in 3 John shows how one part of our lives has an effect on another. Our inner world, in this case a soul that overflows in abundance, has an effect on our outer world in areas of health and finances. There is wisdom to be learned in paying attention to these principles. This really is remarkable as God wants me to be healthy on the inside, knowing it will take care of many of the things I look for on the outside. Our soul is most commonly defined as our will, our mind, and our emotions. Those three areas are to experience and discover what prosperity looks like from God's perspective.

> *My heart is that your will would be free of the fear of man, obeying My
> voice only—prospering. I want your mind to be free of fear and the lies
> of the enemy, saturated in My love and My voice—prospering. I long to
> see your emotions free from any past mistakes, standing firmly in your
> new identity with Me—prospering.*

September 8th

For the kingdom of God is not eating and drinking,
but righteousness and peace and joy in the Holy Spirit.

—Romans 14:17 NASB

RISE: Revealing the heart of the Father is the key for building a culture with a value system that reflects the culture of Heaven. It's impossible to succeed at this endeavor if we ignore what God doesn't ignore. And in this case, we need to pay attention to the fulfillment of our personal purpose and design. This becomes clearly manifested through the hearts of the surrendered believers. One of the areas for which we have a high value is joy, fun, and pleasure. I know it doesn't sound Christian to many, but I believe it is when done correctly. Those are things He designed us for, and in doing so He is glorified by us when we live according to design. I discovered a long time ago if I'm not having fun, I need to reevaluate what I'm doing. That's not to say that everything we experience in life is fun. It isn't. But there's always joy to be found in the journey, as joy is an expression of the Kingdom of God. And the Kingdom is always at hand—joy is always within reach.

Thank You, God, that You are the author of joy and fun! What could I do today to increase my value for fun?

REST: Our relationship with God must bear the fruit of His nature, which is a perfect and complete delight in us as His creation. It is recorded that Jesus had more joy than everyone around Him put together (see Heb. 1:9; John 15:11). And that joy was expressed by Him on the way to the Cross. If anyone has ever had an excuse for not having joy, it would have to be Jesus about to be crucified. He set the standard, and He is the only one worth following.

I am not so somber and stern as religion would have you believe. I am the creator of beauty, of laughter, of delight. I celebrate with joy. I dance with gladness!

September 9th

Hope deferred makes the heart sick, but desire fulfilled is a tree of life.

—Proverbs 13:12 NASB

RISE: The quest for personal fulfillment often takes people in every direction but the right one. The stories of tragic pursuits surround us daily. And yet the Father, who is perfect in every possible way, has designed us for a life of personal fulfillment. But it only works His way. His rules are not confining in the sense of punishment or unhealthy restrictions. They are empowering, as they connect us with His original design. You could probably build a table by using a crescent wrench as hammer, but it's not according to design and would no doubt take longer with many mistakes. The point is, our basic trust must be in the one who designed us for pleasure—His and ours.

> *God, I trust You more than I trust myself. I submit every single one of my dreams and desires to You, knowing that You will fulfill the right ones at the perfect time.*

REST: The picture that comes to mind of this reality is when a person frantically tries to catch a butterfly. They are so erratic in flight that they are difficult to catch. But if you remain still, it just might land on you. Personal fulfillment happens by pursuing the right things in God's value system. A better way to put it is personal fulfillment is not found in the pursuit of personal fulfillment. It is the product or fruit of pursuing God's heart and purposes for our lives. It becomes the butterfly that lands on the person of rest, who is not frantically driven by their own needs or agendas but instead becomes increasingly hungry for God and His Kingdom—His divine order. This really is another way of practicing *"seek first the kingdom of God...and all these things shall be added to you"* (Matt. 6:33).

> *I know you more than you know yourself, and I am completely for you. That is why I know your fulfillment will be found in submission to My vision. It is at the very core of your design.*

September 10th

You are not restricted by us, but you are restricted
by your own affections.

—2 Corinthians 6:12 NKJV

RISE: I don't know if there's anything that thrills me more than experiencing the glory of God. We were designed by the Lord, as a part of our original creation, to dwell in His glory. The glory is the manifest presence of Jesus. Heaven is a presence-based culture, a relational environment. The glory of God is the source of life itself. And to live in His glory means to explore the great delight of who God is. Daily, there is an ever-increasing insight, revelation, and experience of His goodness, of His kindness, of His greatness. This exponential growth in realization continues throughout all of eternity because God is unlimited. We don't wait for Heaven; it starts now. We direct our affections toward Him in ways that literally draw us into encounter with the person of Christ.

Holy Spirit, will You remind me throughout my day today to turn my affection to God? I want to train my affections to remain on Him, so that every moment is encountering Him.

REST: If my affections are sent in wrong directions or I'm all entangled in worry, then I am robbed of the delight that I can have in my journey with Christ. But when my affections are truly anchored into Him, that also affects me. Let me explain it this way. Many times throughout the day, in the middle of whatever I'm doing, I'll just turn my affection toward the Lord. Whenever I do that, the presence of God begins to manifest in such a simple but profound way. It recalibrates my thoughts, my values, and my perception of circumstances. In the glory, everything takes on a different hue. Everything is changed by my time in His presence.

Anchor yourself in Me. Let My peace, My stability, My joy wash over you no matter what storm is raging. Keep yourself in the shelter of My presence through the focus of your affection.

September 11th

*It was in the year King Uzziah died that I saw the Lord. He was
sitting on a lofty throne, and the train of his robe filled the Temple.*

—Isaiah 6:1 NLT

RISE: Dwelling in the glory of God is the great invitation for every believer. Some have voiced concern that if people spend too much time in God's presence, nobody will want to practically serve. But that's really not true. In Isaiah 6:1, Isaiah sees the Lord. It's such an incredible story of an encounter between Isaiah and God. In that story, God says to Himself, *"Whom shall I send?"* (Isa. 6:8). Now picture yourself in this moment. You're in the presence of the Almighty God. You see what you've never seen before. You are overwhelmed with presence. You are overwhelmed with insight. You are overwhelmed with glory. If there were ever a chance that you would want to set up a permanent camp, it would be in that moment. Yet when God says, "Whom shall I send?" Isaiah, in the middle of this glorious experience, answers, "I'll go. Send me."

> *Lord, I want to be so filled with Your glory that my only response is to pour it out to the world around me. Dwelling in Your presence motivates everything I do.*

REST: When we are truly abiding in the glory, we want to do anything to represent His heart well. Serving, then, is not a departure from the glory—quite the opposite. When I have seen His heart, I have a responsibility to make His heart known. I've seen His countenance. I have to let people know what He's like. Because of what I've seen, I cannot stay. I must go out and represent Him well. The New Testament Church has this privilege. The Scripture says that God has given us His glory that we might be one, and then He described the Church as the glorious Church. We are meant to be known for the glory that rests upon us as a people.

> *Be My apostles on the earth. Spread the news of My goodness, release the redemptive strategies of Heaven, and reveal the wisdom of My Kingdom.*

September 12th

*And God called the light day, and the darkness He called night. And
there was evening and there was morning, one day.*

—Genesis 1:5 AMP

RISE: When I go to sleep at night, I turn my heart of affection toward Him. As I'm lying there, I just give Him thanks. I express how deeply I love Him, and then I'm quiet. I'm quiet because I don't want to stay up all night and pray. There are days and moments for that, for sure, but that's not what this moment is. This is my nightly exercise. I turn my affection toward Him, and then the Spirit of God begins to rest upon me. I'm there, face to face with the Lord in that embrace, and that's how I want to fall asleep. I'm not in that moment to sing songs. I'm not there to intercede for the nations. There are times for that, but when I'm going to sleep, I want to go to sleep in the embrace of God.

*Thank You, Papa, that You are always willing to embrace me with Your
presence when I turn my affection toward You.*

REST: Genesis says there was night and there was day, which made the first day. The day began at night, and if we could turn our affection to Him during the night, I think we would find Him doing even greater things throughout our day. We are a people designed to shape the course of history. This is the moment in history that all the prophets pointed to, all the prophets spoke of. There are billions of people on the planet. We are in the beginning of a one-billion-soul harvest. And that's just counting the young people. We are going to see masses of people come into the Kingdom. I love a good strategy, and I'm all for filling stadiums, but in reality, a harvest of this magnitude doesn't come about because of our intelligence. It comes about because of the presence of God upon His people. We have to become a people who are yielded to Him. When we learn to turn our hearts of affection toward Him, we become people whom the Spirit of God can rest upon.

*Your day was meant to begin from rest. Your week was designed to be
anchored in the Sabbath. Settle your affection on Me and, from there,
great things will arise.*

September 13th

This miracle in Cana was the first of the many extraordinary miracles Jesus performed in Galilee. This was a sign revealing his glory, and his disciples believed in him.

—John 2:11 TPT

RISE: How then is the glory of God to fill the earth? One of the ways the glory of God is to fill the earth is by the people of God doing the works of God. Picture it like this: You pray for a neighbor who injured his back, and he is healed. The glory of God is made manifest. When you give bold proclamation of your faith in Christ, telling of the miracle that took place in your life, the glory of God is manifested. When the people of God use the wisdom of God to illustrate who He is, the glory becomes manifested. I'm not certain that the glory of God is going to fill the earth because of a military invasion of Heaven to earth. I think, at least in part, it is going to be through the obedient acts of faith of His people as we see the impossibilities of life bow to the name of Jesus through our lips.

I want Your glory to be manifested in my life, Father. Show me, today, what obedient act of faith You would have me do in Your name.

REST: So here it is. We are facing an opportunity to reap the greatest harvest of all time. There are more people who are about to be saved than have been saved in all of human history. But it's not going to happen simply because we have new strategies. It's going to happen because the people of God on a daily basis carry Him, His presence, and His Kingdom into our world of responsibility and influence. Generations of people will be working together to bring the power and purity of God into society. The world has such a hunger for answers, and they are not finding them in their own structures. This is an opportunity for the people of God—those who know how to believe God for the impossible and who can stand in a place of faith—to bring the King and His Kingdom into that place of influence with great hope.

Don't lose sight of the influence I've given you at this moment. Steward My presence as you move about your daily life. I will not leave you empty-handed.

September 14th

Yet I know that you are most holy; it's indisputable.
You are God-Enthroned, surrounded with songs, living
among the shouts of praise of your princely people.

—Psalm 22:3 TPT

RISE: Everything is focused around this one thing—to give Him glory. It's not just singing songs. It's not just rejoicing. All those are wonderful tools for giving Him glory, but worship is the goal. I can stand in silence, in awe. I can shout and I can dance, in awe. Whatever the manifestation, I am overwhelmed by the One who is so kind and so good. Being a worshiper changes everything. Scripture says that God inhabits the praises of His people, so if we're going to be a presence-based culture, we have to be a worshiping culture. We have to be people who place worship as the top priority.

Your kindness in my life will be at the forefront of my mind today, God.
I worship You with all that I have because of who You are!

REST: We don't worship so that we can get things from Him; we worship because of His worth. We worship because we acknowledge who He is. Another translation of Psalm 22:3 is that He is "enthroned" upon the praises of His people. Believers who come daily before the Lord with lifted hands and a voice of praise, ministering to Him deeply and profoundly, are interacting with the presence and the glory of God in such a way that they are discipled to recognize the Holy Spirit. We are being discipled in worship. God is mentoring us. He's mentoring us to be able to recognize His presence when He comes. Knowing how to recognize Him is vital so that we don't operate out of principle instead of presence. God wants us to sense the moving of His Holy Spirit. Otherwise, we can do a lot of well-intended things for God, based on principles of Scripture and really, at times, miss what He's actually doing.

I love spending time with you. Set your gaze on Me, and let My presence
work within you to draw you even nearer to Me and My ways.

September 15th

This is why I wait upon you, expecting your breakthrough,
for your word brings me hope.

—Psalm 130:5 TPT

RISE: We are to bring transformation to the world, but we do so because we are people of the presence. We're people of the glory. The Lord is raising up an army of people who have the heart of God and can display His power. He is raising up an army of people who live with hope, knowing that Jesus has a purpose and a plan on the earth. He will be successful, and He's chosen to be successful through His people who have said yes to Him, through those who have learned to recognize His leading.

Thank You, Lord, that I get to partner with Your plan of redemption
for the world. You have won the victory, and I get to be a part of it all.

REST: We all love the will of God. But in order to make that value practical, I have to recognize His presence. And there are times when the Spirit of God, the presence of God, is so strong that we must accommodate Him. We don't make Him fit into our plan. Instead, we adjust everything to what He is doing in that moment. I see that happening in this move of God. People of great faith, of great hope, people who believe that nothing is impossible are rising up. And God is training us to be stewards of the presence. It's amazing that I get to host the Spirit of God, to walk into different environments in this world and let it be the Holy Spirit that brings about the change. Yes, I speak. Yes, I act. I declare God's nature is goodness, testify of Him, and then follow with risk and prayer for people. But really, it's the presence of God that makes all the difference.

Let any weight of over-responsibility slide off of your shoulders now. The
Savior of the world has already come, and you have been invited into
My victory over sin and destruction. Come and share this victory with
Me, but don't worry—I have the plans; I know what I'm doing.

September 16th

Then it came to pass the seventh time, that he said, "There is a cloud, as small as a man's hand, rising out of the sea!" So he said, "Go up, say to Ahab, 'Prepare your chariot, and go down before the rain stops you.'"

—1 Kings 18:44 NKJV

RISE: This one-billion-soul harvest is going to happen not because there are great churches in the world. I believe in that. I want all churches to thrive in what God has called them to do. But this great move of God in the glory is going to happen because the people of God, the everyday believers, are released into the earth to be like Jesus. It will be because there are people who believe for the impossible, confront the things that are out of order, and stand as a witness in testimony for what our Father is like. This is the great privilege, and this is the great outpouring of the Holy Spirit that, I believe, has already started.

> *Thank You, Jesus, that I am becoming more and more like You every day. I give You complete access to every area of my life—shape me into Your likeness so that I can more powerfully release Your presence on the earth.*

REST: There is a great story where Elijah is praying for rain. He puts his head between his knees and cries out to God. Elijah's servant goes up on the hill and then comes back, saying, "I don't see anything. There's no sign of rain at all." Finally, the last time he comes down, he says, "I do see a cloud the size of a man's hand." That is not a cloud to be impressed with, but Elijah knew it was the beginning. He ran for cover because he knew small beginnings explode into great expressions when we respond in faith. Jesus did something very similar. He took bread and he broke it and gave thanks for it, and then it was multiplied (see Luke 22:19). It's an unusual but amazing illustration that small things can become great with gratitude. Increase and greatness are brought about when we steward the portion that He has given to us.

> *I don't require from you more than you have to give. Offer up to Me—in tender faith—that which is in your hands, and I will increase what you've given me until it is more than enough.*

September 17th

At this I fell at his feet to worship him. But he said to me, "Don't do that! I am a fellow servant with you and with your brothers and sisters who hold to the testimony of Jesus. Worship God! For it is the Spirit of prophecy who bears testimony to Jesus."

—Revelation 19:10 NIV

RISE: The revelation of the power of the testimony goes beyond the immediate context of ministry. It is a foundational Kingdom principle with implications for every area of our lives as believers. What I have discovered is that our ability to fulfill our calling and commission depends largely on one vital thing—remembering. Our capacity to remember what God has said and done in our lives and throughout history—the testimony—is one of the primary things that determine our success or failure in sustaining a Kingdom lifestyle of power for miracles.

> *Father, thank You that You have given me the tool of memory to help align my reality with Yours. I am going to take several minutes, right now, to gratefully recall specific instances of Your supernatural intervention in my life.*

REST: As we explore the nature of the testimony and the priority of remembering, I believe we will see that the Church must begin to establish core truths and practices in our culture in order to unlock the heavenly resources God has put in the testimony. We must have these resources in order to accomplish all we are called to become and to do, releasing His miracle power into our world.

> *I do not forget. Remembering is for you, and for My Body on the earth, to submerge yourself in the reality of who I am and all that I long to do with you on the earth.*

September 18th

And since we are his true children, we qualify to share all his treasures,
for indeed, we are heirs of God himself. And since we are joined to
Christ, we also inherit all that he is and all that he has. We will
experience being co-glorified with him provided that we
accept his sufferings as our own.

—Romans 8:17 TPT

RISE: Christians must learn how to discover and spend their inheritance. This basically means that we learn to use the unlimited promises given to us by God to bring about a manifestation of His dominion for the sake of humanity. It is always recognized through purity and power and is motivated by God's love. For the most part, the Church has left the riches of Heaven sitting in the bank, thinking that we only get them when we die and go there. The belief that Heaven is entirely a future reality has reduced far too many of God's declarations in Scripture about the believer's identity and calling to "positional" truths that are acknowledged but never experienced. It is time for that to change.

> *I don't want to leave one thing "in the bank" that You have intended for*
> *me to inherit here on earth. Jesus, help me to pursue Heaven on earth*
> *here and now.*

REST: Understanding our inheritance begins with discovering the deeper purpose for our salvation. Many new believers stay immature because they never progress beyond the revelation that they are sinners saved by grace. By progress I don't mean "to leave behind" but "to build upon." Those who progress are those who understand that God's highest purpose for the Cross was not merely to forgive us of sin. It was so that, by forgiving us on the basis of Christ's blood, He could invite us back into an intimate family relationship with Him, our heavenly Father. John 1:12 says, *"But as many as received Him, to them He gave the right to become children of God, to those who believe in His name."* This legal standing of relationship to God as His sons and daughters is precisely what gives us an inheritance.

> *You have a right to pull on Heaven, pursue access into Kingdom realities,*
> *and to anticipate even more of My goodness manifested in your life.*

September 19th

For he knew all about us before we were born and he destined us from the beginning to share the likeness of his Son. This means the Son is the oldest among a vast family of brothers and sisters who will become just like him.

—Romans 8:29 TPT

RISE: The fact that we are heirs of God is mind-boggling. But we must not be content to read these verses and be awed by them. They prophesy our potential, a potential that we must pursue throughout our entire lives. When God invites us into relationship with Him, He is inviting us into a process of becoming, of transformation. This transformation can be measured in our lives because in Jesus Christ we have the model of who we're becoming as the children of God. We have the right to become like Christ, our Elder Brother. We are destined to be fully restored to the image and likeness of God, in which we were originally created.

I never want to stop being amazed by You, Jesus. Your sacrifice allowed me to be reconciled with God's original plan. I am a child of God, becoming more and more like You every single day!

REST: Through salvation we are also restored to our original purpose—the purpose that flows naturally from our restored identity and relationship with God. Ephesians 2:10 says, *"For we are His workmanship, created in Christ Jesus for good works, which God prepared beforehand that we should walk in them."* Works cannot save us, but without the fruit of good works in our lives, we lack the evidence that identifies us as new creations in Christ. Just as God's nature is revealed in what He does, the evidence that we are being transformed into His likeness is that we reveal His nature in what we do.

Step out of any restricted thinking that limits your works to that which you could do on your own. You are My child. You are never on your own. I long to empower your endeavors just as I am empowering your transformation.

September 20th

*"But if You can do anything, take pity on us and help us!" And Jesus
said to him, "'If You can?' All things are possible to him who believes."
Immediately the boy's father cried out and said,
"I do believe; help my unbelief."*

—Mark 9:22-24 NASB

RISE: We, as sons and daughters of God, are destined to reveal our Father to the world by bearing His likeness. We do this as Christ did, by communing with the Father, walking in the anointing of the Holy Spirit, and bringing the Kingdom of Heaven to earth through demonstrations of power and authority, all in the context of showing the love of God. We must learn to spend our inheritance by drawing on the great promises of God for the benefit of the people around us. We can't forget that it was Jesus' death that allowed the essence of God's will to be released to the rest of His family, the saints ("on earth as it is in Heaven"). We must not wait until we die to use our inheritance because our purpose on earth requires heavenly resources to fulfill it.

> *Stir my heart to such compassion for those around me, Father. I need the provision of Heaven, the restoration of Your Kingdom, to counteract the devastating effects of sin.*

REST: The anointing to heal and bring deliverance will be of no value in Heaven. These graces must be used here and now as part of the package of tools used to bring the nations to Jesus. After all, He is called "the desire of the nations." Everyone desires Jesus. They just don't know it. We must become like Him more fully so that the harvest becomes all that God desires and has provided for.

> *Death is not the way to Heaven; I am. And I have given you all access to Me right here, right now. Don't let death be your savior when I have brought salvation to change your life.*

September 21st

*With all my heart I have sought You, [inquiring of You and longing
for You]; do not let me wander from Your commandments [neither
through ignorance nor by willful disobedience]. Your word I have
treasured and stored in my heart, that I may not sin against You.*

—Psalm 119:10-11 AMP

RISE: The testimonies of the Lord are our inheritance. And what is a testimony? A testimony is the written or spoken record of anything God has done in history. Everything God has said and done in history is your eternal possession, and that record holds all the resources you need to be transformed into the image of Christ and become a transformer through demonstrating His good works.

> *Increase my awareness of my access to every single testimony of God's goodness and miraculous intervention, Holy Spirit. Help me to remember to share my own testimonies so that others can grab ahold of the truth that they carry.*

REST: The first thing to see in the definition is that a testimony is about what God has done. When believers hear the word *testimony*, they often associate it with the story of how they came to know Christ, or perhaps a story about someone who experienced a miracle. But we are never the main characters in a testimony. Our stories are testimonies because they tell of what God has done. The corollary to this statement is also true—that we don't have a testimony unless we have experienced a divine invasion of God in our lives! We are His witnesses only to the degree we have encountered His power.

> *My anointed Scripture is full of testimonies that reveal My nature. Read them, allowing them to prophesy to your life about all of the things I desire to do for you and those around you.*

September 22nd

It's not sacrifices that really move your heart. Burnt offerings, sin
offering—that's not what brings you joy. But when you open my ears
and speak deeply to me, I become your willing servant,
your prisoner of love for life.

—Psalm 40:6 TPT

RISE: The testimonies of God are an invaluable inheritance because in each story of what God has done, there is a revelation of His nature. But giving us a better theology is not the primary purpose of that revelation. A revelation of God through a testimony is always an invitation to know God experientially in that revelation. Such encounters transform us. And transformed people transform people. David knew the heart of the Father and understood that they held a revelation of the nature of God. Jesus came to earth knowing that God did not want animal sacrifices and burnt offerings; He wanted a man who would do His will. Jesus embraced His assignment, and it led Him to experience His Father's delight as He fulfilled the Father's desire.

I want to know so much more about who You are, Lord, about what
breaks Your heart and what blesses You. Bring me into encounters with
Your nature through each testimony I hear.

REST: This reality is the same source of life and power for every believer. Knowing the testimonies of God is a crucial part of "seeing what the Father does." Experiencing God through what He has done in the past correctly positions us to experience God in what He is doing in the present. The more we come to know God experientially by responding to the invitations in His testimonies, the more we can become like Him. And the more we become like Him, the more we can do what He does and manifest His nature and power to the world around us.

Your experiences of Me will shape your expectations of Me. I have made
you to encounter My presence, to bring your understanding of Me out
of the theoretical and into the tangible testimony of your experiences.

September 23rd

It is he who made the earth by his power, who established the world by his wisdom, and by his understanding stretched out the heavens.

—Jeremiah 10:12 ESV

RISE: Power is a huge part of your inheritance, but the way to walk in power cannot be separated from personally encountering the God of power. You will grow in your relationship with Him through that experience. The testimonies of God are the key to walking in power because, in unveiling who God is, they teach believers to pursue a relationship with Him more than gifts or answers to prayer. God is longing for His people to love Him along with His gifts. He is longing for them to encounter His incredible love so they will be motivated by passion more than duty. Then He can trust them with His power in unprecedented measure.

> *God, forgive me for any time that I rationalized away a power encounter with You. I don't want a fear of being "overly spiritual" to blind me from the miracles You perform in my life every day.*

REST: The anointing that empowers us to be like Christ and do good works is not an impersonal force. The anointing is a Person. It is the Holy Spirit Himself, and He is passionate to accomplish something very specific in us—to conform us to the image of Christ. The more room we make for Him in our lives, the more He puts His power and revelation to work for that purpose. He is the One who reveals what the Father is doing and saying and then equips us to do and say it.

> *The places of dependence on Me in your heart make room for Me to move in your life. Don't fight against your weaknesses. Instead, open them up to Me. In your places of weakness, I will show up with My strength, transforming You with My grace.*

September 24th

My mouth shall tell of Your righteousness and Your salvation all the day, for I do not know their limits. I will go in the strength of the Lord God; I will make mention of Your righteousness, of Yours only.

—Psalm 71:15-16 NKJV

RISE: The family of God inherits His testimonies just as members of a royal family inherit their family history. Royals study and rehearse the record of their ancestors because it is their connection to that past that gives them their identity and purpose for their lifetime. It lays on them a responsibility of doing something significant during their reign in order to pass the legacy on to the next generation. If one generation fails to live in such a way that honors their family history or fails to pass that history on to the next generation, that line is broken and the inheritance is potentially lost.

Holy Spirit, I want to think of a creative way to keep my own testimonies and the testimonies of my family accessible and easily rehearsed. I want my history with You to sit at the forefront of my mind.

REST: We have been adopted into the royal family of God. When Christ Jesus purchased us through a payment in blood and brought us from death to life, our history was changed. We were on a trajectory to hell. But after we said yes to Jesus, our entire past, present, and future were brought into the history of God and His people. We can't walk in that transformation unless we learn to live from our family history. I'm not talking merely about studying the lives of past believers, or even studying Scripture, though those activities are certainly important. But they are important because they teach us God's version of history and help us gain insights on reality from His perspective, which enables us to live supernaturally.

Bring your memories to Me, My child—the painful ones, the happy ones, the confusing ones—and let Me show you My perspective. I have rewritten your history, grafted you into My family, and given you an entirely new trajectory.

September 25th

For the wrath of God is revealed from heaven against all ungodliness
and unrighteousness of men who suppress the truth in unrighteousness,
because that which is known about God is evident within them;
for God made it evident to them.

—Romans 1:18-19 NASB

RISE: Romans describes the fall of man explicitly as a fall from the truth. Paul says that the reality of God's eternal power and nature are "clearly seen" in the visible realm. That phrase literally means "seen from above." When Adam and Eve fell, they fell from God's perspective on reality. Before they "suppressed the truth," they had unbroken access to the truth of God's nature and His intentions for history. Because they were made in the image of God, they could look at each other and see what God is like. But when they suppressed the truth of who God is, their own image was distorted, separating them from their identity and purpose. From this point on, the human race inherited a distorted perspective on reality and history.

> *Thank You, Papa, that You have restored my access to the truth through the blood of Jesus. I stand in my new identity as Your child, and I will pursue Your perspective always.*

REST: Now that the breach of sin has been healed by the Cross, believers must allow the testimonies of God to teach us the truth that was lost to Adam and Eve—both His plan for history and our identity and role in it. God's plan for mankind has never changed, because He has not changed. But the Church has not yet understood that plan to the degree that we begin collectively walking in it, I believe, because our minds have not yet been sufficiently renewed by the testimonies of God.

> *I am not scared by what I see on the earth today. The evil breaks My heart, but it doesn't surprise Me. I have had a plan for absolute redemption before the beginning of time. The world rests in My hands.*

September 26th

So I will turn toward you and make you fruitful and multiply you,
and I will confirm My covenant with you.

—Leviticus 26:9 NASB

RISE: The covenant vows that God made with Noah, Abraham, Jacob, and the Israelites all reiterated the same promise and commission God gave to Adam and Eve. Why would God still want His earth filled with people when He knew they were sinful and enslaved to the enemy? It can only be because He knew that, through the blood of Christ, He would be able to call out a people for Himself from among the nations of the earth to follow Christ's—the Last Adam's—commission to live in intimacy with God and subdue the earth.

> *Jesus, Your death and resurrection did so much to change my reality forever. Thank You that I have now been trusted to carry out Your divine commission on the earth.*

REST: The fall of man failed to diminish God's interest in having an earth filled with people who live in relationship with Him, people among whom He dwells and walks, as He walked with Adam in the Garden. These testimonies tell us that God's nature and His purposes for mankind have not changed! After all, history is *His story*. He still intends to establish His Kingdom on the earth by co-laboring with His children. He could easily take dominion of the earth in a moment, but His glory and love are most fully expressed when His rule is extended through His covenant relationship with those He made in His image, who worship Him by choice.

> *I have written every chapter of history before it occurs. There is no problem that I haven't already developed a solution to address. Trust Me, walk with Me, and choose to partner with My vision for creation.*

September 27th

Hilkiah the high priest said to Shaphan the court secretary, "I have found the Book of the Law in the Lord's Temple!" ...When the king heard what was written in the Book of the Law, he tore his clothes in despair.

—2 Kings 22:8,11 NLT

RISE: If the Cross made it possible for us to have the same relationship with God that Christ had and bear the same fruit, then why don't we see a glorious Church ruling and reigning with Christ already? I believe it has to do in part with how the Church has failed to use her inheritance, the testimony, to release His power into the earth. When there is a failure to "keep the testimony," the revelation of the nature and will of God cannot be sustained from generation to generation. Revivals have come along periodically when, as in the reign of Josiah, the testimony has been found again and has called believers back to the truth of God's nature and their calling.

I don't want to live in a one-time revival, Lord. I want to be among the generation that lives in a sustained revival because we know how to steward and honor Your presence. Help me to learn how to sustain revival.

REST: But since the first century, I am not aware of any generation that burned with the conviction that the testimony of God's activities among men from the past has been their inheritance to equip them for the present. Therefore, these moves of God have not been sustained beyond a single generation. In response to this, some people have proposed a version of history based on the failure of humanity rather than the nature of God. Many seminarians and historians are taught that Christian revivals typically last two to six years. Revivals, this view suggests, occur mainly to give the Church a shot in the arm, after which everyone should expect business as usual to resume. Historically this is accurate. But the conclusion that this is the purpose for revival is inaccurate. The will of God then becomes defined through what the Church has done instead of what God has made available.

Don't diminish your expectancy just because a lack of revival has become a normalized experience. Take My miraculous testimonies and set those as your precedent instead.

September 28th

And even if our gospel is veiled, it is veiled to those who are perishing.
The god of this age has blinded the minds of unbelievers, so that they
cannot see the light of the gospel that displays the glory
of Christ, who is the image of God.

—2 Corinthians 4:3-4 NIV

RISE: When Christ ascended, He sat down on the throne of David. On the Day of Pentecost, the Father sent the promised Holy Spirit to empower the disciples to establish the Kingdom on earth and fulfill Christ's commission to make disciples of all nations. What most people miss about the Day of Pentecost is that the harvest of 3,000 converts was not simply the fruit of Peter's preaching. Certainly, the Gospel was declared with boldness, but people heard it and were convicted because there had been a shift in the spiritual atmosphere caused by the outpouring of the Spirit.

God, I need to see a shift in the spiritual atmosphere over my city and my
nation. I know You don't change, so I yearn to see the mass conversions
that they saw on the day of Pentecost.

REST: In other words, when believers allow the Holy Spirit to have His way, the atmosphere is transformed, making it easier for people to come to God. Such a change in mindset doesn't just happen. It is the impact of the presence of God doing as He pleases with His people. The co-laboring role brings exponential increase to the impact of the Holy Spirit's activities among men.

My desire to pour out My Spirit has never diminished. Pentecost was
not the high point of My movement on the earth, but just the beginning.
I have poured out My Spirit to equip and empower you into all boldness.

September 29th

Suddenly they heard the sound of a violent blast of wind rushing into the house from out of the heavenly realm. The roar of the wind was so overpowering it was all anyone could bear!

—Acts 2:2 TPT

RISE: At Pentecost, the "god of this age" was bound, and the light of Christ pierced through the spiritual darkness over Jerusalem, where the crowds had crucified Him weeks earlier. It was as though the wind of God that filled the upper room made a distinct sound as it blew across the hearts of yielded people. The sound drew people. It was a roar, a sound from Heaven that arrested the hearts of a people who had previously celebrated His death. They were now asking what they must do to be saved. The sound from Heaven released the atmosphere of Heaven until the prevailing powers of darkness gave way to the superiority of light.

Do it again, God! Thank You that Pentecost was not a one-time outpouring, but rather a manifestation of Your new covenant with mankind.

REST: That is the normal Christian life. Anything less is going backward. This spiritual shift is precisely what happens in true revival. In revival, the outpouring of the Holy Spirit brings an invasion of the presence of the King of Heaven, which displaces the prince of darkness. The result of this displacement is that people experience the life and power of the Kingdom. Bodies are healed, souls are delivered and saved, believers grow in unity, and ultimately society and the earth are transformed.

No darkness can stay in My presence. Come under the shelter of My wings and, together, we will release the Kingdom of Heaven. Increase your expectation of My power and My presence.

September 30th

*But we all, with unveiled face, beholding as in a mirror the glory of the
Lord, are being transformed into the same image from glory to glory,
just as by the Spirit of the Lord.*

—2 Corinthians 3:18 NKJV

RISE: True revival not only calls people to pursue God, but also to pursue their purpose in history and to partner with Him in establishing His dominion over all things. The Holy Spirit doesn't come to give us a shot in the arm; He comes to help us run the race to the end and pass the baton to the next generation with the intent that Kingdom momentum will increase with each succeeding generation. True revival is an outpouring of the Spirit that brings the Kingdom until there is transformation unto reformation. The nature of the Kingdom is continual advancement. It follows, then, that revival is meant to be sustained throughout the generations, until "the knowledge of the glory of God" covers the earth "as the waters cover the sea" (see Hab. 2:14).

*Thank You, Lord, that I get to be a part of an advancing army. I will
declare Your increasing authority, right now, over the areas of my life
that need to see Your redemptive power at work.*

REST: Redefining the nature of God and the nature of revival is simply not an option for the Body of Christ. The problem is never on His side of the equation; it is always on ours. We have not renewed our thinking by defining ourselves according to His truth; thus, we live with limitations that He has not given for us. You and I have the chance in our generation to repent from seeing history through a finite perspective and to increase our experience of the transforming power of the testimonies of God—our inheritance. Our family history in God is one of the primary things that God has established to train us up to walk in our destiny in this hour. If we will embrace the challenge to study, teach, and experience it, we will enable this generation to step into their identity and purpose as the children of God.

*Let Me take you into My arms as I show you the legacy of faith-filled
believers who have gone before you. Don't be overwhelmed; you were
born to bring My perspective into this very moment.*

October

October 1ˢᵗ

You study the Scriptures diligently because you think that in them you
have eternal life. These are the very Scriptures that testify about me,
yet you refuse to come to me to have life.

—John 5:39-40 NIV

RISE: Because of the nature of His Word, God's primary purpose in delivering the Scriptures to us, as Jesus points out in this passage, is to train us to anticipate and recognize Him when He reveals Himself through His divine acts. Jesus said that the evidence that the Pharisees did not have the Word abiding in them was the fact that they didn't believe Jesus and come to Him to receive life. The implication is that the primary purpose of the abiding Word is to prepare and position us for divine encounters that we might respond with faith. Faith is the primary evidence of the Word abiding in us.

I love Your Word, Father. Open each verse to me so that I can encounter
You there, increasing my faith the more I get to know You.

REST: It is sobering to realize that if we have unbelief in our hearts, we can read the Scriptures, but we will fail to hear the voice of the Father giving testimony to who He is in its verses. Unbelief literally blinds and deafens our hearts to His voice, thereby effectively blocking the most powerful thing in the universe from being active in and through us. If we fail to hear His voice, we cannot help but fail to respond to God in the way He desires—with faith that reaches out to know by experience the God revealed in the testimony. This is what the example of the Pharisees proves. Without faith that gives us an understanding of how God's testimony works, we will miss Him when He shows up right in front of us!

The world is full of invitations into My presence. Let My Word, inspired
by My Spirit, beckon you into an even greater intimacy with Me. Let
My voice penetrate your spirit as you get to know Me even more.

October 2ⁿᵈ

Therefore, brethren, having boldness to enter the Holiest by the blood
of Jesus, by a new and living way which He consecrated for us,
through the veil, that is, His flesh.

—Hebrews 10:19-20 NKJV

RISE: Christ was the living Testimony of God to the world. Everything He was, said, and did revealed the nature of the covenant that God desired to have all along with His sons and daughters. With His life and in His death, He created the context for us to approach God, know Him, and walk with Him. Being "in Christ" means that we actually get to participate in both dimensions of Christ's priestly ministry. In Christ, we minister to God with spiritual worship in the Holy of Holies, which we enter through the "new and living way" Christ Himself has made for us.

> *I want my life to be an offering to You, Lord. It's astounding to me*
> *that, now that I am in Christ, You give me unrestricted access to Your*
> *presence. Nothing stands between us anymore!*

REST: Being in Christ also means that we experience the indwelling of the Holy Spirit. Thus, the Holy of Holies now resides in us. This means that we are now carriers of the Testimony—carriers of the realities of God's New Covenant with man through His Son. Our job is to learn how to release the reality and power of the Testimony in the same way Jesus did. Jesus represented God much differently than the Ark of the Testimony represented Him. There is a significant difference between a box of inanimate objects that points to spiritual realities and a living testimony that interacts with and manifests those realities. While the box could only preserve the relics of what God had done, Jesus declared and demonstrated the works of God for all to see.

> *Throughout the history of mankind, I have been reaching out for*
> *connection, calling My people back to Myself. And now, you carry My*
> *presence within you, intimately intertwined with Me, as you release My*
> *Kingdom to the world.*

October 3rd

"But this is the covenant which I will make with the house of Israel after those days," declares the Lord, "I will put My law within them and on their heart I will write it; and I will be their God, and they shall be My people."

—Jeremiah 31:33 NASB

RISE: Likeness and agreement are the heart of covenant. It was this perfect agreement with God that enabled Jesus to release the Spirit of God whenever He spoke. In His words and works, He literally represented the God of the Testimony. Christ has given us access to this superior covenant relationship with God and called us to represent Him in the same way. Thus, keeping the testimony is not a matter of preserving what God has done in our memories, but of revealing what God is like to those around us through declaration and demonstration. The very word *testimony* in Hebrew comes from a root word that means "to repeat, to do again." The testimony is something to be repeated, both in word and in deed.

Thank You, Father, that You are the same always. Your heart for restoration, purity, and connection is constant. Help me to see and understand more of You with every testimony of Your goodness.

REST: When we declare the testimonies of the Lord, we are actually describing who He has promised to be in relationship with us; and more, we are putting a demand on Heaven for that covenant to be renewed and demonstrated in the present as it was in the past. We carry the mercy seat of Christ wherever we go. When we declare the testimonies of God to people, we are setting them up to meet God in the same way we are declaring. This is a powerful reality, but one that we only anticipate and access consistently when we learn to follow in the footsteps of David and make the testimonies of the Lord our delight and our counselors. If we are going to fulfill our role in this covenant relationship, we must learn to keep the testimony and, in doing so, learn to release His power to the world around us.

Delight in Me and begin to raise your expectations of My goodness. Review constantly your own testimonies of My miraculous power, and share them freely.

October 4th

In the future, when your children ask you, "What do these stones
mean?" tell them that the flow of the Jordan was cut off before the ark
of the covenant of the Lord. When it crossed the Jordan, the waters of
the Jordan were cut off. These stones are to be a memorial to the people
of Israel forever.

—Joshua 4:6-7 NIV

RISE: Human beings have an astounding capacity to forget. We are capable of forgetting things that seemed so entirely unforgettable when they happened. On the other hand, we often find that we forget things that didn't seem monumental at the time, but in retrospect were actually terribly important. Both cases reveal our need for some kind of external mechanism that helps us to remember. When Israel crossed into the Promised Land through the Jordan River, Joshua commanded the elders of the tribes to go back into the river and take out twelve stones from the riverbed and create a pile of them on the bank.

Forgive me, Jesus, for every time I've let the greatest miracle of my life—
my salvation because of Your sacrifice—become overshadowed by worry
or fear. I want to be constantly aware of all that You've done for me.

REST: The piles of stones were to be signs and memorials, which are similar in nature. Signs are realities that point to greater realities. Memorials are things that are meant to remind you of other things. In this case, these piles of stones reminded the people of the testimony of how God held back the waters of the Jordan and brought His people into the land of promises. But the supernatural interventions of God in human history are in themselves signs, in that they are realities that point to the greater revelation of God Himself. So, the pile of stones was a memorial and a sign that pointed to another sign, which pointed to the reality.

Strengthen yourself with your memories of My provision, My love, and
My faithfulness. I will give you tools to keep My nature in front of you
always. You only need to ask.

October 5th

*Knowing what they were thinking, Jesus said to them, "Why all
this fussing over forgetting to bring bread? Do you still not see or
understand what I say to you? Are your hearts still hard? You have
good eyes, yet you still don't see, and you have good ears, yet you still
don't hear, neither do you remember."*

—Mark 8:17-18 TPT

RISE: The renewing of the mind allows the Spirit of God to shape our perception, and
our minds become an instrument of righteousness. Our history with God should shape
our perception. Miracles erase options for the believer. This is what the renewed mind
looks like. It no longer starts with lack. A miracle contains the spiritual nutrients that
are to be released into our system to make us think like Christ. In this case they fortify
us with grace to never start a train of thought with what we don't have. But as we see
with the twelve, it is possible to be unaffected by the experience of a miracle.

*I am laying down any area of my thinking that is rooted in lack, Holy
Spirit. I have seen too much of God's goodness for that to have any
influence on my perspective anymore.*

REST: Too many times I am faced with a problem, and I immediately start looking at
my resources as though I were the answer to my dilemma. Jesus asked His disciples how
many times they had to experience the miracle of supernatural provision in order to see
from divine perspective. Jesus was talking about the perception of their legal access to a
Kingdom that never ends and does not have limited resources. They were given a place
of faith to see the limitless resource to draw from for any situation. Perhaps they knew
the gift on them was for others, but they didn't see that it was also for them. Miracles
are supposed to change our perspective on reality.

*I am abundance. Don't look to your own pockets for what you need.
That will only lead to discouragement. Look up, look to Me; I want to
show you the lavishness of Heaven.*

October 6th

This Book of the Law shall not depart from your mouth, but you shall meditate in it day and night, that you may observe to do according to all that is written in it. For then you will make your way prosperous, and then you will have good success. Have I not commanded you? Be strong and of good courage; do not be afraid, nor be dismayed, for the Lord your God is with you wherever you go.

—Joshua 1:8-9 NKJV

RISE: When God brought the children of Israel into the Promised Land, He gave them a very clear assignment. The Israelites were to displace the pagan peoples living in their promised territory, spread their own tribes throughout it, and ultimately establish cities of refuge in each region. Likewise, Christ commissioned us to go into our promised territory—all the world—and make disciples of the nations, displacing the influence of the kingdom of darkness and releasing the reality of the Kingdom of Heaven. As it is for us, the Israelites' success in fulfilling each part of the assignment was entirely dependent on their ability to do that which God had been training them to do in the wilderness—to follow His manifest presence and do what He said, when He said to do it.

I want to meditate on who You are, Papa. I want my mind to be so filled with Your thoughts that they become my thoughts.

REST: When we increase our awareness of God's presence, the commands that God gives us become more doable. "God with us" must become the platform for all of life. Joshua received a key principle of victory in the exhortation to "be strong and very courageous." This exhortation was obviously important, as God repeated it three times, but the final repetition is the most significant, because God makes a link between it and the promise. The truth He gave to Joshua and gives to us in this exhortation is simple but profound: Our strength and courage to do what God has told us to do flow directly from our awareness that God is with us.

I will not send you into a battle that you are not equipped to win. When I invite your thoughts to make a home in Me, I do so for your benefit. My strength will meet your needs and fill them.

October 7th

For I tell you the truth, throughout history there has never been a man who surpasses John the Baptizer. Yet the least of those who now experience heaven's kingdom realm will become even greater than he.

—Matthew 11:11 TPT

RISE: The role of every believer is one of leadership. Not every person has a position with a title, but all lead. There will always be generals in the army. But even a private in the New Testament army has access to more than the generals of the Old Testament army did. Jesus made the point in Matthew. The least person in the Holy Spirit-filled life has access to more in God than the greatest of all the Old Testament prophets. That is why each believer must think of him or herself as one who has influence as a leader. Doing so shifts our priorities and changes how we learn, what we think we need to learn, and how we process the challenges before us.

Holy Spirit, will You show me right now the areas where You have given me influence as a leader? I want to be fully aware of the arenas You have placed me in to release Your love and power.

REST: It is interesting to note that the greatest responsibility for us as leaders has nothing to do with leading. It has to do with following. I am designed to live under the influence of the King and His Kingdom, and I must make sure the right things impact me so that my impact on the world around me is what God intended. In doing so, I must ensure that it is the works of the Lord that impact me most, for history testifies that the ongoing effect is an increased supernatural invasion of the Kingdom of God.

Jesus, the greatest of all, came to serve mankind and lay His life down. Don't misunderstand what I mean by influence, leadership, or dominion. Follow the example of My Son.

October

October 8th

*He alone is your God, the only one who is worthy of your praise, the
one who has done these mighty miracles that you have
seen with your own eyes.*

—Deuteronomy 10:21 NLT

RISE: Testimonies keep us encouraged and aware. When we share these stories, we are releasing the anointing of the spirit of prophecy over one another, saying, "This is our God. This is what He's like. This is what He's doing, and this is what He's going to do." It gives us grace to face whatever impossibilities we are currently facing. Sadly, it is possible to lose a sense of awe and gratitude for the miraculous. It is almost hard to imagine, but Israel grumbled frequently to God in the wilderness in spite of the fact that every day for 40 years they experienced divine health, manna on the ground, and shoes that didn't wear out—plus the visible sign of God's presence among them with the cloud and pillar of fire.

Keep my heart like a child's, Lord, full of wonder and appreciation. I never want to grow calloused to Your miraculous intervention on the earth.

REST: Our joy should not depend on the size of the problem but on the actual invasion of Heaven. I've seen thousands of miracles in my life, and some of them have been more dramatic than others. But the truth is I am responsible to celebrate the goodness of God in all of them. As long as we steward our hearts before the Lord and allow His works to point us to Him, we will find that His works cannot fail to inspire awe, thanks, and celebration. And when I can be trusted to steward my heart in the seemingly simple things, I become qualified for the more critical. When I focus my attention on what God has done and is doing, I remain or become thankful. That one attitude of the heart changes my impact on the world around me, perhaps more than any other. It is that one characteristic that enables me to live aware of God.

Look for My face in every miracle—whether it be the healing of a deadly disease or a surprising moment of beauty. Search for the revelation of My heart, and I will encounter you there.

October 9th

After He had removed him, He raised up David to be their king,
concerning whom He also testified and said, "I have found David the
son of Jesse, a man after My heart, who will do all My will."

—Acts 13:22 NASB

RISE: King David towers above all other Old Testament figures in this sense—he is remembered not so much for the greatness of his actions but for the greatness of his heart for God. His passionate heart set him apart in God's eyes long before he ever won great military victories, before he revolutionized the nature of worship in Israel, or even ushered in Israel's Golden Age of economic and spiritual prosperity. While David was still in obscurity, God saw that he was a man after His own heart.

> *Mold me and shape me, God. I long to be called one who is after Your*
> *own heart! Thank You for the examples of men and women who bless*
> *Your heart with their devotion.*

REST: What was the evidence of David's heart after God? Scripture indicates two primary aspects of David's life before he was anointed king. First, when nobody was looking, when nobody was calling prayer meetings or leading a revival in Judah, David was pouring out his heart in worship and prayer to God in the fields where he tended his father's sheep. With no one around, his pursuit of God was motivated by nothing but a desire to know God for His own sake. Second, David's battles against the lion and the bear revealed his heart for God because he relied completely on God for victory. This trust indicated that David's heart for the Lord was not something that changed according to his circumstances. He had integrity of heart.

> *Keep your focus on your relationship with Me. Everything else—*
> *the miracles, the anointing, the manifestations—is the fruit of our*
> *intimacy. Set your compass by that marker only.*

October 10th

Now David was greatly distressed, for the people spoke of stoning him,
because the soul of all the people was grieved, every man for his
sons and his daughters. But David strengthened himself
in the Lord his God.

—1 Samuel 30:6 NKJV

RISE: God did not bring the man after His heart straight from the pasture to the palace. Incredibly, David did not assume the throne until 10 to 13 years after Samuel had anointed him to be king. In those interim years, David endured more difficulty, persecution, and rejection than many of us face in a lifetime. He probably didn't expect it to take so long to become king. In contrast, Saul, the previous king, had no such difficulty; he was crowned very shortly after being anointed by Samuel. But God did not want another King Saul. While Saul was truly the best man Israel had to offer when they demanded a king (see 1 Sam. 8:6), his heart had not been groomed through testing before he assumed the throne.

Thank You, God, for the things you have built in me during my seasons
of waiting. I know the promises You have spoken over my life, but I don't
want to miss the value of building my trust in You.

REST: David, even though he already possessed a heart for the Lord, was led into years of testing that groomed him to handle the glory and responsibility of the throne. The scriptural account of this season in David's life is filled with lessons on the kinds of character tests we all face on the road to fulfilling our destiny in God. But the real question—what is it about David that ultimately qualifies him to become king? What brings about the moment in which God says, "OK, now you're ready"? I would like to suggest that it was David's ability to do something in the face of the deepest betrayal and rejection imaginable. When he stood completely alone, that is when David "strengthened himself in the Lord his God."

Let your understanding of My faithfulness build a foundation in you
that cannot be shaken. Then, I'll know that I can lead you anywhere,
and you will be firmly planted in Me.

October 11th

Then David and the people who were with him lifted up their voices
and wept, until they had no more power to weep. And David's two
wives, Ahinoam the Jezreelitess, and Abigail the widow of Nabal the
Carmelite, had been taken captive.

—1 Samuel 30:4-5 NKJV

RISE: Facing a volatile group of men ready to stone him caused David not to look to himself for strength but to the Lord his God. His faith gave him the courage to essentially say, "Come on, guys! We've got wives and kids to bring back!" Amazingly, this was all it took to knock the sense back into his men. He simply called them back to the purpose and vision for their lives— demonstrating the true character of a strengthened leader. God gave him the strength to master his own distress, look past the offense of his men's rejection, and rally them together to get their families back.

God, give me the strength to speak identity into people who have shown
me fear and rejection. I will look to You for my help in these times.

REST: When he turned to the men in strength, they pulled themselves together, went after the Amalekites, and retrieved every person and possession that had been taken. But David's personal breakthrough in this moment, his ability to strengthen himself and be faithful to his purpose instead of collapsing under pressure, not only saved his life, it also enabled him to lead his men to victory. His breakthrough kept him standing in front of an unseen door that was just about to open—the door to the throne room. The very battle the Philistines had just prevented him from fighting was the battle in which Saul and Jonathan died. Only a short time later, Israel crowned David king. His darkest moment led him to the back door of the throne room.

Don't set your confidence by the approval of those around you. You were
meant to set the atmosphere, to shift the tone of the room, and to lead
others to freedom. Only your total dependence on Me will give you the
perspective you need.

October 12ᵗʰ

Because you were slaughtered for us, you are worthy to take the scroll and open its seals. Your blood was the price paid to redeem us. You purchased us to bring us to God out of every tribe, language, people group, and nation. You have chosen us to serve our God and formed us into a kingdom of priests who reign on the earth.

—Revelation 5:9-10 TPT

RISE: The true significance of David's promotion from the field to the throne is seen in his kingly legacy. It would be stunning enough if David had only written the Psalms, established an unprecedented form of worship in Jerusalem, designed the Temple, and brought Israel into its Golden Age; but King David was so important to God that he was named the forerunner of the Messiah. Jesus, throughout eternity, will be identified as the Son of David and sit on David's throne. David was promoted to a place of such favor and influence with God that he altered the course of history forever.

Lord, I want my love for You to leave a legacy that impacts the future generations. Thank You that You let Your heart be impacted by the devotion of Your kids.

REST: David's life was not set down in Scripture merely to inspire us. We only need to read the accounts of his sins to know that he was not some kind of superhero. David's life is really a call to every believer. If one man who was a sinner who lived hundreds of years before the blood of Jesus was shed could come into that place of favor with God, then how much more should those who are covered by that blood be able to come into an even greater destiny—to be like Christ and finish His work on the planet? If Jesus is currently seated on the throne of David, then so are we!

I don't call the ones who are already qualified to serve Me. Like David, I equip and qualify those who are willing to lay down their life—in the midst of their messes—to pursue Me wholeheartedly.

October 13th

And Jesus kept increasing in wisdom and stature,
and in favor with God and men.

—Luke 2:52 NASB

RISE: Some of us who have been raised in a democratic society may struggle with the idea that God gives more favor to some people than others. God's favor is not the same as His love. You cannot do anything to change the vastness of God's love for you. But even Jesus Himself had to grow "in favor with God and man." This verse amazes me. I can understand the fact that He needed to grow in favor with man, but why did He have to grow in favor with God? He was perfect in every way. The answer lies in the fact that Jesus did everything He did as a man, laying His divinity aside, in order to be a model for us. Therefore, He, like David, had to be tested. At His baptism, He received His anointing as the Spirit descended on Him and remained, and He was declared by the Father to be the Son of God. But instead of launching right into His ministry, He was led by the Spirit into the wilderness. There He was tested by the enemy, specifically in the area of the Word that had just been spoken over Him.

Jesus, teach me how to grow in favor with both God and man. I need
Your favor to do what I am called to do on the earth.

REST: The "favor" that Jesus grew in is the word *charis*, which refers to the divine grace and ability of God Himself that comes upon and enables a person to accomplish His purposes. As Jesus modeled, each of us must grow in favor if we are going to fulfill our destiny in God. But favor, because it is so glorious and powerful, is a weighty thing. Thus, God, in His mercy, gives you His favor in the measure your character can handle, taking you from glory to glory, faith to faith, and strength to strength.

It is not greedy to pray for My favor, My empowering and enabling
grace, to increase in your life. But pray also for the strengthening of your
character, the wisdom to steward My favor.

October 14ᵗʰ

He who dwells in the secret place of the Most High shall
abide under the shadow of the Almighty.

—Psalm 91:1 NKJV

RISE: David's life shows us that the ability to strengthen and minister to ourselves is a vital skill that we must learn if we are going to develop the character to fulfill our potential as kings and priests. It is impossible for anyone to reach his ultimate destiny in life without learning to minister to himself. We can best appreciate the significance of this ability by understanding the nature of the role to which we are called. When Scripture says *"we shall reign on the earth"* (Rev. 5:10), the implication is that every one of us has a destiny to stand in a position where we influence people around us. Each of us will have a different size and kind of sphere of influence, but we are all called as leaders in society. We are not called to "rule over others" in the sense of domination. In God's Kingdom, the power of rule is the divine enablement to serve, protect, and bless others more effectively.

Holy Spirit, would You show me one area of my life right now where I need to learn how to strengthen myself in the Lord? I don't want any area of my life to be under the shadow of discouragement.

REST: God knew David would succeed as a leader because he took the initiative to seek Him in the secret place. This is the same quality of maturity that He is looking for in us. To experience the positive peer pressure and momentum of a move of God in a corporate group is wonderful. But those who seek God's face and pursue His destiny for their lives when nobody is around are the people who possess the initiative required to strengthen themselves. If they learn to sustain their initiative to seek God by strengthening themselves in testing, they will be the people who will experience the personal breakthroughs that release a corporate blessing to those around them.

Develop a history with Me in the quiet moments when no one is watching. Dig a well of My presence and faithfulness in your life that you can draw from whenever you need.

October 15th

So above all, guard the affections of your heart, for they affect all that
you are. Pay attention to the welfare of your innermost being, for from
there flows the wellspring of life.

—Proverbs 4:23 TPT

RISE: The Western mindset compartmentalizes human beings when it comes to feelings and thinking—the heart feels and the mind thinks. In fact, the Hebrew definition of the word *heart* encompasses the entirety of your "inner man." Your heart is the seat of your mind, imagination, will, desires, emotions, affections, memory, and conscience. It is also the center of your communion with the Spirit of God and possesses the faculties that perceive spiritual reality. Scripture refers to this spiritual perception as "the eyes of your heart." Thus, your heart is what enables you to have faith, which is the "*evidence of things not seen*" (Heb. 11:1). Your faith grows as your heart, led by the Holy Spirit, perceives and understands the invisible realm of spiritual reality. That unseen realm governs the visible realm and brings your mind and will into agreement with the reality of the Kingdom.

> *Open the eyes of my heart, God, so that I can see more clearly who You*
> *are, what You value, and how You operate. I want to align my thinking*
> *with Yours.*

REST: Our internal focus on and agreement with spiritual reality—either the reality of God's Kingdom, established on the truth, or the destructive reality of the enemy's kingdom, established on lies—gives permission for that reality to flow into the "issues of life." This power of agreement with spiritual reality through our focus adds another dimension to the principle that life flows from the heart—you become what you behold. We are becoming kings and priests of the planet, following the lead of our Elder Brother, Jesus. This is why Hebrews tells us to fix our eyes on Jesus (see Heb. 12:2). Our goal is to sustain our focus on Him. The degree to which we understand our identity and purpose—who we are becoming—is always determined by the degree of our revelation of Jesus.

> *There is no fear in Heaven. If it sneaks into your thinking, you can be*
> *sure that it is not of Me. Find the truth, fight for a new way of thinking,*
> *align yourself with the reality of My Kingdom.*

October 16th

So that the tested genuineness of your faith—more precious than gold
that perishes though it is tested by fire—may be found to result in
praise and glory and honor at the revelation of Jesus Christ.

—1 Peter 1:7 ESV

RISE: The tests that David endured were tests that specifically addressed his ability to keep his focus on his identity and purpose. He was tested by coming into circumstances that directly contradicted God's Word over his life. David's actions prove that He believed God's promises over his life. Likewise, the difficulties in our lives expose the degree to which we really believe that God is for us and that His words about our destiny are true. This is the essence of faith—not intellectual assent to truths, but the practical trust we express in God based on who we know Him to be through our relationship with Him. We express that trust when we choose to listen to Him in the midst of our circumstances more than any other voice and then respond to our circumstances in light of what He has said.

I am holding out the hardest circumstance in my life right now—the
one that tries to tell me that Your promises are insecure—and I choose
to stand firm in who You are and what You have said. Amen!

REST: The things David did to strengthen himself were some of the very same things that he did to connect with the Lord before he was brought into the time of testing. He did not go into the wilderness without tools to face the tests he would meet there. God took him there because he was ready—not yet ready for the kingship, but for a series of tests that increased in difficulty as he proved strong enough to handle them. This reveals a truth about the nature of God that should give us good reason to trust Him when we experience challenges in life. That truth—always be prepared for the moment in which you're standing, because God never fails to give you the tools you need beforehand.

Wrestle your dreams out of the tight grip of fear and hold them up to
Me. Let My presence bathe them in My gentle love, My unwavering
ability, and My uncompromising faithfulness.

October 17th

*God made them very fruitful, and they multiplied incredibly until
they were greater in number than those who ruled them. God turned
their hearts to hate his people and to deal treacherously with his
servants. But he sent them his faithful servant, Moses, the deliverer,
and chose Aaron to accompany him. Their command brought down
signs and wonders, working miracles in Egypt.*

—Psalm 105:24-27 TPT

RISE: This verse is basically saying that God sent Israel to Egypt so He could pick a fight. He blessed and multiplied His people until they were a threat to the enemy, then went to the enemy, hardened their hearts, and provoked them. This divine setup justified His rising up on behalf of His people, displaying His wonders, pouring out plagues on the Egyptians, and bringing the Israelites out loaded with spoils. What a strategy! So God not only prepares us for conflict, He leads us right into it.

Father, help me to see the conflicts in my life from Your perspectives—as divine setups to reveal Your grace, love, and mercy through my life. I need Your view on things!

REST: He is not the cause of difficulty in our lives. He is not, nor has He ever been, the sort of Father who brings torment, sickness, or persecution into the lives of His children to teach them how to be more Christlike. The point is that when we are pursuing our God-given purpose, every situation in our lives works together to accomplish it. We never have to live in a moment of conflict without divine purpose because God can win with any hand, even a pair of twos. In reality, He already has won. Our job is to align our hearts with the reality of the victory of the Cross so that we can see His purposes and redemption at work around us. Then we can recognize how to partner with Heaven in our circumstances.

Your decision to trust in My victorious stance in every area of life is the issue. You cannot outsmart Me, but you can exclude yourself from My redemptive plan by clinging to your own strength instead of Mine.

October 18th

And from the days of John the Baptist until now the kingdom of heaven suffers violence, and the violent take it by force.

—Matthew 11:12 NKJV

RISE: The safest place for us to be at any point in our lives is passionately pursing God and the purposes to which He has called us. Passionate pursuit positions us for advancement. To live in the defensive posture protecting what we have is quite dangerous. Just ask the man who buried his one talent (see Matt. 25:18-28). Our assignment and destiny is to advance the Kingdom, and it comes with an umbrella of grace and favor that works to preserve our lives, no matter what's going on around us. The moment we take a back seat in our pursuit of the Kingdom is the moment we become exposed to fiery darts of deception.

> *Lord, I repent from any area of my life where I have fallen back into a defensive posture. I am changing my tune! I want to be at the forefront of the battle, bringing Your Kingdom.*

REST: The more we establish these truths about reality in our thinking, the more we will understand the priority of stewarding our hearts. Your destiny begins in your heart. The more you gaze on the face of Jesus with the eyes of your heart, the more you see who you are becoming. The more your energies and thoughts are focused on your destiny, the more your passion and conviction grow. Your passion and conviction give you a momentum to pursue this one thing, from which all other passions and purposes flow. Your pursuit is the thing that attracts Heaven to bring you into that destiny. So as I navigate the various challenges and obstacles, I must sustain my connection with the Source of life. I can't afford to have a moment in my life when the circumstances distract me from tending that fire in my heart—even a situation when I must tend the fire by myself.

> *More than your prayer needs, more than the areas of your life still waiting for My fulfilled promise, even more than the hurting people around you, set your sights on Me. From your devotion to Me, the rest will overflow.*

October 19th

*Rejoice always and delight in your faith; be unceasing and persistent
in prayer; in every situation [no matter what the circumstances] be
thankful and continually give thanks to God; for this is the will of God
for you in Christ Jesus.*

—1 Thessalonians 5:16-18 AMP

RISE: First of all, the will of God is not merely focused on whether we become a doctor or a teacher or whether we're supposed to have tuna or peanut butter for lunch. It is focused on what we do to position our heart in relationship to God at all times, in all circumstances. Second, rejoicing, praying, and thanksgiving are all acts of our will that, particularly in times of difficulty, weakness, and uncertainty, require faith. They are activities that draw our focus to Heaven so we can agree with what is true, no matter what we feel or perceive with our physical senses and emotions. And since our agreement is what attracts the strength and reality of Heaven into our lives and circumstances, it makes sense that these activities fulfill the will of God expressed in the Lord's Prayer—on earth as it is in Heaven. The transformation of the heart is the first step in bringing Heaven to earth.

*Thank You, God, for the incredible freedom that is found in Your will.
Give me the strength to give thanks to You no matter what I am facing.*

REST: Because rejoicing, prayer, and thanksgiving attract Heaven, they are vital tools for strengthening ourselves in the Lord. You'll notice that all of them are meant to be continuously ongoing in our lives. They're not reserved for crises or holidays. They're a lifestyle—as are all the tools that we use to minister to ourselves. A big reason for this is that in the midst of crisis and difficulty, it is usually hard if not impossible to sit down and reason out how we should respond. Difficulty has a way of exposing the degree to which our lives and minds have been truly transformed by a heavenly perspective for certain responses to be habitual. The things we practice as a lifestyle equip us for difficulties.

*It is not merely for My benefit that I reveal My will for your life. When
you live from My will—rejoicing, praying, thanksgiving—you live the
most authentic, vibrant version of yourself.*

October 20th

In reality, the truth of God is known instinctively, for God has embedded this knowledge inside every human heart. Opposition to truth cannot be excused on the basis of ignorance, because from the creation of the world, the invisible qualities of God's nature have been made visible, such as his eternal power and transcendence. He has made his wonderful attributes easily perceived, for seeing the visible makes us understand the invisible. So then, this leaves everyone without excuse.

—Romans 1:19-20 TPT

RISE: When God tells us to give Him thanks, He's not insinuating that He gives in order to get something from us. He doesn't manipulate us with His gifts. He wants us to thank Him because thankfulness acknowledges the truth about our lives. And when we agree with the truth, then the truth sets us free to see and manifest the greatness that He has put in us as the ones He has made in His image. When we withhold thanks from God, we actually cut ourselves off from who we are.

I will pause in this moment, God, to turn my heart toward thanksgiving to You for all that You've done in my life. I want my endless gratitude to You to spill from my heart.

REST: God has not kept who He is a secret. Knowing God is not hard. It's actually the most obvious thing in the world. All you have to do is glorify Him as God and be thankful. This response, because it agrees with the truth, gives you open access to the vast treasures of the knowledge of God. But without that response, your thoughts become futile and your heart is darkened. *Futile* means "purposeless." When we fail to sustain the response of thanksgiving for everything in our lives, our thinking is cut off from our purpose in God. When we lose sight of our purpose, we will inevitably make choices that are outside of God's intentions for our lives, and this can only be destructive because it works against His design for us.

There is nothing too small to evoke gratitude from you. Let your heart pause in moments of thanksgiving. Train your heart toward appreciation for Me, and you will experience My presence.

October 21st

The Lord your God is in your midst, a victorious warrior. He will
exult over you with joy, He will be quiet in His love,
He will rejoice over you with shouts of joy.

—Zephaniah 3:17 NASB

RISE: Why does God seem to want radical, physical expressions of worship more than silent, awed reverence? While there is certainly a time for the latter, acts of celebration get way more press in the psalmist's descriptions of how we approach God. The reason—God is a God to celebrate. His every action and thought toward us is an extravagant expression of His love, kindness, goodness, and delight in us; and He gives it all not only to bless us for a moment, but to invite us into the deeper blessing of knowing Him. He delights in us, so He wants us to delight in Him. He rejoices over us with singing, so He wants us to rejoice in Him with singing. When we give to Him what He gives to us, we step further into relationship with Him, deepening our heart-connection with the source of life.

Father, can You show me one act of physical worship that would delight
Your heart this morning? I long to know the ways to reveal my love and
devotion to You.

REST: Not only that, but when we do what He is doing, aligning our bodies as well as our spirits and souls with what He has said, there is a release of His nature that flows to us in that place of intimacy. The Holy Spirit is the most joyful person in existence, and joy is one of the primary expressions of His Kingdom in our lives (see Rom. 14:17). His command to "rejoice always" is really an expression of His desire for us to have joy! He is simply telling us how to receive it. We not only rejoice because we have joy—we rejoice in our pursuit of joy.

I am not shy about expressing My delight over you. I want all of Heaven
to know of My love. I dance over you, I sing over you, I leap and spin
with My joy!

October 22nd

I will jump for joy and shout in triumph as I sing your song
and make music for the Most High God.

—Psalm 9:2 TPT

RISE: Thanksgiving should naturally lead to rejoicing when we follow James' instruction to "count it all joy." As we count up all that God has done, we shouldn't stop at merely thanking God. In every one of the acts of God is a revelation of His nature. And as we see God's nature—His extravagance, joy, love, faithfulness, goodness, and power—the only sensible response is to praise Him. Praise and rejoicing are two sides of the same coin. It's hard to praise effectively without rejoicing, without bringing our body, soul, and spirit into an expression of celebration. We can't rejoice without having a reason, and that reason is God's nature, revealed in His relationship with us, that we declare in our praises. When God says to "rejoice always," the implication is that we are to establish praise as a lifestyle.

> *The more I understand the depths of Your goodness, the more I am*
> *overwhelmed with gratitude. No façade of dignity is worth withholding*
> *the praise in my heart for who You are.*

REST: The praise that flows from thanksgiving is described in Hebrews 13:15 as a "sacrifice." This verse gives us a guideline for what kind of activities genuinely qualify as praise. First of all, praise should cost us something. Only then is it a proper response to the God who has given us the costly gift of His own Son. Second, a sacrifice of praise should always require faith because it's impossible to please Him apart from faith.

> *You are able, because of My Son, to offer up the sacrifice of praise before*
> *the breakthrough comes. Because you know Me, because you have*
> *witnessed My faithfulness, your lifestyle of praise is possible no matter*
> *what the circumstances.*

October 23rd

*You also, like living stones, are being built into a spiritual house to be a
holy priesthood, offering spiritual sacrifices acceptable
to God through Jesus Christ.*

—1 Peter 2:5 NIV

RISE: One of the most powerful metaphors for the people of God throughout the Scriptures is that we are the house of God. The reality that the blood of Jesus made a way for the Spirit of God Himself to dwell inside us is absolutely mind-boggling. But God moved into a house that needs to be gutted and remodeled, so to speak. Thus, the moment we choose to follow Christ, we sign up for an ongoing process of transformation in our lives that works to change us into a house that can truly express the glory and nature of God in the world. Paul explains in Romans 12:1-2 that this ongoing transformation is taking place primarily in the dimensions of our mind, which must be renewed, and our body, which must be given as a "living sacrifice." The reason—without a yielded heart, a renewed mind, and surrendered body, we can't fully cooperate with the Holy Spirit, who is the Architect and Builder at work in our lives.

> *Renovate my life, Jesus. Remove anything I've built that is not to Your
> plans, take me back to the foundation of my trust in You, and build
> something beautiful.*

REST: We must come to understand God's purposes in transforming us. If our minds are not renewed to cooperate with His purposes, we will still be using the "stinking thinking" of our carnal man, which, as Paul tells us, is *"enmity against God"* (Rom. 8:7). It is a sobering thing, but we either have our minds renewed and become co-laborers with the Lord, or our minds are set against Him. There is no neutral ground. Rejecting the mind of Christ quenches the Holy Spirit and sabotages the building He is doing in our lives. He is transforming a decent little cottage into a palace He can live in!

> *It's up to you whether you let Me take the reins in constructing your
> life or not. But I am the Creator of the entire universe, and I have a
> beautiful design for your life—come and see!*

October 24ᵗʰ

Anyone who speaks in a tongue edifies themselves,
but the one who prophesies edifies the church.

—1 Corinthians 14:4 NIV

RISE: The word *edify* means to build up. We get the word *edifice* from the same root. When we speak in tongues, we are using our voices to give utterance to the expressions of our spirits as they commune with the Holy Spirit. This is powerful because our spirits pray in perfect agreement with God because they speak from the new nature we received when we were born again. By engaging our soul along with our physical body in what our spirits are saying, we come more completely into agreement with the Holy Spirit. As we sustain this prayer, it leads to the same breakthrough we experience when we physically express praise—we become aware of the manifest presence of God. Or, you could say that our bodies and minds begin to experience an increased measure of the reality that our spirits already experience in the Lord's presence.

> *Holy Spirit, I want this kind of constant connection with You. Build*
> *up the gift of tongues in my life; I long for You to teach my spirit how*
> *to pray.*

REST: When we move into praying with understanding as well as praying with the Spirit, we further increase the level of our agreement with God in prayer. The fact that praying in the Spirit increases our ability to agree with God in prayer is the key to understanding how praying in the Spirit builds our faith. Praying in tongues bypasses the human intellect and immediately activates our Spirit-born faith—for faith does not come from the mind. The link between our level of agreement with Heaven and the level of faith we demonstrate is seen most clearly in Jesus' ministry and in His explanation for how He did what He did. Because everything Jesus did and said was in complete agreement with His Father, everything He did and said was done with faith that released the reality of His Father's Kingdom into the circumstances around Him.

> *My desire is to be constantly connected with you. I want to bring you*
> *even deeper into understanding My nature so you can move in every*
> *way with Me.*

October 25th

*If My people who are called by My name will humble themselves, and
pray and seek My face, and turn from their wicked ways, then I will
hear from heaven, and will forgive their sin and heal their land.*

—2 Chronicles 7:14 NKJV

RISE: For this reason, the most effective life of prayer to which God has called us is not a life of throwing up prayer requests and hoping that one will bring an answer. The prayer of faith that always gets results is the kind we can pray because we have drawn close to His heart and heard Him talk about what He wants to do. Then we can stand in the place of delegated authority as a co-laborer and declare what He had said over our circumstances. Asking God to swoop down and fix the problems in our lives does not take the kind of faith God is looking for.

> *Yes, God! I want to be so intimately connected to Your heart that my
> prayers are agreements, releasing Your rhema word onto the earth.*

REST: If we'll cooperate with the Holy Spirit, we'll start to look just like Jesus. For this reason, I believe God desires every believer to mature to the place where we increasingly see what the Father is doing, hear what He's saying, and step out in faith to agree with Him, just as Christ did. And one of the first gifts the Spirit gives to believers to release the hidden things is the ability to pray in tongues because He knows we need this tool to train our hearts, minds, and bodies to perceive and agree with what He's doing. As you learn how to "build yourself up on your most holy faith" (see Jude 1:20) using this tool, you'll find yourself in situations that simply will not shift until you lean into His voice, hear what He's saying, and stand in faith. And as we learn to do this, we find that while getting answers to prayer is wonderful and important, hearing His voice in the intimacy of prayer is the true source of our strength and life.

> *I have opened up My heart to you, inviting you to work alongside Me
> to see Heaven manifest on this earth. But it requires that our hearts are
> connected in vision, so you can declare My will with confidence.*

October 26th

*Sarah's faith embraced the miracle power to conceive even though she
was barren and was past the age of childbearing, for the authority of
her faith rested in the One who made the promise,
and she tapped into his faithfulness.*

—Hebrews 11:11 TPT

RISE: The tools we use to strengthen ourselves in the Lord are designed to keep us connected with our identity and purpose. Perhaps this is obvious; we only know our identity and purpose because God tells us what they are. Renewing our minds requires us to learn how to let His words over our lives completely cancel out our old beliefs about who we are—even before we see His word manifesting fully in us. This is how we demonstrate faith.

*Papa, will You tell me right now some of the things You think about
me and some of the gifts You have built into me? I need Your word to
cling to.*

REST: David's destiny to be king did not begin with his ascent to the throne but with God's declaration of that destiny through the prophet Samuel. There were probably days in the wilderness when the only evidence he could present as proof that the word was true was his memory of what Samuel said and the oil dripping from his head. But the fact that David pursued his destiny to its fulfillment, without quitting and without taking shortcuts, is clear evidence that he believed what God had said. His faith was not based on circumstances but on who he knew God to be from his history with Him.

*Fill your heart with My words over your life; return to them often to
meditate on who I have called you to be. I am more faithful than the
sun rising each morning.*

October 27th

As a result of this, he has given you magnificent promises that are
beyond all price, so that through the power of these tremendous
promises you can experience partnership with the divine nature, by
which you have escaped the corrupt desires that are of the world.

—2 Peter 1:4 TPT

RISE: When you are born again, you inherit every promise of God for the believer. These promises unlock our potential to become like Christ. But we don't truly possess these promises until three things happen. We first begin to possess a promise when it is spoken into our hearts by the Holy Spirit who takes what is Christ's and declares it to us, telling us things to come (see John 16:13-14). The declaration of the Spirit is what places the promises of the Kingdom into our account.

Forgive Me, Papa, for any time my fear has supplanted Your Lordship,
placing my own ability on Your throne. You are My God. I trust the
fulfillment of my dreams in You alone.

REST: Whenever God speaks to us, His prophetic anointing is released in what He says. That word may come to you through another person or an anointed prayer that is being prayed over you, a passage of Scripture that leapt out at you as you read, a dream or vision, or by the still, small voice of the Spirit in your inner man. That anointing does not just tell you what will be; it is creating what will be. It's as if a railroad track is being laid down before you that leads directly to the fulfillment of the word.

I spoke one word and light entered the earth, the waters parted, and
land was formed. Do not misunderstand My authority on this earth—
whatever I speak will come to pass.

October 28th

For with God nothing will be impossible.

—Luke 1:37 NKJV

RISE: It is impossible for God to lie. His Word is always in complete agreement with His nature and character, and therefore His very words release His power to accomplish what He has said. This is what the angel declared to Mary. The word for *word* is *rhema*, which is the freshly spoken word of God. The word *impossible* means without ability. An expanded literal translation of this verse could be, "No freshly spoken word from God will ever come to you that does not contain its own ability to perform itself!"

> *Thank You, Father, that You create whole universes, entire realities, when You speak. I grab ahold of all that You've said over my life and surround myself with Your truth.*

REST: This latent power in the promises of God increases our understanding of why we can trust the faithfulness of the One who promises. And a practical demonstration of trust is precisely the next thing that needs to happen for you to possess your promises. Thankfully, you don't need to understand the word in order to show the Lord that you trust His word as truth. You start moving down that railroad track to your destiny by simply receiving the word. The third thing that must happen for you to possess your promises is that your faith in the promise must be tested and proven. When the Holy Spirit declares a promise into your account, He has also put a weapon into your arsenal. This tells us two things. First, you will often have to contend for that word against someone who will try to steal it from you. Second, if you contend for the promise by using the promise, you will be victorious.

> *I am not a distant god that you must placate and hide from. I will not speak a word over your life and then leave you to contend for it alone. I wrap around you with My love; I am within you, closer than your breath.*

October 29th

But Jesus replied, "It is written and forever remains written, 'Man
shall not live by bread alone, but by every word that
comes out of the mouth of God.'"

—Matthew 4:4 AMP

RISE: The only way we can position ourselves to see our promises fulfilled is by refusing to define ourselves according to anything but what God has said about us. Jesus rebuked the Pharisees in Mark 7:13, for *"making the word of God of no effect through your tradition which you have handed down."* In other words, the Pharisees insisted on defining themselves and their world according to human interpretation and practice rather than the Word of God. The words *of no effect* mean "to render powerless," giving the picture of pulling the plug on the most powerful thing in the universe—the Word of God. Nothing can diminish the fact that His Word comes fully equipped. But we can shut off our access to that power by choosing to define our lives outside of what God has said.

> *It is sobering to me that You have given me the ability to render Your*
> *Word—that which created the heavens—powerless. Teach me, Holy*
> *Spirit, how to steward God's Word over my life, protectively and*
> *effectively.*

REST: Defining ourselves by the Word of God requires that we constantly train our minds to think in agreement with that Word. This means we have to remind ourselves of His promises often. But don't stop there! Learn to meditate on them. Like Mary, we must treasure them up and ponder them in our hearts (see Luke 2:19). While Eastern meditation tries to get people to empty their minds, biblical meditation focuses on our filling our minds—and our mouths—with the truth.

> *Provide a healthy soil for My Word to land on, and it will grow. Choose*
> *to agree with the seed that I have planted in your heart, and My Word*
> *will bear fruit in your life.*

October 30th

He is the image of the invisible God, the firstborn of all creation.

—Colossians 1:15 NASB

RISE: As kings and priests of the planet, we have a dual responsibility: first to act as representatives of man to God through intercession, and second to act as representatives of God to man by proclaiming and demonstrating the Gospel of the Kingdom. Christ is our model in both of these roles. In His death, He represented sinful humanity to God and took our judgment. And He acted as a representative from God to man. That means that Jesus is perfect theology. If we are tempted to believe something about God that we can't see revealed in Christ, then we'd better reject it. In His life and ministry, Jesus perfectly represented the Father by doing what His Father did and saying what His Father said.

> *Jesus, help me to follow in Your footsteps as I reveal the Father to a world who does not know Him. I want to speak the truth in love like You did so perfectly while on earth.*

REST: One of the primary truths that Jesus proved is that it is simply impossible to represent God accurately without demonstrations of power. Miracles are not something that only Jesus and a small number of highly anointed ministers are expected to produce. The anointing that was on Christ is the same Holy Spirit who has been given to every believer. He is the One who qualifies us as members of the royal priesthood of God and calls us to continue the ministry of Christ by demonstrating what God is like through the miraculous.

> *My love is not passive or weak; it is bold, it intervenes, it reveals the brokenness for the purpose of healing, it changes everything. You have been given the authority to reveal My love to the world.*

October 31st

Everyone will say, "Come and see the incredible things God has done;
it will take your breath away! He multiplies miracles for his people!"
He made a highway going right through the Red Sea as the Hebrews
passed through on dry ground, exploding with joyous excitement over
the miracles of God.

—Psalm 66:5-6 TPT

RISE: Keeping the testimony is a responsibility that God gave to every man and woman in Israel, not merely their leaders. The fact that each individual is accountable for keeping the testimony as a lifestyle defines this as one of the primary tools we must use to strengthen ourselves. We can't expect others to keep the testimony for us. Beyond keeping testimonies in our conversation, we are also to meditate on them. Meditation is powerful because it involves our imagination, which actually can lead us into a significant level of experience, and experience is a vital part of renewing the mind.

Thank You for the ways You have moved in my life, Lord. I am going to
spend the next ten minutes remembering specific instances of Your love
intervening in my story.

REST: This psalm writer could not have possibly seen God part the Red Sea and the Jordan River. But through inspired imagination, he was able to come into a level of experiencing these miracles that enabled him to own these events as his own history. If you are someone who feels like you haven't seen very many miracles, you first need to remember that you possess every story of God's as your own. Then, because they're yours, you should study the testimonies of Scripture and collect the testimonies of both historical saints and the saints around you so you can meditate on them. Meditation on the testimonies trains your mind to think from the realm of faith.

Each example of My works on the earth points to who I am, and I
never change. Grab ahold of each revelation of My nature as your own
inheritance.

November

November 1st

*"Consider carefully what you hear," he continued. "With the measure
you use, it will be measured to you—and even more."*

—Mark 4:24 NIV

RISE: As I have developed a lifestyle of feeding on the promises and prophecies of God over my life and meditating on His testimonies, something interesting has happened. People with testimonies now constantly find me, like heat-seeking missiles. Because the nature of the testimony carries a prophetic anointing, it's as though I am prophesied over on a continual basis. As a result, I have a steady supply of encouragement and strength that shows up wherever I am, all over the world. It's amazing. When we value what God values, His blessings will hunt us down.

> *Holy Spirit, help me to be conscious of what, and who, I am allowing
> to affect my spiritual atmosphere. I want to surround myself with hope
> and testimonies of Your faithfulness.*

REST: Clearly, in Mark Jesus is not referring merely to the physical act of perceiving sound. He's talking about hearing that involves listening. When we listen, we allow what we are hearing to gain our attention and focus, which in turn influences our beliefs and values. These beliefs and values set a standard for our ears that ultimately determines the voices that we pick up in our environment. This standard is also what draws us to certain people more than others. Because I've set a standard for my ears by valuing the testimony, I attract people with the same standard. Our values communicate something in the spiritual realm that alerts others with the same values to our presence.

> *Take a stance of authority over that which influences how you think,
> how you perceive Me, and what you expect to happen. Your peace and
> anticipation of My goodness are worth fighting for.*

November 2nd

And He is the radiance of His glory and the exact representation of
His nature, and upholds all things by the word of His power. When
He had made purification of sins, He sat down at the
right hand of the Majesty on high.

—Hebrews 1:3 NASB

RISE: The standard we set for our ears also determines our ability to strengthen our-selves because strengthening ourselves begins with our choice to listen to God's voice more than any other. Learning to strengthen ourselves does not imply that we are the source of our strength. Every tool in our arsenal is designed to help us draw from the strength made available to us by hearing His voice. Listening is what enables us to establish agreement with Him through obeying His voice, and our agreement is what releases heavenly strength and resources into our lives and circumstances. However, as I just described, the standard we set for our ears can attract heavenly strength that comes through interactions with other people who speak and live from a heavenly per-spective. Therefore, by purposefully associating with people who share our values and controlling our interactions with people who don't, we strengthen ourselves.

Thank You, God, that You are my strength and provision. I will give
love to everyone, but only give influence to Your truth.

REST: I strongly believe that we are all called to minister to anyone and everyone to whom the Holy Spirit would lead us. We're to accept them unconditionally and show them the love and power of God. Certainly, there will also be individuals whom God calls us to do business with, to befriend over a period of time in order to introduce them to Jesus, or to disciple in the faith. But these kinds of relationships are a completely different ballgame from friendships in which we open ourselves to the influence of our friend's perspective and values. We need to be careful about who is close to us and gives input into our lives.

Surround yourself with those people who call you higher—to a greater
faith in Me, to a greater hope in what I am doing on the earth.

November 3ʳᵈ

It takes a grinding wheel to sharpen a blade, and so one person
sharpens the character of another.

—Proverbs 27:17 TPT

RISE: Our close friendships, especially with our spouses, are powerful, because they are built on covenant. Covenant establishes an agreement that allows the spiritual reality that governs your life to flow to the other person and vice versa. This is why it is so vital to develop friendships with people whose lives consistently display the fruit of the Kingdom. When we steward covenant friendships with people of faith, we stay connected to a growing source of strength that often greatly determines our ability to persevere through difficult times.

> *Father, can You show me one tangible expression of Your love that I can*
> *pour out on one of my covenant relationships today? I want my value for*
> *them to be expressed in a way they can experience.*

REST: Our love and honor for one another creates an exchange of life whenever we interact. Because my friends are people of faith, they naturally exude hope, promise, and joy. It doesn't take long when I'm with them for their attitude and spirit to be infectious. But even more, covenant friendships, when they're built on knowing each other after the Spirit, have the effect of calling us back to who we truly are in Christ. They refresh our connection to our purpose and identity, and when our vision for those things is renewed, usually our strength is too. For this reason, I know that one of the best ways to strengthen myself when I'm tired or discouraged is to grab hold of a friend and spend some time with him.

> *Lean on My Word over your life when you feel weak, but don't isolate*
> *yourself. I never meant for you to walk this journey without the loving*
> *support of your brothers and sisters. I have placed both gifts and chances*
> *for growth in their hands.*

November 4th

Don't befriend angry people or associate with hot-tempered people, or
you will learn to be like them and endanger your soul.

—Proverbs 22:24-25 NLT

RISE: When I am in an emotionally vulnerable place, or even if I'm just physically tired, I have to be careful to make sure I am not around people who like to complain or be critical. I have always had strong personal boundaries in place for discerning and interacting with people who speak from a place of negativity or unbelief. Normally I will minister to them, but I will not give them access to my life. When I'm lacking strength, however, I will intentionally avoid them. It may not sound very compassionate, but I am the only one who is responsible for keeping my heart free from doubt and judgment, and I alone can recognize when I am vulnerable to the influence of people who agree with those spirits.

Holy Spirit, will You guide me as I connect to my own inner world.
I want to be aware of those moments when I'm feeling worn out and
vulnerable so that I can steward my heart well with You.

REST: Not all ungodly counsel comes from the ungodly. While they mean well, some people lack the faith perspective that I strive for and tend to work to make me more like them than they do to actually try to help me to become stronger in my trust in God. My job is to protect myself from such an influence, especially when I am vulnerable. My heart is a garden. Some people are good at planting weeds, while others plant the Kingdom. My job, and yours, is to know the difference.

Look for the people I have placed in your life who operate with even
more faith than you do. Let them remind you about the reality of My
Kingdom and then be that reminder for someone else.

November 5th

But when you pray, go into your room, close the door and pray to your
Father, who is unseen. Then your Father, who sees
what is done in secret, will reward you.

—Matthew 6:6 NIV

RISE: The gospels specifically mention occasions when Jesus took His disciples away from the crowds to rest and be together. The testimony of revival history teaches us that very few men and women of God really learn how and when to do this. In case after case, the same person who carried a marvelous anointing that brought salvation, healing, and deliverance to thousands of people lacked the wisdom to see that he wouldn't be able to sustain that ministry if he didn't learn to get away from the crowds long enough to get physical rest and cultivate life-giving relationships with family and friends who would reaffirm his or her focus on the Kingdom. As a result, many of these revivalists died young, and many of their family members suffered physically and spiritually.

> *I want to be emotionally healthy, physically healthy, and spiritually*
> *healthy, Lord. Give me the wisdom to operate from a place of balance*
> *even when my season is full.*

REST: The strength of our intimacy with the Father and with the close covenant relationships in our lives is what will largely determine our ability to minister from a place of faith and obedience to God rather than a place of striving to please or help people. The people who are most vulnerable to overextending themselves on behalf of ministry relationships are people who struggle with intimacy—both with God and others. Ministry can be a great place for them to feel connected and loved, but the truth is, without the accountability that only comes from covenant friendships, they are just being set up for burnout or compromise. This is why God will pull many ministers out of ministry for a time just to learn how to be friends with Him apart from working for Him. All true fruitfulness flows from that intimacy with Him.

> *I created you as a triune being—spirit, soul, and body. Learn to value*
> *all three, as I do. Come into the quiet place of My presence, and let My*
> *love restore any areas of your heart that have been depleted.*

November 6th

*Then he said to them, "Go your way, eat the fat, drink the sweet,
and send portions to those for whom nothing is prepared; for this
day is holy to our Lord. Do not sorrow, for the joy of the Lord is your
strength." So the Levites quieted all the people, saying, "Be still,
for the day is holy; do not be grieved."*

—Nehemiah 8:10-11 NKJV

RISE: For many who were raised in church, weeping over the fact that we don't measure up to God's standard for life as taught in the Scriptures is considered the one legitimate sign of conviction and repentance. And holiness is something generally associated with somberness and tears and not with joy. But in Nehemiah's story of rebuilding the fallen city of Jerusalem, we discover that holiness is more connected to joy and rejoicing. Israel was forbidden to weep when the priest publicly read God's Word, even though they fell far short of what God required from them. They were, instead, to rejoice and celebrate with a feast. Sinners were to celebrate with joy because they understood God's call to holiness!

> *Thank You, God, that Your Word brings life. My heart is open to Your
> correction. I want to experience the fullness of Your joy!*

REST: The idea that the best response to conviction is getting depressed derives from wrong beliefs that blind us to the Holy Spirit's purpose in exposing the places where we fall short of our high calling in Christ. There is a place for tears, as it is godly sorrow that leads us to repentance. But when we have a wrong view of God as a legalistic father, we distort what was supposed to lead us to an encounter with Him that brings transformation. Instead, many develop attitudes of somberness in a fleshly attempt to be holy. Consequently, we've misunderstood and misappropriated the fullness of His grace, which does not merely forgive our sin but empowers us to live like Him.

> *My goal is never to see you hang your head. It is for freedom that I have
> set you free from sin. I am drawing you, convicting you, encouraging you
> as you step into greater measures of My freedom every day.*

November 7th

For there is no difference; for all have sinned and
fall short of the glory of God.

—Romans 3:22-23 NKJV

RISE: The real problem is not in what we lack but how we respond to what God has said. Focusing on our problems more than God's answers should be a dead giveaway that we're really dealing with condemnation, not the Holy Spirit's conviction. Focus on God's answers, not your problems. When the Holy Spirit shows us where we are falling short, the bigger reality is not the areas where we're not yet walking in our destiny but the destiny itself. All have fallen short, yes, but we are destined for glory! The conviction of the Holy Spirit is actually a call to turn our focus away from our sin and our limitations. Such a renewed perspective is supposed to seem overwhelmingly impossible. That way we're more likely to draw near to Him and allow His grace to bring us into our destiny.

> *Thank You, Jesus, that You have made it so my destiny is to experience*
> *and live from the glory of God. I am absolutely dependent on God to*
> *bring me there.*

REST: When we recognize the purpose for the Holy Spirit's conviction, we start to understand how we need to interpret the kinds of tests He allows us to face in our lives. It's obvious that the real tests are not the situations that challenge our strengths but the ones that expose our weaknesses. David's biggest test was not facing Goliath; it was overcoming his own vulnerability to distress by strengthening himself. In fact, most of the warfare we deal with in the Christian life is really internal. As we realign our wrong thinking and transform our old behavior patterns, it is amazing how we find that the devil and the world pose less and less of a threat to the flow of the life of God through us. God prepares us for all of our battles. When our weaknesses are exposed, it is because God has already given us the tools we need to overcome them.

> *Trust Me to know the timing of your breakthroughs. Don't go searching*
> *out your weaknesses, hoping to tackle them in your own strength. Let*
> *My Spirit gently reveal them so you can walk into My freedom.*

November 8th

All these with one mind and one purpose were continually devoting
themselves to prayer, [waiting together] along with the women, and
Mary the mother of Jesus, and with His brothers.

—Acts 1:14 AMP

RISE: The disciples were strengthening themselves in that upper room. Strengthening ourselves in the Lord is all about being prepared to receive and steward the fulfillment of our promises. Think of "invading Heaven" in the physical sense. In order for an astronaut to venture beyond the earth's atmosphere, he must be covered in a pressurized suit that can resist the vacuum of outer space. Without it, his body would instantly explode. If you and I are going to touch the realm of God's glory—and the word *glory* literally means "weight"—we are going to have to exert some internal pressure in order to build enough strength to live in that atmosphere and be carriers of that glory on earth.

Yes, Father! I want to increase my capacity for carrying Your glory.
Build within me—whatever way You choose—an unshakable strength
in You.

REST: To carry His glory is exactly what we are made to do—the Christian life is not only about getting saved so we go to Heaven when we die. Rather, it's about learning to live in Heaven's reality now so that we can co-labor with Christ to establish His Kingdom on earth. The reason the Church has "dumbed down" the Great Commission of discipling nations and seeing the knowledge of the glory of the Lord cover the earth has everything to do with our failure to pick up the baton of the early Church by contending for the authentic ongoing baptism of the Holy Spirit. As the Book of Acts testifies, this baptism was never meant as a one-time event but as an ongoing series of encounters that enable us to walk in increasing levels of power, fulfilling the assignment Jesus gave to His Body.

You were never meant to bring Heaven to earth on your own. I have
given you My most precious gifts—My Son, My Spirit—to empower
and equip you to do the thing that you were called to do, that thing
which will bring you life more than any other.

November 9th

"Well done, my good servant!" his master replied. "Because you have
been trustworthy in a very small matter, take charge of ten cities."

—Luke 19:17 NIV

RISE: At one point, Jesus picked up on His disciples' misunderstanding of how the Kingdom would come. After witnessing thousands of miracles and signs and wonders confirming His message that "the kingdom of heaven is at hand," the disciples expected that *"the kingdom of God would appear immediately"* (Luke 19:11). So, Jesus told them a parable about a nobleman who left the country and entrusted his servants with various sums of money to invest while he was gone. When the nobleman returned, he had each person give an account of what he had done with what he was given. In response he gave each person authority over cities in his realm in direct correlation to his ability to invest and manage what he had been given to steward.

> *I want to be a good steward of Your Kingdom, God. Guide me, stretch*
> *my capacity, put me in situations that will develop my character. I trust*
> *in You completely.*

REST: This is how the Kingdom of God comes—not all at once, but little by little as the people of God steward the anointing they received in their last encounter. We can't take cities and nations for God because He already possesses them. That's why in the second psalm it says to ask God for the nations, and He'll give them to us as our inheritance. Our job is to become ones to whom He can entrust His authority until entire cities and nations come under the righteous influence of those who serve well, carrying God's agenda. This kind of increase comes to those who are faithful with what they've been given.

> *I won't withhold any good thing from you. That is My promise. But I*
> *will only give you those things that you are ready to manage victoriously.*
> *Lean into My guidance and trust Me to release things at the right time.*

November 10th

But just as we have been approved by God to be entrusted with the
gospel, so we speak, not as pleasing men, but God
who examines our hearts.

—1 Thessalonians 2:4 NASB

RISE: So how do we steward what's been given to us? We use the tools we've been given to contend for the promises and desires that God has birthed in our hearts through the Holy Spirit. We also take other specific steps of faith and obedience in order to line up our thinking and behavior with what we've heard. If you have a longing to preach the Gospel, a first step might be preaching to yourself in the car. It may be a small beginning, but we can't despise it because faith says that it's not where you are but where you're going that is important. And faith understands that spiritual release comes through physical obedience.

> *Jesus, will You show me one step that I can take today toward my*
> *dreams? I want to develop the muscle of stewardship so that I can carry*
> *all that You have for me.*

REST: Faith must conquer our fear of failure if we are going to fully embrace a journey of transformation. As the lesson from Nehemiah teaches, our promises and desires are usually connected to the places where we need to grow in our character and in our capacity to think and live like God. If there were no power to change, it would be cruel for God to give us promises that we could never qualify to receive. But because the Spirit of the resurrected Christ lives in our bodies, His promises and desires are the keys to our breakthrough. We have to come to see the places of lack in our lives as the very places where God intends to bring us into our greatest victories—if we will take the risk to step out on our promises.

> *I am delighted when you take a step, in faith, toward stewarding your*
> *dreams. Open the soft spots of your heart to Me—those places of fear,*
> *insecurity, and weakness. They are not shocking to Me, but rather*
> *invitations for My presence to invade.*

November 11th

And he who does not take his cross and follow after
Me is not worthy of Me.

—Matthew 10:38 NKJV

RISE: Jesus made the requirements to follow Him very clear. Jesus doesn't say that we have to experience punishment for our sins. That Cross was His alone to bear. Taking up your cross means embracing the truth that your life is not about you. Romans 14:7 puts it this way: *"For none of us lives to himself, and no one dies to himself."* Jesus' Cross was not about Him. His Cross was about pleasing His Father and redeeming us. Likewise, our cross is not about us but about living our lives for Christ and doing our part to make His mission succeed on earth.

> *Thank You, Jesus, for this reminder. My life is no longer my own, and I am so grateful that that is the case. Help me to live my life in accordance with this truth.*

REST: Jesus suffered by resisting the very things He would overcome through His death and resurrection—the kingdom of darkness and its reign of sin and death over the human race. Likewise, the cross we take up and the suffering that we endure as believers is the resistance of the enemy forces that we have been delegated to displace from the land that we have inherited with Christ. Exercising the power and authority we've been given to take our territory from the enemy is what strengthens our character to stand in a place of influence in that territory to establish the Kingdom. We're not merely to bind the strongman, kick him out of the house, and take back what he has stolen from us. We're supposed to become Kingdom strongmen who can release the blessings of Heaven to fill the house.

> *My Spirit is in you, empowering you and guiding you as you remove every last trace of sin's influence on this world. Your authority over darkness begins with your submission to My light.*

November 12th

*From the moment John stepped onto the scene until now, the realm of
heaven's kingdom is bursting forth, and passionate people
have taken hold of its power.*

—Matthew 11:12 TPT

RISE: Spiritual giants have the habit of rising up during history's darkest moments to
meet the challenge. They look into the storms of their day—the manifestations of the
kingdom of darkness in the territory they are convinced is the rightful inheritance of
the Lord—and rise up with faith to displace the storms, declaring, "Not on my shift!"
Jesus never intended that only a few special believers would walk in a great anointing
like His to change the spiritual climate over regions. It is time for a whole generation of
believers to embrace the opportunity before them—to take up their cross and contend
for the breakthroughs that will allow God to entrust them with measures of anointing
great enough to take back the inheritance we are invited to share with Him.

*Thank You, Father, that You poured out Your Spirit on all of us so that
we could rise to the challenge and manifest Your authority in every area
of the earth.*

REST: To do this, we will need great courage because we will be required to take risks
when we step out in faith into what we've seen and heard from the Lord. We will never
take that step if our hope rests on experiencing another great event, like waiting for the
next wave of revival to sweep in or a prophet to call us out and give us a word. We must
take personal responsibility to strengthen every weak place and break our agreement
with fear. We must become the ongoing manifestation of revival and stop waiting for
outside circumstances to line up with our dreams. We do this by giving thanks and
rejoicing, praying as He prays, meditating on promises and testimonies, and associating
with people of faith—not just when others around us are doing so, but continuously,
as a lifestyle.

*You are conduits of My presence on the earth and the ones who can allow
or destroy those things that would block our connection. Everything I do
is for the restoration of our connection and the redemption of the world.*

November 13th

*Then suddenly there appeared with the angel a multitude of the
heavenly host (angelic army) praising God and saying, "Glory to God
in the highest [heaven], and on earth peace among men
with whom He is well-pleased."*

—Luke 2:13-14 AMP

RISE: The greatest shift of seasons in the history of planet Earth came with an announcement given by angels—peace and goodwill toward men! This plan had been in waiting since before the worlds were made, but it needed to be withheld until the right moment. Sin filled the earth, people were out of touch with God's perspective for their lives, and there was little passion to know the one true God throughout the world—the timing was perfect.

*Thank You, thank You, God, that Your plan for the earth was restoration
and intimacy all along! Thank You that You designed us to live within
Your pleasure.*

REST: Most of us celebrate this message at Christmastime every year. This decree revealed God's heart more clearly than ever before. It redefined God's intent for humanity, which so far has lasted two thousand years. But after all these years, many of us have not shifted our thinking to be consistent with His announced plan—one of peace and goodwill. Without a shift in thinking it will be all too easy to misrepresent this magnificent One by expecting and allowing things to take place on our watch that Jesus never would have allowed.

*Peace, My shalom—everything in its right order—is My desire for the
world. I didn't come to punish or shame, but to spread My delight and
the peace of My dominion to you.*

November 14th

*The same way a loving father feels toward his children—that's but a
sample of your tender feelings toward us, your beloved children, who
live in awe of you. You know all about us, inside and out.*

—Psalm 103:13-14 TPT

RISE: If I were to do to my children what many people think God does to His children, I'd be arrested for child abuse. People say God is good, yet they credit Him with
causing cancer and natural disasters and even blame Him for terrorist activities. Some
try to escape the pain of such shameful reasoning by stating, "He allowed it" instead
of "He caused it." In my way of thinking, there's little to no difference. If I abuse my
children or "allow/approve" a neighbor to do it, it's obvious I have a very serious problem. And when we sweep the abusive misdeed under the carpet called, "God works in
mysterious ways," we add insult to injury.

*Papa, I'm so sorry if I ever attributed events to You that were never in
Your plan. Expand my understanding of Your goodness, Father. I need
a greater understanding of Your heart for me and for the world.*

REST: There is a common thought among many that God causes or allows evil to take
place so He can display His mercy. That would be like me breaking my child's arm to
show my ability to give him comfort and then using my skills to reset the broken bone.
People ask, "What about Job?" My response is, "What about Jesus?" Job provides the
question. Jesus gives the answer. The story of Job is about holding to our faith in the
midst of trials and seeing God restore everything brilliantly. But the story of Jesus is the
only one I follow.

*I long to wrap you in My arms of love, to restore those places in your
heart that have been injured, to empower you to life a life of incredible
freedom and purpose. Look at My Son if You wonder about My will for
the earth.*

November 15th

Now, Lord, consider their threats and enable your servants to speak your
word with great boldness. Stretch out your hand to heal and perform
signs and wonders through the name of your holy servant Jesus.

—Acts 4:29-30 NIV

RISE: There's no question that God can turn any situation around for His glory and
for our benefit—this of course includes the most evil conditions known to humanity
around the world. But that is the testimony of His greatness and His redemptive purpose. It does not represent His design. To attribute evil to Him tragically undermines
our purpose on the earth, as it cripples our ability to represent Jesus as the manifestation of God's goodwill toward men. Our boldness to declare and demonstrate who He
is in a given situation is seriously impaired if we're not confident of what He is like.
When the boldness that is normal to the one filled with the Spirit of God diminishes,
it costs us dearly. It is often our boldness that draws Him into an impossible situation.

> *Fill me with Your boldness, God. I want to look on every example of*
> *pain, sickness, and brokenness with the absolute confidence in Your*
> *heart for restoration and redemption.*

REST: What might be even more devastating in this view of God causing evil is that it
ultimately compromises our ability to discern the difference between God's discipline
and an actual demonic assault. And that is a weakness that we cannot afford to carry
around any longer. People constantly embrace a hellish situation in their lives because
of the thought that God intended it for good. That way of thinking infects the God-
given ability to discern the works of the devil with a human reasoning that is demonic
in nature. In fact, it's not just discernment that is in question. This kind of breakdown
in our assignment to spiritual maturity causes us to forget who the enemy really is and
what we're actually fighting against.

> *You are My light-filled army, battling against the darkness that has*
> *already been defeated. Spread the word! I have conquered death,*
> *sickness, division, and despair. Don't let any trace of darkness stand*
> *unopposed.*

November 16th

*But the one who indulges in a sinful life is of the devil, because the
devil has been sinning from the beginning. The reason the Son of God
was revealed was to undo and destroy the works of the devil.*

—1 John 3:8 TPT

RISE: It's not complicated. Loss, death, and destruction are the things left behind when the devil has had influence in a given situation. Jesus is the Good Shepherd. And what does that goodness look like? He gives abundant life. Here it is—loss, death, and destruction vs. abundant life. One is bad; the other is good. It shouldn't be that hard to distinguish between the two. Jesus taught us how to recognize the works of the devil and then modeled how we destroy them. Do we have the right to set a new way of life and ministry that doesn't do what Jesus commanded us to do? No. Absolutely not!

*Jesus, thank You for bringing abundant life to me. Help me to never lose
focus on why You came and how much You love me.*

REST: Most every believer confesses that God is good. We have to. It's in the Bible. It's not the belief in His goodness that threatens us. It's our definition of this goodness that has brought much debate and sometimes conflict and turmoil into the family of God. If He is as good as many claim, how we respond to this truth will require massive change in how we do life. Instead of creating doctrines that explain away our weakness and anemic faith, we'll actually have to find out why the "greater works than these" have not been happening in and around us (see John 14:12). Creating doctrines of no miracles today not only contradicts His Word, it is a sneaky way to avoid responsibility. Instead of changing the standard for life given by Jesus, who walked the earth two thousand years ago, we are to embrace it and follow His model.

*You can find your definition of goodness through Me, not the other way
around. I have set the standard of My love through My Son. Let Him
teach you what goodness looks like.*

November 17th

Truly, truly, I say to you, he who believes in Me, the works that I do,
he will do also; and greater works than these he will do;
because I go to the Father.

—John 14:12 NASB

RISE: The Pharisees saw Jesus as a threat to their positions of power and influence. In a similar way, many leaders today feel threatened over a possible shift in theological positions that implies we've not been as successful in ministry as we could have been. We empower the lie we believe. The fight to protect the sanctity of our history has kept us from a more significant future. I'm thankful for my past. I'm thankful for what our forefathers fought for so that we might live in greater liberty in Christ. But there is more.

> *I never want to limit what is possible with You just because of my pride.*
> *Keep me humble and hungry for **all** You have paid for, God. I don't*
> *want to miss a thing.*

REST: His goodness is beyond our ability to comprehend, but not our ability to experience. Our hearts will take us where our heads can't fit. Understanding is vital, but it often comes through experiencing God. Faith for the journey of walking with God leads to encounters with God. It results in a growing knowledge and understanding of truth, as in, "*By faith we understand that the worlds were framed by the word of God*" (Heb. 11:3). Having said that, one of the great commands of Scripture pertaining to the experience of His goodness is, "*taste and see that the Lord is good*" (Ps. 34:8). If you'll taste it for yourself, you'll see it more clearly. Your perception of truth will increase as you experience truth more deeply.

> *I created every neuropathway in your mind. You cannot contain Me*
> *with that same mind, but I am inviting you into encounters with*
> *Me. Set down control and let your heart and spirit be pulled into*
> *experiencing My goodness.*

November 18th

Now to him who is able to do immeasurably more than all we ask or imagine, according to his power that is at work within us, to him be glory.

—Ephesians 3:20-21 NIV

RISE: Changing our theology doesn't change Him. Either He is authentically good or He is not. I would never suggest that we pretend He is different than He is. Nothing is accomplished by allowing our imagination to create our own image of God. He would then be no better than the gods made out of wood or stone, also created by human initiative. Inventing Him in our minds or building Him with our hands is a similarity that is both vain and ultimately destructive. Discovering who He is and what He is like in reality is the only possible way to discover His true goodness. This eternal journey into His infinite goodness is the one we are privileged to embrace.

I want to know the truth of who You are, Father. Forgive me for the assumptions I've made about Your nature. My theories about Your goodness cannot contain You!

REST: It's impossible for us to create a concept of what He is like that is greater than He really is. He is either greater than we can understand, perceive, describe, or imagine, or He is not God—we are. Neither can we exaggerate His goodness. We can twist it, pervert it, dilute it, and misrepresent it. But the one thing we cannot do is exaggerate the goodness of God. It will take us all of eternity just to broach the subject of His goodness. What God does for us is beyond the reach of our biggest prayer on our greatest day with our highest level of faith—He exists in that realm to work for us. His commitment to us is to function beyond the limitations of our imagination and perform the unthinkable on our behalf. These are expressions of His goodness, which come from His being. He is perfect goodness personified.

Watch how children learn and follow their lead. Stay curious and open to learning more about Me. There is more to know than a lifetime can contain. Let your wonder guide you into more of My presence.

November 19th

*You will know me as "I AM" after you have lifted me up from the
earth as the Son of Man. Then you will realize that I do
nothing on my own initiative, but I only speak the
truth that the Father has revealed to me.*

—John 8:28 TPT

RISE: If someone calls me on the phone and tells me that the sickness I am suffering from has been given to me by God to teach me to trust Him, I need to examine his word to see if it is an authentic word from God. God, the Chief of all artists, has left us with many masterpieces throughout Matthew, Mark, Luke, and John. The stories of the Master's touch abound as person after person is healed and delivered by the love of this perfect Father. As I study these four Gospels, I must take note that I can't find any "painting" with the same strokes or colors. There's not one example of Jesus giving a disease to anyone. In fact, His lifestyle was the opposite. What the person claims is an authentic word from God contradicts the examples of His known works. The renewed mind is able to conclude that what was given to me with God's signature at the bottom is in fact a forgery.

*Thank You for leaving us Your Word, Papa. Thank You for sharing
Your heart in the shape of Your Son.*

REST: Tragically, many forgeries are accepted by believers day after day and then sold to others in the Christian marketplace as authentic revelations of the will of God. They in turn distort the revealed will of God throughout the Scriptures, perverting our sense of what He is like. The biggest forgery of all just might be the teaching that Jesus no longer heals people from sickness and delivers them from torment. Simple examination of Scripture proves that such a concept is a devilish misrepresentation of the One who gave Himself to reveal the Father and redeem humanity. Perhaps it's these forgeries that have been marketed for decades by well-meaning believers that have contributed to the single greatest vacuum in human consciousness—the knowledge of the goodness of God.

*I am not hiding; I want you to see My heart and My intentions for the
world that were revealed by My Son. Set your standard by Him.*

November 20th

Then the Jews said among themselves, "Where does He intend to go that we shall not find Him? ...What is this thing that He said, 'You will seek Me and not find Me, and where I am you cannot come'?"

—John 7:35-36 NKJV

RISE: Because God is better than I think, I must adjust my thinking and the tenderness of my heart until I live conscious of both His nature and His presence. And that awareness then becomes the reality I live from. His nature defines who I am and what I do. This greatest reality of all realities is to become my spiritual, emotional, and intellectual home. In the same way I travel from my home to my office, or from my home to minister in another country, so His nature is to become the home I travel from—it is the reference point for all of life. And though I travel great distances from my home, I am never to be away from the awareness of His goodness. That is the home or the abiding place of my heart that goes with me everywhere.

Father, I want my experience and expectation of Your goodness to become the bedrock of my life. Remove anything that stands in the way of me living from the truth.

REST: Revelation is seldom given to those who are merely curious. You'll never see Him reveal truth just to make us smarter or more capable of debating with those who see differently. Truth by nature is the transforming power of God to instill freedom in the life of those who embrace it. It could be said that freedom exists in a person's life to the degree he embraces truth from the heart. It's more than a mental agreement to a concept called truth. It is the heartfelt yes to a way of life. That way of life becomes measurable in our lifestyle of freedom. Who He is is revealed in what He says. He identifies Himself as the Word. In other words, He says nothing apart from who He is. His Word reveals His nature and manifests His presence. Jesus was never a broadcaster of truths He didn't live.

Open your heart to My voice; let it sink in deep and transform you. Shed those layers of fear, performance, and doubt. Come into the fullness of My freedom.

November 21st

"You won't die!" the serpent replied to the woman. "God knows that
your eyes will be opened as soon as you eat it, and you will
be like God, knowing both good and evil."

—Genesis 3:4-5 NLT

RISE: Lies are costly, as they steal life from all who embrace them. Tragically, if I believe a lie, I empower the liar. The devil is the enemy of our souls. He works to trip us up through lies, intimidation, accusation, and seduction. His aim is to get us to question who God really is. His first interaction with Adam and Eve was to get them to question God's motives for giving a command not to eat the forbidden fruit, which was from the Tree of the Knowledge of Good and Evil. He accuses God of using His commands to protect Himself from humanity by keeping people from becoming like Him, knowing good and evil. Such nonsense was the tool used to poison humanity at its core.

> *I can see in my life where the enemy has tried to get me to doubt my*
> *identity as a new creation and Your faithfulness, God. I refuse to give*
> *those lies an audience from now on.*

REST: Adam and Eve ate the forbidden fruit to become like God. They tried to obtain through an act what they already had by design—they were created in the image of God. Entertaining a lie still can have an effect on us—spirit, soul, and body. It's a poison that works into our being to destroy our identity and purpose. I can't afford to have a thought in my head about me that He doesn't have in His head about me. Thinking independently of God is not freedom. In fact, it is the worst possible bondage imaginable to think outside of the purpose and design set in place by the greatest creative genius ever to exist. The greatest gift we can give ourselves is to require that our thought life work in tandem with His goodness. Being tethered to His goodness is the most wonderful illustration of freedom and liberty possible.

> *I am not holding anything back that would be for your good. Trust Me*
> *that I know the best way for you. Let Me pour out My love into your life.*

November 22nd

And I will put enmity between you and the woman, and between your
seed and her seed; he shall bruise you on the head,
and you shall bruise him on the heel.

—Genesis 3:15 NASB

RISE: Satan didn't come into the Garden of Eden and violently take possession of Adam and Eve. He couldn't—he had no dominion there. Dominion empowers. And because man was given the keys of dominion over the planet, the devil would have to get his authority from man. The suggestion to eat the forbidden fruit was simply the devil's effort to get Adam and Eve to agree with him in opposition to God, thus empowering him. To this day it is through agreement that the devil is able to kill, steal, and destroy. He is still empowered through man's agreement.

I repent for any time that I've handed over my authority to the enemy,
Lord. I am reclaiming Your gift of dominion, agreeing only with Your
truth.

REST: Mankind's authority to rule was forfeited when Adam ate the forbidden fruit. Paul said, "*You are that one's slaves whom you obey*" (Rom. 6:16). In that one act, mankind went from ruler over a planet to the slave and possession of the evil one. All that Adam owned, including the title deed to the planet with its corresponding position of rule, became part of the devil's spoil. God's predetermined plan of redemption immediately kicked into play. Jesus would come to reclaim all that was lost.

Sin has never caught Me off guard. It doesn't scare Me, worry Me,
or leave Me without a plan. Sin grieves Me because there is so much
more available to you. Come and experience the fullness of My original
design for your life!

November 23rd

For the Son of Man came to seek and to save the lost.

—Luke 19:10 NIV

RISE: God's plan of rulership for man never ceased. Jesus came to bear man's penalty for sin and recapture what had been lost. The Father wanted satan defeated by man, one made in His image. Many make the mistake of thinking that the devil is the opposite of God. He's a created being and would be more likely compared to the opposite of Michael, also an archangel. The devil has never been a threat to God in any possible measure. He can be removed forever with a simple word. But God, in His wisdom, has chosen to use the devil as a chess piece on a chessboard. He uses him at will, so that the devil's best attempts to destroy are always placed into the hands of the One who causes *"all things* [to] *work together for good to those who love God, to those who are the called according to His purpose"* (Rom. 8:28).

> *You have the final victory, God, and I get to join in on Your triumph. I am already on the winning team, reclaiming now what rightfully belongs to Your Kingdom.*

REST: We must remember God is building for eternity—that is where the ultimate vindication and restoration will be seen. Thankfully, there is a great measure of victory in this life that is far beyond what any of us could earn. But it would be a great mistake to ignore eternity, as eternity is the cornerstone of all logic and reason. Jesus, who would shed His blood to redeem mankind, emptied Himself of His rights as God and took upon Himself the limitations of man. While Jesus never stopped being God, He took on flesh to complete the assignment that we failed to finish. Satan was defeated by a man—the Son of Man—who was rightly related to God. Now, as people receive the work of Christ on the Cross for salvation, they become grafted into that victory.

> *Pull on the reality of Heaven, releasing the restoration of My Kingdom onto the earth. There is so much more available than what you are seeing now, so much more of My goodness that I want to reveal.*

November 24th

The God of peace will soon crush Satan under your feet. The
[wonderful] grace of our Lord Jesus be with you.

—Romans 16:20 AMP

RISE: In redeeming man, Jesus recovered what man had given away. God's original plan was never aborted; it was fully realized once and for all in the resurrection and ascension of Jesus. We were then to be completely restored to His plan of ruling as a people made in His image. We were born to rule—rule over creation, over darkness—to plunder hell, to rescue those headed there, and to establish the rule of Jesus wherever we go by preaching the Gospel of the Kingdom.

> *Thank You, Lord, for creating me in Your image and calling me to rule*
> *with You, restoring the earth to its original design. Help me to see the*
> *world around me how You meant it to be, not simply how it is now.*

REST: In the original purpose of God, mankind ruled over creation. Now that sin has entered the world, creation has been infected by darkness, such as disease, sickness, afflicting spirits, poverty, natural disasters, and demonic influence. Our rule is still over creation, but now it is focused on exposing and undoing the works of the devil. We are to give what we have received to reach that end. If I truly receive power from an encounter with the God of power, I am equipped to give it away. The invasion of God into impossible situations comes through a people who have received power from on high and have learned to release it into the circumstances of life.

> *Let your spirit connect with My vision for the earth; allow your*
> *imagination to roam, exploring what total redemption would look*
> *like for your family, your city, the land that you live on, and even this*
> *evening's headlines.*

November 25th

You are worthy, O Lord, to receive glory and honor and power; for
You created all things, and by Your will they exist and were created.

—Revelation 4:11 NKJV

RISE: It's time for a revolution in our vision. When prophets tell us, "Your vision is too small," many of us think the antidote is to increase whatever numbers we're expecting. For example: if we're expecting ten new converts, let's change it to one hundred. If we were praying for cities, let's pray instead for nations. With such responses, we're missing the sharp edge of the frequently repeated word. Increasing the numbers is not necessarily a sign of a larger vision from God's perspective. Vision starts with identity and purpose. Through a revolution in our identity, we can think with divine purpose. Such a change begins with a revelation of Him.

> *Holy Spirit, I need You to fill me up with Your power and Your purpose.*
> *I need to encounter You yet again so that I can properly dream in line*
> *with God's vision for my life.*

REST: We are often more convinced of our unworthiness than we are of His worth. Our inability takes on greater focus than does His ability. But the same One who called fearful Gideon a "valiant warrior" and unstable Peter a "rock" has called us the Body of His beloved Son on earth. That has to count for something. The very fact that He declares it makes the impossible possible. Those who walk in arrogance because of how they see themselves in Christ don't really see it at all. When we see who He is, what He has done on our behalf, and who He says we are, there is only one possible response— worship from a humble and surrendered heart.

> *My spoken word set the planets into motion. I created the oceans and the*
> *land with one utterance. Don't you think that I can bring you to exactly*
> *where I need you?*

November 26th

If you think I've come to set aside the law of Moses or the writings of
the prophets, you're mistaken. I have come to fulfill and bring
to perfection all that has been written.

—Matthew 5:17 TPT

RISE: I remember growing up thinking that God the Father was angry, and it was Jesus who calmed Him down. The stories of the Old Testament only seemed to confirm that misguided idea. It almost seemed like there were two completely different deities in charge of each dispensation. While that is not true, we've been left with a challenging task of reconciling the unique approaches to problems that couldn't be more diametrically opposed to each other than they are in the Old and New Testaments. While there are glimpses of grace in the Old, it is the ongoing judgments, diseases, curses, and the like that all seem to have God's blessing, that become a theological nightmare.

Father, forgive me for any misunderstanding I've had about Your
nature that has left me hiding behind Jesus to protect myself from You.
You have always been for me. Your love has written my entire story.

REST: I absolutely love *all* of Scripture! I have a special fondness for the Old Testament. If you can read and embrace it without being offended at God or using it to replace the standard that Jesus set in the New Testament, then it becomes a most glorious journey. Discovering the role of the Old in the days of the New is absolutely needed so that we might live in wisdom. There are four main things that the Old Testament does for us that are helpful in recognizing and living in the goodness of God: It reveals the severity of sin; it exposes the absolute hopeless condition of humanity; it shows us our need of a savior; it points to Jesus as the only possible solution to our lost condition.

I am love—consistent, patient, pursuing My children despite continuous
rejection, empowering, celebratory, kind, forever offering redemption to
the world. My nature is unchanging.

November 27th

Therefore the Law has become our tutor to lead us to Christ, so that we
may be justified by faith. But now that faith has come,
we are no longer under a tutor.

—Galatians 3:24-25 NASB

RISE: The Old Testament Law is the teacher that leads us to Christ. It first reveals that we are sinners; but, thankfully, it doesn't leave us there. Jesus not only satisfied the appetite of the Law in bearing our judgment upon Himself, He was the One the Law was pointing to, much like a sign on a restaurant points to what's inside the building. The Mosaic Law pointed to Jesus. As you read and reread Old Testament Scriptures, it becomes obvious that the Father wanted us to realize that His answer was on the way. The Savior was on the way.

> *Thank You, Jesus, that You did not leave me with just the awareness of*
> *my sin but offered a complete and permanent solution. Help me to see*
> *Your presence throughout the Scriptures.*

REST: Because the Old Testament leads us to Jesus, it automatically points to the Kingdom that this King of kings rules over. The Kingdom is the realm of His rule, displaying His will for all He has made. Page after page carries the wonderful picture of the Kingdom of God that was to come. Throughout the time before Christ, there were events, prophecies, and laws that spoke of life under grace. There were unusual moments of grace that gave insight into what was coming through types and shadows. And while Israel expected the Kingdom to show up through the military rule of their Messiah, Jesus revealed it as a Kingdom that first touched the heart.

> *I have sown the desire and recognition of My Kingdom into the hearts*
> *of people throughout time. I have been beckoning My people home,*
> *chasing down their stubborn hearts, since the Garden. It's who I am.*

November 28th

The law and the prophets were until John. Since that time the
kingdom of God has been preached, and everyone is pressing into it.

—Luke 16:16 NKJV

RISE: Wonderful revelations are gained about life under the New Covenant from the Old Testament through types and shadows, meaning there are natural illustrations of spiritual truths. For example, we know that the Jews were required to offer a spotless lamb as a payment for their sin. But we also know that Jesus is the actual Lamb of God who takes away the sin of the world. Once the actual comes in answer to the Old Testament type or shadow, there's no more need to go back and embrace the symbol. Otherwise, animal sacrifices would still have merit.

Your sacrifice fulfilled so much, Jesus. There wasn't a more perfect way
for our Savior to come. You answered everything, once and for all.

REST: The entire Old Testament points to Jesus. He is the central figure of *all* Scripture. Both the Law and the prophets declared His role as Messiah, showing how Jesus would fulfill God's redemptive plan. The stories, prophecies, and laws all pointed to Him at various levels in the same way that a highway sign points to an upcoming city from varying distances. The sign is real and significant, but in itself it is not the reality we are looking for. It points to something greater than itself. In this case we must not worship the sign of the Old Testament. Neither can we afford to be distracted by it, as though in some way it contained a greater reality than the message of the Messiah Himself. These signs serve their purpose by taking us to Jesus. The nature of His life and purpose is clear and must not be diluted or dismantled by unresolved questions from the Old Covenant. Why did He come? He came to destroy the works of the devil.

Can you imagine the celebration in Heaven when the perfect time had
finally come to send your Savior to the earth to fulfill every promise? The
angel armies praised Me to announce His birth to the shepherds—My
plan of redemption cannot be halted.

November 29th

"The time has come," he said. "The kingdom of God has come near.
Repent and believe the good news!"

—Mark 1:15 NIV

RISE: The nature of the message we carry determines the nature of the reality we will live and minister in. Those who fully embrace our God-given assignment for the message of the Kingdom will see the ever-increasing government of God displayed in the affairs of mankind. This is the only message that creates an environment suitable to the display of God's love, His uncompromising purity, and His unfathomable power. This is the message that Jesus preached and in turn taught His disciples to preach. It remains the now word.

> *Thank You, God, that Your Kingdom is not difficult to access, hard to find, or impossible to enter. You offer Your presence—Your domain— freely to Your sons and daughters!*

REST: The Church has largely replaced the Gospel of the Kingdom with the Gospel of salvation. It's the beauty of the salvation message that makes it so easy to miss the fact that it is only a part of the whole message that Jesus gave us. The Gospel of salvation is focused on getting people saved and going to Heaven. The Gospel of the Kingdom is focused on the transformation of lives, cities, and nations through the effect of God's present rule—this is made manifest by bringing the reality of Heaven to earth. We must not confuse our destiny with our assignment. Heaven is my destiny, while bringing the Kingdom is my assignment.

> *There is nothing in the world more powerful than My Word over your life. Don't hide behind walls, protecting your salvation. You are a conqueror! Take My Word and release My joy, My righteousness, and My peace wherever you go.*

November 30th

From the four corners of the earth, the peoples of the world will
remember and return to the Lord. Every nation will
come and worship him.

—Psalm 22:27 TPT

RISE: Don't skip over the bigger promises of Scripture simply because they are hard to believe because of their size. Whenever He declares something this big, He's hoping to capture people's hearts, making it impossible for them to be satisfied with mediocrity. The promises are there, in a sense waiting for adoption. Instead of trying to figure out the season for the promises to be fulfilled, why not come before God and see if God might want to fulfill them in our time? After all, how many times did the disciples get the timing right in their understanding of God's prophetic promises? I don't consider myself any better than they were. These promises are not given to us to help us to know the future as much as they are given to create hunger for what might be.

> *Holy Spirit, sometimes the promises I read in the Bible are hard for me*
> *to fully digest, they seem so big. Challenge my faith with these promises,*
> *stretch my understanding of Your will for the earth.*

REST: The promises of God are clearly seen when the people of God get hungry and cry out to God for their fulfillment. When you declare the right message, you create the atmosphere where everyone is able to press in. No matter the need, there is an answer now. The right message marries the truth of Jesus as the desire of the nations with the nations themselves. The right message changes the atmosphere to make the manifestation of His dominion realized. Perhaps this is the context in which the irresistible grace of God is embraced, thus fulfilling the desire found in the heart of every person alive.

> *You don't have to convince the nations to want My presence; you merely*
> *have to reflect My heart with truth and love. I am the source of all life,*
> *truth, and joy. Every heart hungers to find its home in Me.*

December

December 1ˢᵗ

A jar of wine vinegar was there, so they soaked a sponge in it, put the sponge on a stalk of the hyssop plant, and lifted it to Jesus' lips. When he had received the drink, Jesus said, "It is finished." With that, he bowed his head and gave up his spirit.

—John 19:29-30 NIV

RISE: It is a mistake to think that when Jesus cried out, "It is finished," He was merely proclaiming that His life as a man living on earth was over. Both the Law and the prophets had rightfully made a judgment on humanity, for God Himself declared, "The person who sins shall die!" (see Ezek. 18:20). The power of this judgment was so strong that if Jesus had not come for one hundred thousand years, and trillions of people had lived during that time, it rightfully would have damned every single one and still not have been satisfied in its demands. Jesus came to quench the appetite of that unquenchable fire by meeting the requirements of the Law and the prophets. When He said, "It is finished," He was declaring, "The appetite of the Law and Prophets has been satisfied once and for all! It's a new day."

Even before I knew how much I needed You, Jesus, You had already gone before me to release me from sin and satisfy the Law. I'm so grateful for my freedom.

REST: It's too easy to complicate the Christian life. For example, we are told to put on the full armor of God, which includes the helmet of salvation, breastplate of righteousness, and so on (see Eph. 6:10–18). The apostle Paul gave us this important instruction, but most of the time we miss the point. God is my armor. He's not saying, "Put something on that is a reality that is separate from Me." He's saying, "I'm it. Just abide in Me. I become your salvation. I am your righteousness, the breastplate over you. I am the Gospel of peace. I am the Good News. I am the sword of the Spirit."

All that you need is found in Me. I'm not asking you to find righteousness within yourself with which to guard your heart; I am offering you Myself as the source of unlimited righteousness, grace, and love.

December 2ⁿᵈ

*For whatever was written in earlier times was written for our
instruction, so that through perseverance and the encouragement
of the Scriptures we might have hope.*

—Romans 15:4 NASB

RISE: Correct study of Scripture is to give us encouragement that results in great hope—that we might have hope. And yet for many, the study of the Old Testament does anything but give them hope for their own lives. All many see are the judgments of God toward the nations. I believe if we get a different outcome than what this Romans passage said we would have (encouragement and hope), we must learn to approach the Scriptures differently until we bear His intended fruit.

> *Father, I promise never to stop my journey into Your Word feeling
> discouraged. Holy Spirit, help me to see the true hope and promise
> found in every part of the Bible.*

REST: The Old Testament was given for our instruction as New Covenant people. For a season the Old Testament Scriptures were the only Bible that the New Testament Church had. What has been written gives us the backdrop to the truths we enjoy today. But as it is with most things, improper application can also bring death. "*For the letter kills, but the Spirit gives life*" (2 Cor. 3:6). It's a matter of perception. Many Christians' lives have been crippled because of an unclear understanding of what Jesus came to accomplish and fulfill. If I don't understand that, I won't understand my purpose and calling. To put it more practically, through wisdom and revelation we must understand what of the Old Testament ended at the Cross, what was changed by the Cross, and what came through the Cross unchanged.

> *Read the entirety of My Word as a love letter from a Father who longs
> to see His children return to His arms. Don't give up on My Scriptures.
> Ask Me, and I will show You My heart within the verses.*

December 3rd

For as by one man's disobedience many were made sinners, so also by one Man's obedience many will be made righteous.

—Romans 5:19 NKJV

RISE: The sacrifice of animals was required under the Old Testament Law. It was mandated by God to remind us that the penalty of sin is death. And while the blood of animals never actually did away with the record of sin, dealt with the nature of sin in the ones making the sacrifice or dealt with the consequences of sin, it did postpone the penalty for one more year. It became a point of obedience that prophesied of what was coming—the Lamb of God, who would take away the sins of the world.

Thank You, Lord, that I don't have to keep a record of my sins throughout the year or wait for a specific day to become right with You again. I can come before you freely as Your child.

REST: When Jesus offered Himself as a sacrifice on behalf of all mankind, He made it possible for the sacrifice of one to make the many righteous. When Jesus Christ died on our behalf once and for all, it changed everything. He was the Lamb of God, without sin, blemish, or fault of any kind. The requirement of the Law for the shedding of blood for sin was satisfied for all time. We can say with confidence that never again will we be required to sacrifice another animal to postpone the penalty of sin for one more year. It is finished. The Cross brought an end to the sacrifice of animals and, more importantly, satisfied the appetite of the Law for the judgment of humanity. Salvation is now given to all who call upon the name of the Lord.

Leave trying to atone for your own sins behind. The Cross changed it all. I can now welcome you into My righteousness because of My faithfulness. All you have to do is believe.

December 4ᵗʰ

*The Spirit of the Lord is upon me, and he has anointed me to be hope
for the poor, freedom for the brokenhearted, and new eyes for the blind,
and to preach to prisoners, "You are set free!" I have come to share the
message of Jubilee, for the time of God's great acceptance has begun.*

—Luke 4:18 TPT

RISE: The Sabbath was created for the benefit of mankind. It was an important enough part of God's economy that He Himself rested the seventh day from His works in creation. God even required that the land rest every seven years (rest from planting crops). Then every seventh Sabbath year required yet another year of rest, this time marked by what the Bible calls the Year of Jubilee. So that means that both the forty-ninth and the fiftieth year, the land rests again, while at the same time debts are forgiven, slaves are freed, and many other similar things are done to increase the well-being of God's people. But as you can imagine, not planting crops that seventh year requires that His people trust Him to provide for them like He did for Israel in the wilderness.

*Help me to value rest the way You do, God. Sometimes it feels like I have
no time, but You intentionally protected Yours. I want to do the same.*

REST: While I do think the weekly Sabbath rest is essential for mental, emotional, physical, and spiritual health, the Sabbath was also a foretaste of what the daily life of the believer is to be like—without works as it pertains to our salvation. Both the Sabbath and the Year of Jubilee were changed at the Cross. When Jesus announced the beginning of His ministry, He was essentially saying that the Year of Jubilee was the ongoing experience of those belonging to Him. In other words, every day is the Sabbath and every year is the Year of Jubilee—rest and liberty are to be seen on the countenance of all who belong to Him. After the Cross, Jubilee changed from being every fifty years to now being the everyday lifestyle of those in Christ every year.

*It's time to celebrate! You are dwelling in My liberty, My redemption,
and My restoration. Jubilee is now your lifestyle in Me.*

December 5th

But you are a chosen generation, a royal priesthood, a holy nation,
His own special people, that you may proclaim the praises of Him who
called you out of darkness into His marvelous light.

—1 Peter 2:9 NKJV

RISE: King David is known for many wonderful things throughout Scripture. But the one thing that was the primary reference point in all of his life was his passion for the presence of God. I think that his biggest mark on history was the standard he set as a worshiper. It was his worship that sculpted the heart of a nation into a nation who valued the presence of God. As Moses once declared, it was the presence of God upon His people that became the distinguishing mark that separated them from all other nations. The Tabernacle of David changed the focus of life and ministry for all priests in the Old Testament. It's a good thing, too. In the New Testament, we discover that every believer is now a priest unto the Lord.

God, give me the courage of David to follow Your presence, connecting
with Your heart, even at the cost of my dignity. You are my first priority.

REST: We now have the privilege of ministering to God as they did in David's tabernacle. And the beautiful thing for us all is that this worship can and must be done in our homes, our cars, as well as in the corporate gatherings with our brothers and sisters. The Tabernacle of David, and its corresponding role in worship, is unchanged from the Old Testament to the New. Further study will again verify that the ministry of thanksgiving, praise, and worship—all aspects of our ministry unto Him—are all unchanged by the Cross. In fact, it was the Cross that brought this prototype out of the laboratory of an Old Testament experiment into the daily life of God's people, who have become His eternal dwelling place. It has become a norm.

You are a worshiper. It is who I have created you to be, so you will find
the most fulfillment in that identity. Offer up every moment to Me as a
gift, and I will meet you there.

December 6th

As surely as I live, says the Sovereign Lord, I take no pleasure in the
death of wicked people. I only want them to turn from their wicked
ways so they can live. Turn! Turn from your wickedness,
O people of Israel! Why should you die?

—Ezekiel 33:11 NLT

RISE: The law of Moses was but for a season. It was never meant to carry the full manifestation of God's nature to be discovered and enjoyed by His people. While it was necessary and beautiful, it fell far short in representing the Father's heart. That was not its purpose. The Law taught Israel what they needed to know about the Messiah before He came upon the scene. And even then, most missed His coming. And yet riddled all throughout God's dealings with His people in the Old Testament was the revelation of grace. Some of the most beautiful glimpses of God's heart are hidden in the scenes of the Old Testament. There are great differences between law and grace. But for now, this will suffice—law requires, while grace enables.

Thank You, thank You that I no longer have to live under the code of the
Law anymore. You have made Your home in me, and I am enveloped
in Your grace every day.

REST: God illustrated His heart for His people over and over again. God is not an angry tyrant wishing evil people to be punished and die. If that were true, it would have happened long before now, released through a simple decree. Instead, we see Him interceding so that the wicked would turn and live. His passion for all of us is to experience life to the fullest! But it is never forced upon us; otherwise, He ends up with robots, not people made in His image.

I will always meet you where you are, as I did throughout the Old
Testament. But I long to bring you fully into the freedom and grace of
My Kingdom.

December 7th

But without faith it is impossible to [walk with God and]
please Him, for whoever comes [near] to God must [necessarily]
believe that God exists and that He rewards those who
[earnestly and diligently] seek Him.

—Hebrews 11:6 AMP

RISE: God invites us to discover Him—the One who rewards all who join in the journey into the great expanse called the goodness of God. This is the journey of faith. Faith has two parts; the first is a conviction of His existence. But even the devil has that much going for him. It's the second part that launches us into the adventure and distinguishes us from the rest of all that exists—a confidence in His nature. He is a rewarder! In other words, what we believe about Him will have an effect on our lives in a measurable way because He rewards those who have set their hearts on discovering Him.

I won't be so silly as to pretend that I don't want Your blessing, God.
I do! I want my life to radiate Your goodness to the world around me.

REST: God ensures that we find Him if the heart is genuinely searching with a readiness to obey. Jesus also said He would disclose Himself to those who follow Him (see John 14:21). It's as though He is saying that if we seek Him with all of our hearts, He will make sure to put Himself in the middle of the road we're walking on. This invitation comes from the Father of life—the eternal God who loves through sacrifice and giving. The greatest gift we could ever give ourselves is to anchor our intellect and will into the strongest foundation possible—the goodness of God.

Submission sounds scary, but submission to My will is the most freeing,
life-giving, and natural thing you can do. You will become the fullest
version of yourself as you find your identity in Me.

December 8th

*When Jesus saw what was happening, he became indignant with his
disciples and said to them, "Let all the little children come to me and
never hinder them! Don't you know that God's kingdom
realm exists for such as these?"*

—Mark 10:14 TPT

RISE: My faith can go only where I have understanding of His goodness. His goodness then becomes the real estate that I live on and explore freely. He liberally gives us all He is and all He has (see John 16:14-15). Biblical faith explores this realm with the delight and pleasure of a well-loved child. Jesus teaches that the Kingdom of God belongs to those who are like children. Adults tend to manage what they have, taking fewer and fewer risks as they get older. But children tirelessly explore. When our faith explores His goodness, we are most like the children Jesus honored and celebrated.

> *God, I want to learn how to explore Your goodness instead of fearfully
> protecting what I already have. Lead me into to realms of Your love. I
> will eagerly follow.*

REST: Everything about God is extreme in the best possible sense. He is infinitely good, infinitely holy and powerful, infinitely beautiful, magnificent, and glorious. These are just a few terms to describe Him. But none of the endless lists of traits and characteristics confine Him. Religion, which I define as form without power, tends to attempt the impossible task of restricting Him into neat little packages, giving us a false sense of intelligence and ultimately control. But He is bigger and bigger and bigger still. Each virtue gives us a glimpse into that which is beyond measure but is open for observation. You could take one trait and explore it for all of eternity but not come close to exhausting the depths of who He is in that particular virtue.

> *Dive deeply into My presence. Come with wonder and hope to learn
> more about Me. You cannot anticipate too much or imagine too far into
> the realms of My goodness.*

December 9th

Then Moses said, "I pray You, show me Your glory!" And He said,
"I Myself will make all My goodness pass before you."

—Exodus 33:18-19 NASB

RISE: When Moses asked to see the glory of God, he did not choose some random aspect of God's person or nature. He chose the original target for every person alive. We were created and designed to live in the glory of God, which is the manifested presence of Jesus. Sin caused us to fall short of God's intended target. To sin means "to miss the mark." Consider an archer shooting an arrow at a target and then watching that arrow not even reach the target, let alone hit the bull's-eye. That is what our sin has done. We not only missed the mark, we didn't even reach the target. But take note of the target— it is the glory of God. We were created to live in that realm. Moses knew it instinctively and longed to see it more clearly.

> *It's hard for me to even imagine living in Your glory, so I lay down my limited capacity to understand at Your feet. Guide me wherever You would have me go, Lord. Your vision for my life is so much larger than mine.*

REST: Moses asked to see God's glory. God said "okay" and showed Moses His goodness. Take note! It was His goodness that changed Moses' countenance. This, the one time Moses' own countenance was changed, was only after a fresh revelation of God's goodness. Is this not what is missing in the New Testament Church? Is it possible that God intends to change the countenance of His people by a fresh revelation of His goodness? I think so. The world has seen a divided Church, an angry Church, a materialistic Church, and the list goes on. What would happen if they were to see a Church whose very countenance has been transformed by seeing Him, His glory—His goodness? This is what the world is crying for; they want to believe it's true—God is good. How we behold Him is what makes this a possibility.

> *I long to see My Church represent My heart like My Son represented Me on the earth—full of My compassion, My goodness, My purity and power.*

December 10th

These are the things you shall do: speak each man the truth to his neighbor; give judgment in your gates for truth, justice, and peace.

—Zechariah 8:16 NKJV

RISE: If you take someone you love to the doctor to be examined because of a suspicious-looking growth on his arm, you will want that doctor to bring judgment upon the growth and do whatever needs to be done to remove it. There's no feeling of sympathy toward the tumor, nor is there any concern over what others might think. Judgment is the only acceptable response, as your love for that person requires such a reaction toward anything that threatens his well-being. Love requires that I fight for him by seeking for his protection.

> *Papa, thank You that You are not scared to judge sin for what it is. You are full of mercy for the person, but you won't let the diseased thing remain in their life.*

REST: Judgment has to happen because God is holy—He is perfect in beauty, with undefiled purity, completely separate from all that is dark and evil and totally driven by love in all actions, thoughts, and intentions. Sin violates and contaminates all that He has made, creating a breach between Creator and creation. Yet judgment had to be released because He is love. Love requires judgment if it's to be real love. Love without judgment is apathetic, lethargic, and passionless; it really isn't love at all. Any belief system that promotes conviction without emotional expression is more consistent with Buddhism than it is with the Gospel of Jesus Christ. It doesn't rock the boat. That is something that Jesus had no problem doing time and time again. Jesus was far from passive.

> *Judgment is a part of My love because I am a good Father. I protect My children, and I will not allow the carnivorous destruction of sin to eat away at your lives. I love you too much to see that happen.*

December 11th

*Let us then approach God's throne of grace with confidence, so that we
may receive mercy and find grace to help us in our time of need.*

—Hebrews 4:16 NIV

RISE: Standing with people in the midst of their problems seems to be a fading value.
To stand with someone who is in sin is frowned upon, as it makes others think we support their sin. Jesus sure seemed to have a different approach and was called a friend of sinners as a result. On a practical side, it serves no purpose to create an atmosphere that encourages people to freely exhibit their sinfulness without consequences. It's much wiser to stand with someone with issues if he wants to clean up his mess.

Father, teach me the kind of loyalty that pulls someone closer when they make a mess. I want to speak the truth in love. I want to show Your persistent grace to everyone.

REST: Choices have consequences, good and bad. That is life. Our loyalty to one another must be solid, but it must not empower others toward wrongdoing. But as crazy as it sounds, unsanctified mercy has taken the place of true mercy. Unsanctified mercy empowers people toward sin without an awareness of consequences. True mercy is shown to people in trouble by loving them when they don't deserve it, but also by telling them the truth, working to bring them into a freedom that God intended for everyone. True freedom is not doing as we please. It's being enabled to do the right thing well.

Don't forget that My grace is for You too, My child. I will not leave you in the destructive patterns of sin. That is not love. But I will always chase you down with My grace and mercy. There is nowhere that your sin can take you that I can't find.

December 12th

God be merciful to us and bless us, and cause His face to shine upon us,
that Your way may be known on the earth,
Your salvation among all nations.

—Psalm 67:1-2 NKJV

RISE: The conclusion to Psalm 67 is that everyone on earth feared God and experienced His salvation! But what caused them to see the heart of God and His nature to the point that they were convicted of their own sins and turned in repentance to Him? What caused such a miraculous turn of events? Blessings. Blessings are what preceded both statements of nations coming to Christ—bless us so they know what You're like, and God shall bless us, and they'll come to Him (my paraphrase). No wonder the devil works so hard to undermine our confidence in His absolute goodness.

> *God, I need to experience Your blessing in my life. I want to learn how*
> *to increase in Your favor so that I can show the world who You are and*
> *what You're like.*

REST: Blessings are manifestations of increased favor. Yet favor has a purpose. Without discovering that purpose, we are prone to self-promotion and personal kingdom building. The queen of Sheba put it this way when she acknowledged the favor that rested upon Solomon. "*Blessed be the Lord your God, who delighted in you, setting you on the throne of Israel! Because the Lord has loved Israel forever, therefore He made you king, to do justice and righteousness*" (1 Kings 10:9). There it is. Because God loved Israel, He showed favor upon Solomon and made him king. Favor was to benefit those He served as king or it would be misused. It basically comes down to this: favor upon me must benefit the people under my influence, or it is misused.

> *The devil offered My Son the dominion over cities, but even he*
> *misunderstood My purpose on the earth. Jesus came, with all authority,*
> *to lay down His life. My dominion brings freedom, joy, and fullness of*
> *life.*

December 13th

I will ask the Father, and He will give you another Helper,
that He may be with you forever.

—John 14:16 NASB

RISE: Jesus is the exact representation of the Father—His nature and His person. He is that which emanates from the Father's being, manifesting His glory. When Jesus tells the disciples about the Holy Spirit, He calls Him "another Helper." The word used here for *another* means one who is exactly the same. When we look at Jesus, He is exactly the same as His Father. Then Jesus sent the Holy Spirit, who is exactly like Jesus. In other words, God wanted to make sure that there would be no chance of missing the revelation needed to permeate and shift the course of history at this point and time—the revelation of our God as a good and perfect Father.

> *I'm overwhelmed by the ways that You have made yourself available to*
> *me, Lord. Thank You for pursuing me with such tender, persistent love.*

REST: Jesus reveals a Father who is not abusive or self-serving. The Holy Spirit, who now lives in us, reaffirms the wonder and beauty of this perfectly good Father. The work that He is doing in us is all about deepening our connection to the Father, who brings identity, purpose, destiny, and an awareness of unlimited resources to accomplish our purpose in life. When the Holy Spirit is able to do His perfect work in us, our connection to all that is good is strengthened and made clear. This revelation of God as our Father is the ultimate expression of the goodness of God.

> *I have sown attributes of Myself all around you. You can't miss Me! I*
> *am revealing Myself to you constantly, calling you into a deeper and*
> *deeper connection with My heart.*

December 14th

For what children are not disciplined by their father? If you are not disciplined—and everyone undergoes discipline—then you are not legitimate, not true sons and daughters at all.

—Hebrews 12:7-8 NIV

RISE: When I talk about this perfect Father, I'm not talking about someone who refuses to discipline His children. And while the subject of discipline is not what people want to hear, it is real and needed. The truth of the matter is that He loves us too much to leave us as we are. Some of the most significant changes only take place in that context. According to Scripture, discipline proves we belong to Him as sons and daughters. Those who are without discipline are not real heirs and descendants. They are fakes. They may talk the talk, but you can't authentically walk the walk without discipline.

> *You won't leave me stuck in my old ways, and I am so grateful for that! I open myself up to Your discipline, Father. Your pruning gives me hope for my growth.*

REST: In John 15, Jesus illustrates godly discipline by talking about pruning. God rewards all growth with pruning. It doesn't happen only when there's something wrong. It's that, left untended, vines will grow to a place where they bear little to no fruit. All the energy of the vine goes into growing branches and leaves. God is very concerned with fruit from our lives and does whatever is needed to keep that priority in place. If we are left unchecked, our growth is in appearance (religious—form without power). And just as Adam and Eve covered themselves with leaves to hide their nakedness, so we hide our immaturity behind the appearance of growth and not in the substance of Christlikeness. There is to be fruit of being like Jesus—converts, miracles, answers to prayer, and a changed life.

> *My discipline is not harsh, it is redirection. It is the input of a Father into your life. Don't withdraw from My pruning; lean into My affectionate guidance.*

December 15th

So when they continued asking Him, He raised Himself up and said to
them, "He who is without sin among you, l
et him throw a stone at her first."

—John 8:7 NKJV

RISE: Everything Jesus said and did worked to fulfill that one assignment—reveal the Father. When they brought the woman caught in adultery to Jesus to see what He would do, He once again represented the Father. The religious leaders brought stones to kill her according to the Law they lived under. But Jesus came with a different assignment. He bent over and wrote in the dirt, telling those intending to stone her to go ahead, under the condition that they were free from sin. Interestingly, the only one without sin refused to cast a stone at all. Instead, He revealed the Father. In reality, this was a Father/daughter moment.

> *Thank You, Jesus, that every time I sin You reveal the Father's heart*
> *toward me. Help me to show that same grace to others.*

REST: All those intending to stone her to death fled the scene. Whatever He wrote released such an atmosphere of grace that those driven by judgment had to leave. Jesus then did what any one of us would have done if our daughter were lost in such moral failure and humiliating shame. He served her. Jesus didn't care what the religious leaders thought of Him. The opinions of the crowd didn't matter either. The Father had to be seen. And more importantly, the Father had to be known by this one who was lost, this one who was manifesting her orphaned heart. Her sin wasn't ignored or treated lightly. Instead, He disciplined her—with loving words (see John 8:11).

> *Don't hide your sin from Me. Let me gently take your shame from your*
> *hands and wrap you in My love and forgiveness. Sin is so heavy, and I*
> *never meant for you to carry that weight.*

December 16th

He got up, rebuked the wind and said to the waves, "Quiet! Be still!"
Then the wind died down and it was completely calm.

—Mark 4:39 NIV

RISE: There is a deep, personal need in the Body of Christ to see Jesus for who He is. Jesus Christ is perfect in every way. He is perfect beauty, perfect majesty, perfect power, and perfect humility. The list of His wonderful characteristics and virtues is endless. Jesus Christ is perfect theology—He is the will of God personified. Jesus stilled every life-threatening storm that He encountered. God can use any tragedy to His purposes. But that doesn't mean the problem was His design. Jesus didn't deal with storms in that way. Regardless of how or why the storm came about, Jesus was the solution.

I will look to You, Jesus, in moments of confusion or pain. You gave us
the perfect representation of the Father's will. So, I just need to look to
Your example to understand His heart for a matter.

REST: Why did Jesus rebuke the storm instead of just telling it to stop? The implication is that the powers of darkness were involved in the storm, and they needed to be dealt with because they violated the heart and purpose of God on the earth. And if the devil is involved in the storm, we don't want to be found saying the storm is the will of the Father. Whatever you think you know about God that you can't find in the person of Jesus you have reason to question. Jesus Christ is the fullest and most precise revelation of the Father and His nature that could ever be made known.

I was preparing the world for Him, My Son who would show a hurting
and orphaned planet My Father's heart. I am bent on reconciliation,
focused on redemption, and joyously absorbed with bringing My shalom
to the earth.

December 17th

Yet He did not leave Himself without some witness [as evidence of Himself], in that He kept constantly doing good things and showing you kindness, and giving you rains from heaven and productive seasons, filling your hearts with food and happiness.

—Acts 14:17 AMP

RISE: God sprinkled the entire Old Testament with evidence of His goodness, profoundly visible for those hungry enough to see it. He was setting the stage for the greatest revelation of all time—Jesus Christ. Jesus is a revelation of the heart and nature of God the Father. One of my favorite New Testament Scriptures on this theme speaks of how God revealed His heart throughout Old Testament times. It is one that deeply moves me, as it shows the heart of God reaching out to people before there is a relationship. Before we even come to know God as our Father, He is doing things to fill our hearts with gladness. That is amazing. It's His calling card. This simple approach by God is what He calls leaving Himself a witness.

> *I am humbled by Your love, God. That You would pursue me, showing me Your lovingkindness before I would even acknowledge You, overwhelms me with gratitude for who You are.*

REST: A witness to an event of any kind is someone who speaks not from hearsay, but from personal experience, from firsthand knowledge of the subject at hand. When God leaves Himself a witness, He is drawing each person to Himself to experience His favor. His desire is for that favor to awaken a longing in their hearts to know Him as their Father. He will not force Himself upon us, as He continues to work to protect one of the most glorious parts of His creation—the free will of mankind. Yet in His longing for us, He draws us to Himself through the blessings that can only come from a good Father.

> *Ask Me, and I will show you how I was protecting you, guiding you, pouring out My love upon you even before you knew Me. It is My lovingkindness that drew you to a change of heart.*

December 18th

Now this he did not say on his own authority; but being high priest
that year he prophesied that Jesus would die for the nation, and not
for that nation only, but also that He would gather together in one the
children of God who were scattered abroad.

—John 11:51-52 NKJV

RISE: One of the things that is sometimes hard to get used to is that God loves to bless both the righteous and the unrighteous. We celebrate the times when God gives a brilliant insight to a believer. Whether that insight cures a disease, or makes possible a new invention that will serve mankind well, or brings peace between two nations in conflict through His beloved peacemaker, it's something that we are all encouraged to hear about. I believe He is affirming the gifts and callings of this servant of the Lord and is using him or her in a profound way to increase the witness of His heart for people. But it must also be acknowledged that He sometimes chooses to do the same through unbelievers who at times are extremely wicked in lifestyle and even purpose. What is God doing by giving such treasure to the wicked? Leaving a witness.

> *Expand my heart, Lord. I want to be aware of the ways that You're*
> *moving inside the Church and outside. I want to honor the favor You*
> *bestow, no matter where it lands.*

REST: The anointing of God can rest upon ungodly people for divine purposes. We see that again with Caiaphas, the high priest. He prophesied about the crucifixion of Christ and the effects it would have on the nation of Israel. He declared the word of the Lord, not from his relationship with God, but because of his position. There are times when God rests upon a life entirely for the person—the calling card of blessing. And sometimes that grace is upon the person for the sake of the people he serves or influences, as was the case with Caiaphas. It's our job to recognize it if we intend to see the full effect of His calling card upon society.

> *I can see the bigger picture. So, I will rest upon the one who will move*
> *My plan forward. Don't let that turn you toward bitterness; let it stir*
> *up your hunger to see the fulfillment of My plans.*

December 19th

Life came into being because of him, for his life is
light for all humanity.

—John 1:4 TPT

RISE: God is usually blamed for the evils that exist in the world because if He is God, He can remove any problem quite easily because He is big and powerful. But to rid the world of sin and its consequences would require something extremely dramatic— removing all sinners. And apart from being born again, how many of us would be left? C.S. Lewis once made a statement that has helped me quite a bit throughout the years: "Once the author steps on the stage, the play is over." He can fix it all in a moment. But when He does, time stops, eternity begins, and the final line has been drawn in the sand. His answer would be quite painful. His patience, which we see in full operation right now, is so that we can gather as many into the family as possible. His longsuffering is beyond all of our abilities to comprehend and comes at great personal cost.

> *Thank You, Father, for Your incredible patience and grace. I have been*
> *as much a recipient of that as anyone else. Thank You for the time to win*
> *souls for Your Kingdom.*

REST: Fixing this world's problems through a "military invasion of Heaven" is not the answer we want. For then He enforces His will over mankind, destroying the greatest of all creations called the free will. In doing so He would then forfeit the chance to have a people of divine purpose. He chose instead an invasion of love, where the hearts of people are conquered by One who sacrifices fully for their well-being. As a result, we now have a Gospel of power that solves the issues at hand quite well, enabling us to bring that same message to them that changed us forever. We now just need people who believe it, live it, and will risk all to display it.

> *I will not overpower your choice. I came to bring freedom, and it is only*
> *within the context of freedom that your love can manifest. Choose this*
> *day whom you will serve and then walk it out.*

December 20th

He will glorify me on the earth, for he will receive from me what
is mine and reveal it to you. Everything that belongs to the Father
belongs to me—that's why I say that the Divine Encourager will
receive what is mine and reveal it to you.

—John 16:14-15 TPT

RISE: I can die of starvation with a million dollars in the bank. If I don't make withdrawals from what's in my account, my wealth is no better than a dream, principle, or fantasy. Everything in our account in Christ is beyond our wildest dreams. We can't make a withdrawal if we don't know what exists. Jesus models the mere beginning of what's in our account. The promises of His Word give us even greater insight into this superior reality. It's time to see what Jesus has so we can see what Jesus gave us. Here's the bottom line—He gave us everything that belongs to Him. And the Father gave Him everything!

> *Holy Spirit, will You teach me what is truly in my account as a child of*
> *God? I so often forget how much I've been given, but I want to withdraw*
> *it all to release Heaven here and now.*

REST: This really is an amazing passage of Scripture, one for which we bear great responsibility. The Holy Spirit releases what Jesus alone possesses into our accounts through declaration. Every time He speaks to us, He transfers the eternal resources of Jesus to our account, enabling us to complete our assignment. There was never to be a discrepancy between how we live today and His initial standard. Going to Heaven is not my responsibility. He will get me there entirely by His grace. My job is very specific and extremely important—bring Heaven to earth through prayer and obedience. When Jesus declared the Kingdom was at hand, He displayed it by giving life, breaking the powers of darkness, and restoring broken lives, hearts, and homes. He told us to pick up the same message. Why should we expect a different outcome?

> *The beauty of Heaven will be unmatched, but you have a chance to*
> *release Heaven into the dark corners of the earth right now. My light is*
> *more powerful than any darkness; don't wait to experience that reality!*

December 21st

And knowing their thoughts Jesus said to them, "Any kingdom divided
against itself is laid waste; and any city or house divided
against itself will not stand."

—Matthew 12:25 NASB

RISE: One of the most common phrases used in this discussion is that "God is in control." It is true that He is the Sovereign God. He reigns over all, and everything belongs to Him. But is He in control? This is not a question of His ability or His power and authority. If He is, doesn't that make Him responsible for Hitler? Is brain cancer His idea? If He is in control, then we have to credit Him with disease, earthquakes, hurricanes, and all the other calamities in life. I think it's more accurate to say He is in charge, but He is not in control. Every parent reading this should get this point quite easily. While we are in charge of our homes, not everything that happens under our roof is necessarily our idea or is approved by us.

> *Thank You, Father, that You are not the author of pain and suffering.*
> *Even though I don't always understand, I will never stop coming*
> *against the powers of darkness with faith and boldness.*

REST: It has never seemed right to me to hear Christians talk about a tragedy and then say, "It must have been the will of God." Or worse yet, "We don't know why it was God's will for that child to die, but we know God has a reason." As heartbreaking as the disaster is, the response of believers is equally appalling, in my thinking. There's the assumption that if God wanted a different outcome, He would have made it happen. That is lazy theology that somehow releases us from responsibility by shifting the blame to a God who put us in charge. We may not have all the responsibility when there are threats of horrific problems headed our way, but we do have some. And it's time to find out how to use the tools we've been given, how to cooperate with the Holy Spirit in a way that brings glory to the name of Jesus in the earth, instead of making theological excuses.

> *Just keep doing the things—keep praying for the sick, keep seeking out*
> *the brokenhearted, keep loving on those who haven't experienced My*
> *love.*

December 22nd

*Our Father in heaven, hallowed be Your name. Your kingdom come.
Your will be done on earth as it is in heaven. Give us this day our daily
bread. And forgive us our debts, as we forgive our debtors. And do not
lead us into temptation, but deliver us from the evil one. For Yours is
the kingdom and the power and the glory forever. Amen.*

—Matthew 6:9-13 NKJV

RISE: When Jesus taught His disciples to pray, He gave them a list of principles to guide them. They are found in what is commonly called the Lord's Prayer. That's not really a good title for the prayer because in the prayer is the confession of sin, and Jesus had no sin. It could more accurately be called the Disciple's Prayer. As such, it is a profound example of the kinds of things we're to put both our attention and affection on in prayer. Perhaps the most important lesson learned is that the Kingdom of God becomes manifest through prayer.

*Thanks, Papa, that talking to You never has to be complicated. Thanks
for the ways that You've showed us Your love, Your provision, and Your
intention on the earth.*

REST: The prayer begins with, "Our Father," and it ends with, "For Yours is the Kingdom...Amen." Look at the point being made. It's a Father's Kingdom. In other words, all conversation about Kingdom is about family. And once we've left the subject of family, we've left the subject of Kingdom. This, of course, is bigger than our biological families. It is about a Father who lovingly serves the purpose and benefit of all that He has made, all for His glory.

*You have been given a place in My family, a place of honor, of inheritance,
and of responsibility. Extend My heart to those around you. They have
a hunger to share in our family, even if they can't say it yet.*

December 23rd

Be imitators of God in everything you do, for then you will represent
your Father as his beloved sons and daughters.

—Ephesians 5:1 TPT

RISE: Without a conviction of God's goodness, it's not possible to develop the clear focus and the strength of faith to pursue the breakthroughs that the earth itself aches for. How we see Him defines how we think and how we live. The way we understand Him is the way we will represent Him. When I talk about the goodness of God and His greatness displayed in Jesus, I don't forget that He was also the one who chased the money changers out of the temple with a whip. This, too, is love, as Jesus hates whatever misrepresents the Father! The religious leaders of His day used their position for personal gain instead of in service of the people.

> *Holy Spirit, would You disentangle any aspect of my thinking that isn't*
> *securely rooted in God's goodness? I can't afford to have a misconception*
> *of who He is to me and to those around me.*

REST: In the same way, it is a misrepresentation of the Father to say He permits sickness to discipline us. This is not true any more than it is to say He uses sin to discipline His children. For sickness is to my body what sin is to my soul. It's time for those money changers to get chased out of the temple. When we understand the nature of this truth, we see that Jesus is not warring against the Father to reveal Himself as a new and improved standard of God. He is accurately revealing and manifesting the nature of the Father, as He has always been. We can either create a doctrine that allows for lack or seek God until Heaven comes according to promise.

> *Everything I do is rooted in My goodness, and that will never change.*
> *Sink your understanding deep into this truth, and join Me as I release*
> *My goodness upon the earth.*

December 24ᵗʰ

One day when the crowds were being baptized, Jesus himself was
baptized. As he was praying, the heavens opened, and the Holy Spirit,
in bodily form, descended on him like a dove. And a voice from heaven
said, "You are my dearly loved Son, and you bring me great joy."

—Luke 3:21-22 NLT

RISE: Jesus gave us an example. Even though He is the eternal Son of God, He chose to live with the limitations of a man so that He might give us something to follow. Let's face it, if Jesus did all His miracles as God, I'm still impressed. But that is an impossible example for me to follow. I am simply an observer, which I'm very happy with, if that's His purpose for my life. I have no problem celebrating the amazing things that only God can do. But from the beginning, it has been God who continually sets the stage to partner with imperfect people in a co-laboring relationship. When I see that He did what He did as a man following His Father, then I am compelled to do whatever I need to do to follow that example. I am no longer content to live as I am.

Thank You, Father, that You've provided so many ways to encounter Your
Kingdom on the earth. I read Your Word, I hear Your voice, I learn about
Your heart—and all that is available to me—through the miracles of Jesus.

REST: There are two conditions put upon me in Jesus' example. These qualifications are essential for me to emulate the life, presence, and power that Jesus made evident. First is the fact that Jesus had no sin. Without Jesus, I was hopelessly lost in sin. Now I am found in Christ, without sin, because His blood has made me clean. Because of such overwhelming mercy and grace, I have met the first qualification. The second condition is that Jesus was entirely empowered by the Holy Spirit. Jesus' life was an illustration of what one man could do who had no sin and was entirely empowered by the Holy Spirit. The reality of Jesus' success in ministry doesn't change because not everyone I pray for gets healed. He is the standard, not me. He is the leader, and I'm learning to follow. Any discrepancies are on my end, not His.

Read the miracles of Jesus in a new light—they are invitations to you
into the realm of My Kingdom. Keep Me as your standard, and keep
pressing into more of My presence.

December 25th

*A highway shall be there, and a road, and it shall be called the
Highway of Holiness. The unclean shall not pass over it, but it shall
be for others. Whoever walks the road, although a fool,
shall not go astray.*

—Isaiah 35:8 NKJV

RISE: There is an environment created in the outpouring of the Spirit in which holiness becomes the normal expression of a people bathed in His presence. Isaiah speaks of this as the highway of holiness. A highway is a road designed to expedite travel because obstacles have been removed. It usually involves easy access and has fellow travelers. A highway of holiness allows for a momentum to be created for the people of God to live in purity effortlessly. It is so significant that even foolish things get covered. This is not to minimize sin or foolishness. It is just to help us to realize that when many live righteously, it creates a momentum where even the weak succeed.

> *Teach me more about Your holiness, Lord. I want to understand the beauty of Your holiness and experience such an outpouring of the Spirit in my time.*

REST: God is creating such a highway in this time of outpouring that it is going to be hard to wander off the road. This concept is difficult for many to embrace, as we are accustomed to the opposite. We have been quick to speak about the "great falling away" but not the great harvest and city transformation that is also a part of end-time prophecy. A day is coming when there will exist a righteous peer pressure, not based on punishment or the fear of man but on His manifested presence—His glory.

> *My holiness is beautiful, enticing, and fulfilling. A revelation of My holiness does not look like a rigid fence meant to keep people out, but rather an expression that calls people up beyond their human nature and into Mine.*

December 26ᵗʰ

*The secret things belong to the Lord our God, but those things which
are revealed belong to us and to our children forever, that we
may do all the words of this law.*

—Deuteronomy 29:29 NKJV

RISE: What we don't know is sometimes as important as what we do know. While the Scriptures never exalt ignorance, they do honor trust. And trust is proven most in the midst of confusing circumstances with their corresponding questions. In effect, trust means that what we have come to know to be true about God is greater than all the circumstantial evidence that denies it. This is vital for those who display His unfolding purposes in the earth.

> *Father, give me an increased appetite for Your wonder. I want to
> experience the things I don't yet understand with a childlike wonder
> and anticipation of Your goodness.*

REST: Remembering the purposes of God at this point is crucial. He longs to have a people who represent Jesus accurately, in purity and power, becoming those who can be trusted to co-labor with Him in a way that doesn't divide His family or pervert His reasoning. Simply put, this means to reign with Christ. His passion is to bring people into ever increasing manifestation of His presence/glory upon them. That means that the weightiness of God's glory will rest upon a people who live with an undivided heart. The bottom line is that to be a people who can carry the beauty and glory of God in the earth, we must be proven as a people of trust. And the measure of trust we live with becomes the most evident when things turn out differently than what we expected or prayed for.

> *There will be chances for you to build your trust in Me, to dig down
> in the midst of the mess and declare that your hope is found in Me.
> Those moments are treasures, as they build an unshakable foundation
> for things to come.*

December 27th

*"Come now, let us settle the matter," says the Lord. "Though your sins
are like scarlet, they shall be as white as snow; though they are
red as crimson, they shall be like wool."*

—Isaiah 1:18 NIV

RISE: God is more than capable of going head to head with anyone in debate. The thought that God might be intimidated with humanity's questions is quite humorous. He invites us into this dialogue. It's just that He has a different value system than we do, although ours is changing daily in our walk with Him. And to have a relationship with Him is always on His terms. But we know that His terms are always for our best. God has one basic requirement of anyone who approaches Him—faith. That is what He values. Living in the place of trust positions us for breakthroughs—bold faith stands on the shoulders of quiet trust.

> *I want to build my trust in the quiet times, Holy Spirit, so that I will be
> prepared and able to handle the moments that require boldness. Help
> me to build My trust in You, God.*

REST: Faith is an activity of the heart. Real faith comes through yieldedness, not some trumped-up activity of the brain. Faith comes from surrender, not striving. Faith is not mindless. Understanding with the renewed mind (see Rom. 12:2) can often be used to set the context for faith to work in, much like the banks of a river set the parameters for the flow of the water. While faith is not mindless, it is also not mind-full. It is not intellectual in nature. True faith is superior to reason in that it gives our intellect a context in which to grow safely—in the knowledge of God. To know God is the greatest privilege given to anyone. The Cross of Jesus Christ is the ultimate invitation to know God. It is here we can know with certainty He has spared no expense in enabling us to respond successfully to His invitation.

> *I want to engage with you, to hear your heart and your questions. But
> a lack of faith puts distance between us, and we can only truly engage
> through intimacy. Draw near, lean on My chest, share your thoughts
> with Me and let Me share Mine with you.*

December 28th

I would have despaired unless I had believed that I would see the
goodness of the Lord in the land of the living.

—Psalm 27:13 NASB

RISE: Eternity runs through our veins, yet we live in time. We are citizens of earth, but we are already citizens of Heaven. We are saved, yet we will be saved when Jesus comes for us. Our old nature has been crucified with Christ, yet our capacity to sin has not disappeared. We are introduced to a Kingdom that is both here and now, yet this very same Kingdom is coming. We often live in tension between two conflicting realities. That is the life of a believer. And that is why the life of trust is to be built, not upon principles or theories, but upon the solid rock called God's goodness.

> *Thank You that even though I exist in such various tensions, I do not*
> *have to feel tossed about like on a wave. You are my anchor; I will hold*
> *fast to You, choosing to live from Heaven to earth.*

REST: The need for mystery need not be painful or dreaded. It is a part of our ongoing story. We value the outcome—the miracles, the breakthroughs, and the divine interventions—as we should. But He seems to treasure the process—that which takes us to the outcome. It's the process that reveals and demonstrates our devotion to Him. Devotion, that realm of established trust, is something He can build upon. God is the ultimate entrepreneur, building the unexpected in the earth upon and through the lives of His trusted saints.

> *I am not in a rush. You can take as long as you need to build your trust*
> *with Me. I will walk you through every scary thing. Your heart is safe*
> *with Me.*

December 29th

For the word of the Lord is right, and all His work is done in truth.
He loves righteousness and justice; the earth is full of the
goodness of the Lord.

—Psalm 33:4-5 NKJV

RISE: God's goodness is bigger and more valuable than creation itself. It is the most unexplored reality in existence. This that is greater than space and time must be embraced with hearts of surrender, with bold and courageous hearts of surrender. The level of deception even in the hearts of God's people has been so strong that there is an arrogance masquerading as humility teaching us to receive the evil that comes our way as the mysterious hand of God. It's arrogance because it comes from the soulish ideals of people without biblical roots, without biblical surrender. Yielding to God's goodness should be easier than it is. Yet it has become the challenge of the hour—because this surrender is so entirely a grace expression of Heaven that no one could ever take the credit for what God has done in us.

I repent for any time that I've ascribed pain to You, God, because it was
easier to do that than to live with not understanding. You are good all
the time, and I will lean on that truth forever.

REST: One of the definitions for this word *full* is "having no empty space." It's beautiful. The world has no empty spaces untouched by God's goodness. That being the case, no one has to look far to find this treasure. But one may have to look differently. I have a responsibility to steward the knowledge of His goodness. If in fact all of this is true, then my thoughts must be consistent with this reality. I am the one who must change. I must think consistently with who He is and what He is like, or I will feed my soul on the inferior, living with the assumption that what I think I know is true. Anchoring our souls in anything but His goodness is the ultimate waste of time.

Ask Me, and I will show you My goodness in every single place. Seek
it out, expect to find it, and the way you think of My connection to the
world just might change.

December 30th

"Believe in me so that rivers of living water will burst out from within
you, flowing from your innermost being, just like the Scripture says!"
Jesus was prophesying about the Holy Spirit that believers were
being prepared to receive.

—John 7:38-39 TPT

RISE: Living a life filled with the Spirit of God is the only possible way I can consistently bring others into an encounter with God. Maintaining an awareness of Him, with the willingness to do whatever He wants, makes this challenging goal doable. Being filled with the Spirit does not point to an experience we might have had a certain number of years ago. It's not measured by what I contain but by what flows from me. Only in the continual overflow of His presence through our lives are we truly full of the Holy Spirit. And it's in that condition that we are most likely able to bring others into an encounter with God.

> *Holy Spirit, I need a fresh encounter with You today. I don't want to*
> *move forward with a stale understanding. I want to be an open conduit*
> *of Your presence.*

REST: The picture He gives us in this passage is profound. He is teaching us what happens when we minister in His anointing—what happens when God has His way through us. It's like a river flowing from us. And that river is the Holy Spirit. It couldn't be clearer. He flows from us. And this time, the picture is not of a water bottle to contain Him. He is in us as a river to impact the spiritual geography around us. He lives in us, but He wants out—He is in us as a river, not a lake. He is a flowing presence, carrying the heart of the Father, desiring to saturate the land with the works of Jesus.

> *I want to pour My presence out on you, filling Your life with My blessings*
> *and manifestations of My goodness, so that there is a ripple effect from*
> *your life out into the world.*

December 31st

I assure you and most solemnly say to you, whoever says to this mountain, "Be lifted up and thrown into the sea!" and does not doubt in his heart [in God's unlimited power], but believes that what he says is going to take place, it will be done for him [in accordance with God's will].

—Mark 11:23 AMP

RISE: I owe people the message of the Gospel of the Kingdom of God. It must be declared. This wonderful message includes the good news of salvation for lost and broken humanity, which is all of us. But it is much bigger than that. It is the proclamation of God's rule over everything that exists, in the natural realm as well as the spiritual. And all of that is in the here and now. Whatever He rules over has life, freedom, beauty, and order. The decree itself is important because some things don't manifest until they are spoken. If we realized how what we say attracts spiritual reinforcements, angelic or demonic, we'd be much more careful to watch what we say. We'd also be more deliberate in proclaiming what is true—God is in charge and longs to manifest His goodness everywhere.

Holy Spirit, help me to guard my tongue, protecting my understanding of God's goodness, and only releasing that reality with my words. I want to be a part of bringing Heaven to earth!

REST: One of the more shocking discoveries for us has been that God is actually in a good mood. He sees the beginning from the end and is convinced that His plan of redeeming people from their sin, enabling them to rule with Christ, will actually work. He has given us His best—Jesus, the Son of God, and the Holy Spirit—to live in us. In some ways, this statement of God's mood is one of the more alarming statements for many, especially for those who view Him as constantly on the verge of an angry outburst of some sort. My main goal is to at least make people think of how we perceive Him. Because He is better than we think, let's change the way we think and let the whole world know He really is in a good mood.

It is My shalom—My peace, My design, My perspective—that I long to pour out onto the earth. My love is overflowing as I joyously bring the world back into alignment. Won't you join Me?

About
Bill & Beni Johnson

BENI and BILL JOHNSON are the Senior Pastors of Bethel Church in Redding, California, and serve a growing number of churches that cross denominational lines. They are both bestselling authors, Bill, of *When Heaven Invades Earth* and *Hosting the Presence*, and Beni of *The Happy Intercessor*. They have three children and ten grandchildren.

Reflections